Bitasion

Sidestone Press

Bitasion

Archéologie des habitations-plantations des Petites Antilles

Lesser Antilles Plantation Archaeology

Ouvrage dirigé par

Kenneth Kelly & Benoit Bérard

Published by Sidestone Press, Leiden
www.sidestone.com

ISBN 978-90-8890-194-2

Photograph cover: Habitation Fond Moulin, Grand Rivière, Martinique
Photograph by J. Cazassus-Bérard, 2012
Lay-out & cover design: Sidestone Press

TABOUI NO. 1
COLLECTION D'ARCHÉOLOGIE CARAÏBE
DIRIGÉE PAR BENOÎT BÉRARD

Contents

Foreword

This is the first volume in the *Taboui* series, published by the Caribbean history and archaeology laboratory (EA 929) of the Université des Antilles et de la Guyane. This new series is dedicated to the exploration of Caribbean archaeology in all of its thematic, chronological, and geographical diversity. Overseen by an international editorial board, it welcomes contributions in French, English, and Spanish.

The archaeology of the Caribbean islands has witnessed a dramatic development over the past 20 years; a development characterized by growth in the number of researchers engaged in the region, as well as increasingly sophisticated research questions and analytical methods. Unfortunately, the publishing opportunities in Caribbean archaeology have not followed the same growth curve. Thus, today the advancement of Caribbean archaeology is limited by a lack of world-class book series or journals devoted to this subject. Furthermore, cultural resource management archaeology has also witnessed a tremendous growth over the past 10 years, particularly in the French West Indies, Puerto Rico, and the US Virgin Islands. Yet the results of this research are rarely made available in the region as a whole. The creation of this trilingual publication specifically dedicated to Caribbean archaeology will encourace a better dissemination of the important results of this research.

The establishment of the *Taboui* series should be seen as a direct response to this need. This project has been brought about thanks to the support of the French Ministry of Culture and Communication, and the University of the Antilles and Guyane. The word *taboui* signifies the "men's house", the place for the exchange of knowledge and for initiations among the Kalinago of the Lesser Antilles. We can only hope that this series will also be the space shared by all archaeologists working in the Caribbean, and that it will encourage the exchange of knowledge amongst this community of researchers and the wider public in the Caribbean region.

Préambule

Le présent ouvrage constitue le premier volume de la collection *Taboui* éditée par l'EA 929 AIHP/GEODE de l'Université des Antilles et de la Guyane et dont nous assurons la direction. Cette nouvelle collection est consacrée à l'archéologie caraïbe dans toutes ses déclinaisons thématiques, chronologiques ou géographiques. Pilotée par un comité scientifique international, elle accueillera des ouvrages en français, anglais ou espagnol.

L'archéologie antillaise a connu un très fort développement au cours des vingt dernières années. Un développement marqué par une multiplication des chercheurs ainsi qu'un renouvellement important des problématiques de recherche et des méthodes d'analyse.

Malheureusement, l'évolution des supports de publication n'a pas suivi la même courbe de croissance. Ainsi, aujourd'hui le développement de l'archéologie dans les Antilles se trouve limité par un manque de collections ou de revues de qualité qui lui soient spécifiquement consacrées.

Par ailleurs, l'archéologie préventive connaît depuis une dizaine d'années un développement important tout particulièrement dans les Antilles françaises, Porto-Rico et les Iles Vierges américaines. Les résultats de ces travaux ont à l'heure actuelle un très faible taux de publication. La création d'un support de publication trilingue spécifiquement dédié à l'archéologie de la zone devrait favoriser une meilleure diffusion des importants résultats de ces recherches.

La création de la collection *Taboui* doit être conçue comme une réponse à ce besoin. Ce projet a pu être mené à bien grâce au soutien du Ministère de la Culture et de la Communication et de l'Université des Antilles et de la Guyane. Le taboui était la maison collective des hommes, le lieu de l'échange des savoirs et des initiations chez les Kalinago des Petites Antilles. Nous ne pouvons que souhaiter que la présente collection soit, elle aussi, le lieu commun à tous les archéologues travaillant dans la zone et qu'elle favorise la diffusion des connaissances au sein de cette communauté scientifique mais aussi plus largement au sein de la population antillaise.

Introduction

Archéologie des habitations-plantations[1] des Petites Antilles

Benoît Bérard

EA 929 AIHP-GEODE
Université des Antilles et de la Guyane
Faculté des Lettres et Sciences Humaines
Campus de Schoelcher
Martinique
benoit.berard@mediaserv.net

L'étude des dynamiques liées à la mise en place et à l'expansion des espaces urbains a connu un important et légitime développement au cours des dernières années tant sous l'impulsion des historiens que des archéologues. Il n'en reste pas moins que les habitations-plantations constituent le creuset historique et symbolique où fut fondu l'alliage original que sont les cultures antillaises. Elles sont le berceau des sociétés créoles contemporaines qui y ont puisé tant leur forte parenté que leur diversité. Leur étude a donc, tout naturellement, été précocement le terrain de prédilection des historiens. Les archéologues antillanistes se consacraient alors plus volontiers à l'étude des sociétés précolombiennes. En 1991, l'archéologie historique, de façon générale, n'occupe encore que 117 pages sur les 982 que comptent les actes du 13e congrès de l'Association Internationale d'Archéologie de la Caraïbe (Ayubi & Haviser 1991).

Ainsi, en dehors des travaux pionniers de J. Handler et F. Lange à la Barbade (Handler & Lange 1978), c'est surtout depuis la fin des années 1980 qu'un véritable développement de l'étude archéologique des habitations-plantations antillaises a pu être observé. L'incroyable richesse de cet objet historique a permis une multiplication des problématiques et des méthodes d'approches. Trois grands courants peuvent être distingués :

---

1 Concernant la discussion historique et terminologique autour des notions d'habitation et de plantation cf. Begot, 2008.

- Premièrement, on observe le développement par les historiens de l'Université des Antilles et de la Guyane, en particulier Danielle Bégot et Mireille Mousnier, d'études d'archéologie industrielle[2] complétées dans les Antilles Françaises par les premières fouilles consacrées à l'étude de l'appareil industriel (Leton 1989; Vidal 1994). Ces travaux sont menés autour d'approches centrées sur l'histoire des cultures matérielles et l'histoire des techniques participant ainsi activement au mouvement de patrimonialisation des habitations de Guadeloupe et de Martinique.
- Deuxièmement, au sein un programme global d'archéologie historique développé sous la direction de Norman Barka sont réalisées des prospections systématiques et une cartographie des plantations dans les Antilles néerlandaises (en particulier Saint Eustache et dans une moindre mesure Sint Maarten). Les données produites ont soutenu une analyse spatiale de ces plantations (Delle, 1994) ainsi que des travaux sur les élites hollandaises et le cas particulier des marchands de St Eustache (Barka 1991, 1996).
- Troisièmement, dans les Antilles anglophones, à la suite de J. Handler et F. Lange, les fouilles de villages et de cimetières d'esclaves se sont développées généralement sous l'impulsion d'universitaires nord-américains. Initialement consacrés à l'étude des persistances et des transformations des cultures africaines en contexte servile, ces travaux ont abouti à une approche globale des comportements humains et des relations sociales au sein des plantations[3].

Ainsi, quels que soient les angles d'approche, cette multiplication des recherches a largement participé au développement de l'archéologie historique dans l'espace antillais au cours des deux dernières décennies. Dans un premier temps, les principaux programmes se sont concentrés dans les Grandes Antilles et tout particulièrement à la Jamaïque (Armstrong 1990; Delle 1998; Hauser 2008; Higman 1998). Pour les Petites Antilles, il faut attendre la deuxième moitié des années 1990 pour voir se mettre en place des programmes spécifiques importants sous l'impulsion de G. Fox à Antigua et surtout de K. Kelly (Kelly 2002, 2004) dans les Antilles Françaises. Cette dynamique a été renforcée au cours des dix dernières années par l'arrivée de nouveaux chercheurs et par le développement dans les Antilles Françaises de l'archéologie préventive.

Cependant, aucun ouvrage de synthèse ou monographie importante n'avait encore exposé les résultats de ces travaux. C'est donc à la fois pour rendre compte de cette dynamique et en partie pallier ce manque que nous avons décidé avec mon collègue Kenneth Kelly de diriger le présent ouvrage. Il nous faut ici remercier l'ensemble des chercheurs qui ont accepté de participer à cette aventure. En effet, dans ce volume sont regroupés à la fois les principaux spécialistes ayant travaillé dans les Petites Antilles au cours des dernières décennies ainsi qu'un certain nombre de jeunes docteurs ou doctorants dont le dynamisme et le talent permettent d'envisager l'avenir avec sérénité.

---

2 Pour une bibliographie complète de ces travaux se reporter à Bégot, 2011.

3 Pour les références de ces travaux se reporter à la conclusion de ce volume par K. Kelly.

Les questions pouvant être traitées par l'archéologie des habitations-plantations sont extrêmement riches et multiples et ne sauraient être épuisées par la publication d'un unique ouvrage. Les différents chapitres qui composent ce livre n'ont pas vocation à tendre à l'exhaustivité sous la forme d'un catalogue ou d'un bilan de la recherche. Le temps des synthèses n'est d'ailleurs sans doute pas encore venu. Ils nous semblent, par contre, être représentatifs, par la variété des questions abordées et la diversité des angles d'approche, de la dynamique actuelle de ce champs de la recherche. Cette diversité est évidemment liée à celle des espaces concernés: les habitations-plantations de cinq îles des Petites Antilles : Antigua, la Guadeloupe, la Dominique, la Martinique et la Barbade sont ici étudiées. Elle est aussi, au sein d'un même espace, due à la cohabitation de différentes pratiques universitaires. Ainsi, la cohabitation entre une archéologie préventive conduite par des archéologues formés en France et une archéologie programmée essentiellement menée par des universitaires nord-américains constitue, en imposant un indispensable dialogue, une des richesses actuelles de l'archéologie des habitations et de l'esclavage dans les Antilles Françaises (cf. K. Kelly, Chapitre 1).

Cette diversité est aussi bien entendu le fruit de la diversité même de l'objet, chaque habitation-plantation constituant une microsociété originale. Cependant, par delà cette originalité, chaque site étudié est aussi une expression du système de la plantation coloniale esclavagiste dans sa totalité et mérite d'être analysé dans le cadre du système commercial proto-capitaliste qui se met en place autour de l'espace atlantique à l'époque moderne. Ainsi, la fouille de la plantation Betty Hope à Antigua offre-t-elle un regard sur la globalité du système sucrier et ses conséquences environnementales sur l'espace Antillais (cf. G. Fox, Chapitre 2).

L'archéologie des habitations-plantations, est aujourd'hui beaucoup une archéologie des esclaves. Dans ce domaine, les premières fouilles de villages d'esclaves ont beaucoup traité des conditions de vie des populations serviles au travers d'une analyse de l'évolution de la nature et de l'organisation de leur habitat. Si beaucoup reste à faire dans ce domaine, d'autres approches commencent à émerger comme l'étude de leur alimentation au travers de l'analyse des restes de faune découverts au cours des fouilles. Ce recours à l'archéozoologie permet d'aborder des questions telle que la capacité et les modalités d'auto-approvisionnement des esclaves, la dichotomie ayant pu exister entre l'alimentation des populations libres et serviles mais aussi l'importance de l'exploitation des espèces locales, terrestres et maritimes, par rapport à la faune coloniale importée (cf. D.Wallman, Chapitre 3 et N. Tomadini et al., Chapitre 4).

L'approche d'un système aussi complexe que celui des plantations coloniales esclavagistes nécessite le recours à l'ensemble des disciplines archéologiques. Ainsi, dans les Petites Antilles, il a été très précocement fait appel à l'archéologie funéraire (Corruccini et al., 1982). Ces travaux se sont pour l'instant concentrés sur la fouille de cimetières d'esclaves. La contribution de T. Varney (Chapitre 5) aborde donc une thématique tout à fait originale : celle des sépultures de planteurs au travers de la fouille préventive d'un cimetière familial à Antigua.

Les habitations-plantations antillaises s'inscrivent dans un système économique globalisé centré sur l'espace atlantique. Cependant, la nature de chacune de ces microsociétés regroupant planteurs, employés libres et esclaves varie fortement. Le travail de M. Hauser (Chapitre 6) explore ainsi les différences ayant pu exister en Dominique entre la pratique des planteurs d'origine française et celle des planteurs anglais. Il nous montre aussi au-delà des liens coloniaux l'importance des interactions intra-antillaises dans la construction des sociétés créoles et ce au-delà même de la période esclavagiste.

En effet, les habitions-plantations ne disparaissent pas le jour de l'émancipation des esclaves. Ainsi, il est du plus grand intérêt d'analyser tant le devenir de ces structures face aux crises successives et à l'émergence des usines sucrières que celui des populations qui y vivaient et y travaillaient. Ce devenir des nouveaux libres est aujourd'hui un des champs important de la recherche historique mais aussi de l'archéologie antillaises (cf. S. Rebovich, Chapitre 7 ainsi que S. Bergman et F.H. Smith, Chapitre 8).

Ainsi, ce volume nous montre bien que l'archéologie des habitations dans les Petites Antilles est aujourd'hui multidisciplinaire, multiculturelle et plurinationale pour reprendre le titre de la conclusion de K. Kelly.

Nous espérons que cet ouvrage, tout en diffusant une information jusqu'à présent trop dispersée, sera le point de départ de nouvelles recherches. En effet, en y regardant de plus près, l'archéologie des habitations-plantations dans les Petites Antilles est aujourd'hui constituée d'une mosaïque d'approches partielles fonction des intérêts et des pratiques variés des chercheurs. Il serait certainement souhaitable de concevoir aujourd'hui la fouille de ces sites au travers d'approches plus globales : dans le temps long (pré- et post-abolition), prenant en compte l'ensemble des populations libres et serviles (dans la vie comme dans la mort), leurs conditions de vie, leur culture matérielle, leurs relations sociales mais aussi l'analyse des bâtiments industriels et techniques ; le tout dans une vision multi-scalaire articulant sphères locales, régionales et internationales rendant indispensable un dialogue constant entre historiens et archéologues. Nous avons bon espoir que la richesse des contributions qui constituent cette publication contribuera à la conception de ce "programme idéal". Ce développement de la recherche est une nécessité scientifique mais aussi sociale pour les populations antillaises. L'archéologie historique est une voie d'accès privilégiée aux interstices de l'histoire coloniale (contact précoloniaux, commerce interlope, marronnage physique et moral, nécessaires concessions fruits de la négociation permanente entre norme coloniale et réalité quotidienne, etc.). En fouillant la terre antillaise, les archéologues ne peuvent que conter la quotidienneté de la vie au sein de l'archipel. Or c'est aussi (beaucoup ?) de ces interstices, s'inscrivant le plus souvent dans des échelles micro-locales, locales ou régionales, qu'ont émergé les cultures antillaises.

Références bibliographiques

Armstrong, D.V.

1990 *The Old Village and the Great House: An Archaeological and Historical Examination of Drax Hall Plantation, St. Ann's Bay, Jamaica*, Urbana, University of Illinois Press.

Ayubi, E.N. & J.B. Haviser (eds)

1991 *Proceedings of the thirteenth International Congress for caribbean archaeology, Curaçao, July, 1989*, Reports of the Archaeological-Anthropological Institute of the Netherlands Antilles, n° 9, Part 1, Curaçao.

Barka, N. F.

1991 The merchants of St. Eustatius: an Archaeological and Historical analysis. In E.N. Ayubi and J.B. Haviser (eds). *Proceedings of the thirteenth International Congress for caribbean archaeology, Curaçao, July, 1989*, Reports of the Archaeological-Anthropological Institute of the Netherlands Antilles, n° 9, Part 1, Curaçao.

1996 Archaeology of the Dutch Elite: The country estate of Johannes de Graaff. St. Eustatius Archaeological Research Series N°8. Williamsburg, Va.: Department of Anthropology, College of William and Mary.

Bégot, D.

2008 Introduction. In D.Bégot (ed.), (2008), *La plantation coloniale esclavagiste XVIIe-XIXe siècle*, Actes du 127e congrès national des sociétés historiques et scientifiques, Nancy, 2002, Paris, CTHS, 343 p.

2011 L'habitation de l'histoire à l'archéologie industrielle et au patrimoine, In D. Bégot (ed.), *Guide de la recherche en histoire antillaise et guyanaise*, tome I, Paris, CTHS, 275-339.

Corruccini R.S., J.S. Handler, R. Mutaw and F.W. Lange

1982 Osteology of a Slave Burial Population from Barbados, West Indies. *American Journal of Physical Anthropology*, 59, 443-459.

Delle, J. A.

1994 A Spatial Analysis of Sugar Plantation on St. Eustatius, Netherlands Antilles. Master's Thesis, Department of Anthropology, College William and Mary, Williamsburg, Virginia.

1998 *An Archaeology of Social Space: Analyzing Coffee Plantations in Jamaica's Blue Mountains.* New York, Plenum Press, 1998.

Handler, J.S. and F. Lange

1978 *Plantation Slavery in Barbados: An Archaeological and Historical Investigation* Cambridge, Harvard University Press.

Hauser, M.W.

2008 *An Archaeology of Black Markets: Local Ceramics and Economies in Eighteenth-Century Jamaica.* Gainesville, FL, University Press of Florida.

Higman, B.

1998 *Montpelier, Jamaica: A Plantation Community in Slavery and Freedom, 1739-1912.* Kingston, Jamaica, The Press University of the West Indies.

Kelly, K.G.

2002 African Diaspora Archaeology in Guadeloupe, French West Indies. *Antiquity* 76, pp. 333-334.

2004 Historical Archaeology in the French Caribbean: An Introduction to a Special Volume of the Journal of Caribbean Archaeology. *Journal of Caribbean Archaeology* Special Issue No. 1, 1-10.

Leton, C.

1989 Fond Saint-Jacques 1, *Archéologie Patrimoine de la Martinique*, CERA Martinique, Fort de France, 1989.

Vidal, N.

1994 Le fonctionnement et l'évolution du système de chauffe des habitations-sucreries traditionnelles à la Martinique entre le XVIIe et le début du XIXe siècle. *Caribena* n°4, Fort-de-France, 137-152.

Chapter 1

Archaeology, Plantations, and Slavery in the French West Indies

Kenneth G. Kelly

Department of Anthropology
University of South Carolina
Columbia
kenneth.kelly@sc.edu

Abstract

Historical archaeological research on plantations and slavery has been ongoing since the late 1960s in the Caribbean, yet the French West Indies has only recently begun to be investigated. This chapter reviews some of the reasons for this time lag, and also explores the distinct cultural context of the French West Indies as it relates to the politics of archaeological research on slavery. By drawing upon examples from archaeological projects investigating plantation slavery in Martinique and Guadeloupe, some insights are provided to help contextualize the differences, and the similarities, between the experiences of slavery in the former French colonies, and how they compare to the former British colonies.

Résumé

Aux Antilles, les recherches archéologiques sur les habitations et l'esclavage existent depuis les années 1960. Quant aux Antilles françaises, ce n'est que depuis quelques années que ces recherches interrogent les contextes liés à l'esclavage. Le présent chapitre résume les raisons de ce démarrage tardif et étudie le contexte culturel spécifique des Antilles françaises au niveau de la politique de la recherche archéologique sur l'esclavage. L'étude des projets étudiant l'esclavage en Martinique et Guadeloupe, nous permet d'interroger, dans leur propre contexte, les différences et les similarités des expériences de l'esclavage dans les colonies françaises, et de les comparer avec celles des colonies britanniques.

Resumen

Investigaciones arqueológicas históricas sobre plantaciones y esclavitud se vienen realizando desde a fines de los 1960s en el caribe, pero en las Indias Occidentales francesas solamente han sido investigadas recientemente. Este ensayo analiza algunas de las razones por esta demora, y también explora el contexto cultural exclusivo de las Indias Occidentales francesas relacionado con la política de las investigaciones arqueológicas sobre la esclavitud. Tomando como ejemplos proyectos arqueológicos investigando esclavitud en las plantaciones en Martinique y Guadeloupe, se proveen algunas revelaciones para ayudar a contextualizar las diferencia, y las similitudes, entre las experiencias de la esclavitud en las antiguas colonias francesas, y como se comparan a las antiguas colonia británicas.

Key words

plantation archaeology, slavery, French West Indies

Mots-clés

l'archéologie des plantations, esclavage, Antilles Françaises

Palabras clave

arqueologia de los ingenios, la esclavitud, Las Antillas Francesas

Archaeological research into the subject of plantations and slavery in the French West Indies has been slow to develop, when compared with the state of these research programs elsewhere in the Caribbean (Delpuech 2001a; Haviser 1999; see also chapters in Farnsworth 2001). The Anglophone Caribbean has been the undisputed leader in African Diaspora archaeology in the region, with substantive projects underway since the early 1970s in Barbados and Jamaica (Handler & Lange 1978; Armstrong 1990; Higman 1998), and more recently projects on virtually every Anglophone island, no matter how small or peripheral to the primary thrust of the plantation economy (for examples, see Hauser 2011; Lenik 2011, 2012; Pulsipher & Goodwin 2001; Wilkie & Farnsworth 2005; and others). Elsewhere in the Caribbean, the Dutch islands have been the focus of historical archaeology with an African diaspora perspective since the 1980s, if not earlier, and formerly Danish islands have also seen some plantation-focused work beginning at least by the 1990s (see Farnsworth 2001). Formerly Spanish colonies have witnessed African diaspora archaeology since at least the 1980s, with some very early Spanish-era plantations being investigated in Jamaica (Woodward 2006, 2011), the Dominican Republic (Arrom & Garcia-Arévalo 1986; Manon-Arredondo 1978; Vega 1979; Weik 1997), and also in Cuba (Singleton 2001, 2005). Both of these nations have also been in the forefront of maroon research (Agorsah 1993; La Rosa Corzo 2005; Weik 1997, 2012).

Yet when considering the importance of individual nations in the production of wealth through the plantation economies, it is clear that the most important colonial power of the 18th century, by virtually every measure, has been overlooked by archaeologists (Kelly 2009). Alongside England, France began developing its colonial plantation economies in the 17th century, and by the late 18th century France was producing more sugar, rum, coffee, and indigo than its rival colonial power, Great Britain (Blackburn 1997). A measure of this importance can be seen in the fact that France, at the end of the Seven Years War (1756-1763), surrendered her possession of New France (from the Gulf of St Lawrence to the Gulf of Mexico east of the Mississippi River) rather than give up the 2756 sq. kilometers (1065 sq. miles) of Guadeloupe and Martinique (Dewar 2010). Furthermore, the French colonial holdings were players in some of the most dramatic events of the late 18th and early 19th century, including the only successful slave rebellion (in St Domingue), the consequences of the French Revolution and its emancipation, and the re-establishment of slavery in the colonies of Guyane and more importantly, Guadeloupe (Dubois 2004, Bénot & Dorigny 2003, Dorigny 2003, Régent 2004). And yet, although archaeological work had been directed at other sites of the colonial period (Delpuech 2001a; see also papers in Kelly 2004), prior to the 1990s, no historical archaeological work had been conducted on African Diaspora related sites anywhere in the former French colonial holdings of Martinique and Guadeloupe.

1.1 Archaeological research on French West Indian plantations

Beginning in the late 1980s and early 1990s, a few projects began to investigate the archaeology of aspects of plantation economies in Martinique. In Martinique, these include the work by Suzannah England on pottery production at Trois Ilets (England 1994), industrial archaeology inventories and documentation at Habitation Crève Cœur (Barrett 1989a, 1989b, 1990), and the partial excavation of a slave cemetery at Fonds St Jacques (CERA 1989). In Guadeloupe, efforts were similarly sporadic, with the wide ranging industrial archaeology heritage survey led by Danielle Bégot (1991), and limited archaeological work at the coffee plantation of La Grivelière conducted by Gerard Richard (Richard 1998). African-descended people were the subject of archaeological investigations derived from salvage work in Guadeloupe at the beach-front cemetery site of Anse Ste Margueritte (Courtaud et al. 1999; Courtaud & Romon 2004). The 1990s also saw the initiation of archaeological work at the Jesuit plantation of Loyola in French Guyana, started by Yannick Le Roux (Le Roux 1994), and expanded by Reginald Auger and others from Quebec (Le Roux et al. 2009). Work has recently been published by Barone-Visigalli (2010) on the plantations of St Regis and Maripa, also in Guyane. Yet none of these projects was explicitly focused on the same kinds of anthropological issues, such as ethnicity, identity, resistance, and creolization that were being explored by African diaspora focused historical archaeologists elsewhere in the

Caribbean (for example, see Armstrong 1990, 2003; Armstrong & Kelly 2000; Hauser 2008; Higman 1998; Agorsah 1993; Pulsipher & Goodwin 2001; Wilkie & Farnsworth 2005).

Several recent developments have changed this situation. In 2001 I began a long-term archaeological research program investigating the slavery experience in the French West Indies, first in Guadeloupe, and then in Martinique (Kelly 2002, 2008, 2009, 2011). These projects demonstrated that the archaeological vestiges associated with slavery were present, and could be recovered by archaeologists who were aware of their potential and focused on their particular characteristics. Another important development was really a set of events and commemorations: the 200th anniversary (in 1994) of the first abolition of slavery during the revolutionary period in 1794, the 150th anniversary of the 1848 abolition of slavery (in 1998), and the 200th anniversary of the reestablishment of slavery by Napoleon in 1802 (in 2002). These three events, especially the last, led to serious academic and popular reflection in France on the issues of slavery and why they were not more integral parts of the French national consciousness, and what the consequences of these events were (see Dorigny 2003; Bénot & Dorigny 2003, etc.). This has continued to grow with the passage in France of the "Loi Taubira" in 2001 which recognized slavery and the slave trade as a crime against humanity, required the teaching and study of the subject, and implemented the creation of a scientific committee charged with safeguarding the memory of slavery.

Another development with significant impact has been the establishment of Services Regional d'Archéologie (SRA) in each of the overseas departments of the Caribbean region. These offices, only recently established (1986 in Martinique, 1992 in Guadeloupe and Guyane, and only 2011 in Réunion—not Caribbean, but a plantation based colony as well) (Delpuech 2001b), are charged with the oversight of archaeological resources in their respective locations, and based upon the recommendations of those offices, they stipulate the cultural resources management (CRM) archaeological work that must be undertaken (Bérard and Stouvenot 2011). Of the three SRA offices in the broader Caribbean region, only that in Guyane is directed by a specialist in American archaeology. Yet another complicating matter is the fact that in the French system of archaeology, the focus has been by definition on prehistory (Delpuech 2001b; Bérard & Stouvenot 2011; see also Journot & Bellan 2011 and Burnouf et al. 2009); this is why the SRA was not established in Réunion earlier—Réunion was uninhabited prior to colonization and therefore had no prehistoric occupations.

In the last decade, the SRAs of Martinique, Guadeloupe and Guyane have taken an increasingly proactive role in mandating CRM work in locations that have been deemed sensitive through historical research, in particular through the very detailed island maps of the late 18th century (Bérard & Stouvenot 2011, see also the annual bulletins or *Bilans Scientifique* that are published by the Service Régional d'Archéologie in Guadeloupe, Guyane, and Martinique for the work; for one of the detailed 18th century maps, see Bégot et al. 1998). This, coupled with the demonstrable ability to identify, excavate, and interpret slave housing and other aspects of plantations, has prompted several of the archaeologists employed by INRAP (Institut National de Recherches Archéologiques Préventives), an organization charged by the French state with implementing archaeological resource evaluation, to take a particular interest in the colonial period archaeology of the former colonies (for examples, see Casagrande 2007, Casagrande & Serrand 2008, etc.). As a result of increasingly sympathetic SRA directors and motivated CRM personnel employed at INRAP as well as in private CRM firms, the last five years have seen a real elaboration of colonial period archaeological research in the regions, some of which is included in this volume, and the *Proceedings* of the recent IACA conferences. Now, plantation and early colonial sites are regularly sought out for archaeological testing, and aspects of the sites that would not have been investigated earlier, such as slave villages, are systematically explored for archaeological resources.

1.2 Challenges to integrating results

In spite of this excellent turn of events, there remain some challenges for developing cross-Caribbean comparisons between French *départements* and other Caribbean islands. Whereas the overwhelming majority of the colonial period archaeological work conducted in the Caribbean is developed from a research problem orientation where archaeologists have sought out sites that are best suited to their exploration of particular theoretical issues (creolization, resistance, subsistence, etc.--see chapters in Siegel and Righter 2011), in France the relatively undeveloped nature of colonial period archaeological research has meant that there are no university-based scholars who are focused on these sorts of issues. That means that there are no French scholars who are exploring research problem-based approaches to colonial period archaeology in the French Caribbean (this is not the case for prehistoric archaeology however—see Berard 2004; Grouard 2001; others). With this lack of senior research archaeologists engaged in colonial period problem-oriented archaeology, it is very difficult for interested students to receive the training they need to become specialized in this topic. As a result, virtually all colonial period archaeology currently undertaken in the French West Indies by French archaeologists falls within the parameters of Cultural Resource Management archaeology, and this poses some challenges. For one thing, the methodology of French CRM work is very different from that generally employed in seeking out, and excavating, plantation sites elsewhere in the region, most of which is not conducted in the guise of CRM research (see for example the methodologies employed by Armstrong 1990, 2003; Higman 1998; Wilkie & Farnsworth 2005; Pulsipher & Goodwin 2001; Richard 1998; Le Roux et al. 2009). This poses obstacles to developing comparisons between archaeological data from different islands in the region, as the recovery strategies are different.

French CRM strategies in rural or otherwise not built-up areas are overwhelmingly geared toward mechanical testing of properties, using backhoes or similar equipment with wide buckets that open windows 2-3 meters wide, and 7 to 10 meters long, typically to subsoil. If significant remains are identified, such as masonry walls, floors, or the like, the bucket ceases to excavate, and the remainder of the window is opened with shovels. However, if ephemeral archaeological materials are present, such as post-holes and -molds, sheet middens, and other features typically found in slave villages, they may not be identified unless they penetrate to the subsoil or bedrock. To the great credit of the SRA directors and their management of the French system of cultural preservation, it should be noted that very little CRM work is conducted elsewhere in the Caribbean, as Cultural Resource Management legislation is, with very few exceptions (Guadeloupe, Martinique, Puerto Rico, US Virgin Islands are in the forefront) poorly developed, or implemented, throughout the region (see the chapters in Siegel and Righter 2011 for a detailed discussion of virtually all of the Caribbean). In that way, it is important to recognize that French CRM archaeologists, whether they are working for INRAP or for one of the private companies, are recovering archaeological data in systematic ways that are not being recovered in many other Caribbean settings. The problem for comparison lies in the differences of methodology between research problem-oriented strategies employed by university-based archaeologists, and the more rapid CRM strategies.

These strategies of mechanical exposure, while rapid and effective to a certain extent, are also of limited use in many of the areas where slave villages are located. Decades of archaeological research around the Caribbean region has demonstrated that the villages occupied by enslaved people were overwhelmingly located on marginal lands, where they would not compromise economically important terrain (Armstrong & Kelly 2000; Handler & Lange 1978; Hicks 2007; Higman 1988; Pulsipher & Goodwin 2001; Wilkie & Farnsworth 2005). These marginal spaces are typically located on rocky hills or slopes, and often are characterized by shallow soils overlying bedrock. In this setting machine scraping does an excellent job of exposing the postholes, but otherwise destroys archaeological deposits that, precisely because of their marginal location, tend to be well preserved, having never been subjected to deep plowing or other mechanical post occupation disturbance (Armstrong 1990, 2003; Higman 1998; Kelly 2002, 2011). Furthermore, some of these less optimal village locations are very steep and wooded, so mechanical testing is not feasible, and therefore the sites may be overlooked. Having potential development impacts as a primary motivation for exploration also limits the potential of testing archaeologically significant areas such as slave villages. As slave villages were frequently located in the least agriculturally suitable areas, often steep or otherwise unsuitable, these areas may also not be the areas that are likely to be subject to development, especially for housing or other sorts of economic development that prioritize accessibility.

In contrast, strategies employed by other researchers that focus on hand excavation, while certainly slower, and arguably not so well suited to the demands of CRM archaeology, can be more effective at revealing the subtleties of slave village archaeological contexts (Le Roux et al. 2009; Armstrong 1990, 2003; Higman 1998). For example, while working on steep and heavily forested slopes such as characterize the slave village site at Crève Cœur, the vestiges of house platforms, where soil deposits are very shallow and sloping, can be explored to reveal arrays of postholes and other features that constitute the remains of slave housing and activity areas (Kelly 2008, 2011). Likewise, the controlled artifact collection that results from hand excavation permits the recovery of artifacts, such as the locally manufactured ceramics or *coco neg*, that would be less likely to be recovered through opportunistic recovery of artifacts from back dirt piles generated by the mechanical clearing.

Archaeological work on slave village sites in both Guadeloupe and Martinique indicates that the housing built and used by enslaved workers underwent an evolution, with the 17th and 18th centuries being characterized by lightly built housing locally called *kaz en gaulettes* (Guadeloupe) or *ti baum* (Martinique) (Berthelot & Gaumé 2002; Kelly 2008, 2011). This housing is less likely to be identified as slave housing using the mechanical methods due to its ephemeral remains. However, the housing of the 19th century, which is much more durably built, often of masonry, and often laid out in a regular pattern as elsewhere in the Caribbean (Chapman 1991; Denise 2004; Ursulet 2004), is much more amenable to identification by mechanical means (Casagrande & Serrand 2008).

When comparing plantation archaeology in the various locations of the Caribbean, such as elsewhere in this volume, it is clear that in spite of the broad commonalities of the plantation slavery system in the West Indies, there was considerable variability in the manifestation of slavery in different islands and different nations, and at different times. For example, when comparing 18th century access to material culture, particularly that imported from the metropole, we see that enslaved residents of British colonies typically had access to a greater diversity of material than seen in the French colonies (see Armstrong 1990; Wilkie & Farnsworth 2005 for examples of the wide array of imported materials in slave village contexts). However, after the revolutionary upheavals of the early 19th century, at least the enslaved residents of Guadeloupe participated in local market economies that provided access to imported material culture in ways similar to that seen in Jamaica and elsewhere (Gibson 2007). Likewise, we see that some of the general trends of the 19th century, such as the amelioration of housing on plantations seen in the British and Danish islands (Chapman 1991), were not equally manifest in the French colonies. While this amelioration is seen in Guadeloupe in the early 19th century (although perhaps associated with different motivations than elsewhere--Kelly 2008, 2011, 2014), a similar improvement of slave housing in Martinique is generally not seen until the middle of the 19th century, at the point of abolition (Charlery 2004; Denise 2004; Ursulet 2004; Kelly 2014). Other aspects of the archaeological record of slavery in the French West Indies show some of the similarities with the other regions of the Caribbean. For example, zooarchaeological data from Martinique and Guadeloupe show that enslaved people there engaged in many of the same strategies for survival as are seen elsewhere (Armstrong 1990, Wilkie & Farnsworth 2005; Kipple 2001), such as the trapping of small terrestrial animals from the local environment, and the collection of maritime resources from the nearby littoral areas (Wallman, this volume). However, archaeological and historical evidence suggests that plantations may also have employed full time specialist fishermen who exploited pelagic species to feed the slave village (Price 1966).

1.3 The benefits of sharing research results

Important studies by French CRM archaeologists are now contributing to a broader understanding of French colonial slave experiences. An outstanding example of this is presented in Casagrande and Serrand's (2008) evaluative testing of Habitation Guyonneau in northwestern Basse-Terre, Guadeloupe. At this estate (then-called le Vanier), the Carte des Ingenieurs du Roi, an island-wide map dating to the 1760s, indicated the location of the slave village to be adjacent to or underneath a recent *lotissement* or housing development some 300 meters north of the planter's house and industrial complex (Kelly 2002). My visit to the presumed location of this slave village in 2001 resulted in the identification of scattered ceramics and other artifacts appropriate to a slave village dating to the mid-late 18th century. No above ground architectural or other remains were visible, and given the relatively low density of materials, and its presumed disturbed nature, no excavations were conducted on this location. However, several years later, in advance of a proposed development of some land closer to the existing planter's house, the director of the SRA of Guadeloupe required INRAP to conduct archaeological testing of the property. This mechanical testing resulted in the identification of a 19th century slave village characterized by a series of masonry and rubble platforms and adjacent refuse deposits. Since my 2001 survey of the village location shown on the CIR had indicated that the village had been abandoned around the end of the 18th century at approximately the time of the French Revolution based upon the artifacts present at the site, this village that Casagrande and Serrand located must have been its successor. This pattern, of abandonment during the brief Revolutionary emancipation between 1794 and 1802, is a pattern I had noticed elsewhere in Guadeloupe, particularly at Habitation Coquenda in northern Grande-Terre, where two distinct village locations, one dating to the 18th century and indicated on the CIR, and one dating to the 19th century closer to the works, were present (Kelly 2014). At Habitation Guyonneau, Casagrande and Serrand had found the location of the second, later village, and in so doing were contributing data that conform to the pattern identified at Habitation Coquenda. The evidence from Habitation Guyonneau also conforms to another pattern of 19th century slave villages that I identified at La Mahaudière, also in northern Grande-Terre (Kelly 2011, 2014). Here, the slave village did not change locations between the late 18th century and the early 19th century, but the architecture and arrangement of the village underwent a significant transformation that I argue (2008, 2011) is due to the turmoil associated with the re-establishment of slavery in 1802. At La Mahaudière, the earlier village was archaeologically relatively ephemeral, with no remains visible above ground, and only postholes dug into the bedrock to indicate where structures had been. In the earliest years of the 19th century, the village at La Mahaudière was rearranged, with new, "improved" larger and more durable masonry structures being constructed in a set of orderly rows. This is a pattern also seen in the early 19th century slave village at Habitation Grande Pointe, in southern Basse-Terre, Guadeloupe, where I conducted archaeological mapping and testing in 2002. Fortunately, because the authors of the Habitation Guyoneau study, Fabrice Casagrande and Nathalie Serrand, were in discussions with me, and we visited with each other when possible, we each knew of the others work and recognized that our joint data make a stronger case for the pattern I had observed and identified in 2001.

1.4 Collaboration: hybrid vigor through contrasting approaches

Based upon 10 years worth of work on African Diaspora archaeological sites in the French West Indies, and through collaboration with a number of French archaeologists in Guadeloupe and Martinique, it is clear that both French and American methodologies have strengths and weaknesses, yet they can generate comparative, if not comparable, data sets. American methods, emphasizing hand excavation of closely controlled contexts permit the detailed exploration of activity areas and subtle changes through time, whereas the French methodologies employed in Martinique and Guadeloupe are very well suited to the exposure of larger areas of villages and the spatial arrangements within those areas. To use an analogy from biology, hybrid vigor, in our case the extra intellectual and interpretive strength that is achieved through the marrying of contrasting approaches, can be a very real product of our collaboration, and one that leads to increasingly complex and nuanced interpretations of the plantation archaeological data we recover.

Theoretical and methodological approaches are necessarily deeply intertwined, and research questions that drive archaeological work in by American researchers need to be articulated in ways that communicate those goals to non-American colleagues. Similarly, well defined research questions can be a central aspect of CRM oriented archaeological work as practiced in the French West Indies. It remains essential that archaeological research conducted in the French West Indies, whether by French or foreign nationals, takes into consideration the kinds of data that can potentially be recovered from plantation sites, and interrogates those data in light of historical and anthropological questions that require archaeological information for clarification. Only through the continued maintenance of an open dialogue between French and American practitioners can the strengths of these two approaches be brought together to compliment each other.

Acknowledgements

The research discussed in this chapter has been made possible through financial support from the Wenner-Gren Foundation for Anthropological Research (grant for work in Guadeloupe), the University of South Carolina (grants for work in Guadeloupe and Martinique), and through continued support by the Services Regional d'Archeologie in Guadeloupe and Martinique. Special thanks are due to the directors of the SRA in Guadeloupe, Antoine Chancerel, Marie-Armelle Paulet-Locard and Christian Stouvenot, and the directors of the SRA in Martinique, Olivier Kayser, Henri Marchesi, and Annie Noe-Dufour, and their staff. Thanks are also due to the many student volunteers who worked on these projects between 2001 and 2010, and without whom this could not have been completed. Thanks also to my French colleagues at INRAP who have always been very open about sharing the work they have been conducting. Without that open sharing, we cannot advance the state of our knowledge of plantations and slavery in the Caribbean.

References

Agorsah, E.K.

1993 Archaeology and Resistance History in the Caribbean. *The African Archaeological Review* 11: 175-195.

Armstrong, D.V.

1990 *The Old Village and the Great House: An Archaeological and Historical Examination of Drax Hall Plantation, St. Ann's Bay, Jamaica.* Urbana, University of Illinois Press.

Armstrong, D.V. and K.G. Kelly

2000 Settlement Patterns and the Origin of African Jamaican Society: Seville Plantation, St. Ann's Bay, Jamaica. *Ethnohistory* 47(2): 369-397.

Armstrong, D.V.

2003 *Creole Transformation from Slavery to Freedom: Historical Archaeology of the East End Community, St. John, Virgin Islands.* Gainesville, University Press of Florida.

Arrom, J. J., and M. Garcia-Arévalo

1986 *Cimarron.* Santo Domingo, Fundacion Garcia-Arévalo.

Barone-Visigalli, E.

2010 *Histoire et archéologie de la Guyane française: Les jésuites de la Comté. Habitations St. Régis et Maripa.* Matoury, Guyane, Ibis Rouge.

Barret, J.-B.

1989a Creve-Coeur, Sainte-Anne, Martinique--site d'archéologie industrielle. Rapport de fouille no. 2. Août-Sept 1989. Fort-de-France, Martinique, CERA.

Barret, J.-B.

1989b Archéologie historique du site de Creve-Coeur, Sainte-Anne, Martinique. Fort-de-France, Martinique, CERA.

Barret, J.-B.

1990 Creve-Coeur, Sainte-Anne, Martinique--site d'archéologie industrielle. Rapport de fouille no. 3. Janvier, Février, Mars 1990. Fort-de-France, Martinique.

Bégot, D.

1991 Les habitations-sucreries du littoral guadeloupéen et leur évolution. *Caribena* 1: 149-190.

Bégot, D., M. Pelletier and C. Bousquet-Bressolier

1998 *La Martinique de Moreau du Temple, 1770.* Paris, Editions du Comité des travaux historiques et scientifiques.

Bénot, Y. and M. Dorigny (editors)

2003 *Rétablissement de l'esclavage dans les colonies françaises.* Paris, Maisonneuve et Larose.

Bérard, B.

2004 *Les premières occupations agricoles de l'Arc Antillais: Migrations et insularité.* British Archaeological Reports, International series 1299, Paris mongraphs in American archaeology 15. Oxford: Archaeopress.

Bérard, B. and Ch. Stouvenot

2011 French West Indies. *Protecting Heritage in the Caribbean.* P. E. Siegel and E. Righter. Tuscaloosa, University of Alabama Press: 80-89.

Berthelot, J. and M. Gaumé

2002 *Kaz Antiyé jan moun ka rété.* Goyave, Guadeloupe, Editions Perspectives Créoles.

Blackburn, R.

1997 *The Making of New World Slavery: From the Baroque to the Modern, 1492-1800.* London, Verso.

Burnouf, J., D. Arribet-Deroin, B. Desachy, F. Journot and A. Nissen-Jaubert

2009 *Manuel d'Archéologie Médiéval et Moderne.* Paris, Armand Colin.

Casagrande, F.

2007 Saint-Claude "Bélost-La Diotte". Pessac, France, INRAP.

Casagrande, F. and N. Serrand

2008 Deshaies "Guyonneau, Rivière Forban". Pessac, France, INRAP.

CERA

1989 *Archéologie: Patrimoine de la Martinique. Fond Saint-Jacques 1.* Fort-de-France, Martinique, CERA.

Chapman, W.

1991 Slave Villages in the Danish West Indies: Changes of the late Eighteenth and early Nineteenth Centuries. In *Perspectives in Vernacular Architecture, IV* edited by T. Carter and Bernard L. Herman 108-120. Columbia, University of Missouri Press.

Charlery, Ch.

2004 Maisons de maître et habitations coloniales dans les anciens territoires français de l'Amérique tropicale. *In Situ: Revue de Patrimoines* 5: 1-55.

Courtaud, P., A. Delpuech and Th. Romon

1999 Archaeological Investigations at Colonial Cemeteries on Guadeloupe: African Slave Burial Sites or Not? In *African Sites Archaeology in the Caribbean* edited by J.B. Haviser 277-290. Princeton, NJ, Markus Wiener.

Courtaud, P. and Th. Romon

2004 Le Site d'Anse Sainte-Margeurite (Guadeloupe, Grande-Terre): Presentation d'un Cimetière d'Epoque Coloniale. *Journal of Caribbean Archaeology* Special Publication 1: 58-67.

Delpuech, A.

2001 Historical Archaeology in the French West Indies: Recent Research in Guadeloupe. In *Island Lives: Historical Archaeologies of the Caribbean* edited by Paul Farnsworth 21-59. Tuscaloosa, University of Alabama Press:

Delpuech, A.

2001 Archéologie historique en Guadeloupe. Une autre approche du passé antillais. *Bulletin de la Société d'Histoire de la Guadeloupe.* 129: 19-59.

Denise, C.

2004 Une histoire évolutive de l'habitat martiniquais. *In Situ: Revue de Patrimoines* 5: 1-8.

Dewar, H.

2010 Canada or Guadeloupe?: French and British Perceptions of Empire, 1760-1783. *Canadian Historical Review* 91(4): 637-660.

Dorigny, M.(ed.)

2003 *The Abolitions of Slavery: From Léger Félicité Sonthonax to Victor Schoelcher, 1793, 1794, 1848.* New York, Berghahn Books.

Dubois, L.

2004 *A Colony of Citizens: Revolution and Slave Emancipation in the French Caribbean, 1787-1804.* Chapel Hill, University of North Carolina Press.

England, S.

1994 Acculturation in the Creole Context: A Case Study of La Poterie, Martinique. Unpublished Ph.D dissertation, Department of Archaeology, University of Cambridge.

Farnsworth, P.(ed.)

2001 *Island Lives: Historical Archaeologies of the Caribbean.* Tuscaloosa, University of Alabama Press.

Gibson, H.R.

2007 Daily Practice and Domestic Economies in Guadeloupe: An Archaeological and Historical Study. Unpublished Ph.D. dissertation, Department of Anthropology, Syracuse University.

Grouard, S.

2001 Subsistence, technique systems and territoriality management in the pre-Columbian West Indies Islands: Vertebrate and crustacean exploitation during Saladoid and Troumassoid periods in Guadeloupe (400 BC to 1500 AD.). Unpublished Ph.D. dissertation, Université Nanterre.

Handler, J. S. and F. Lange

1978 *Plantation Slavery in Barbados: An Archaeological and Historical Investigation.* Cambridge, Harvard University Press.

Hauser, M.W.

2008 *An Archaeology of Black Markets: Local Ceramics and Economies in Eighteenth-Century Jamaica.* Gainesville, University Presses of Florida.

Hauser, M.W.

2011 Economic Networks and Landscapes of Production: Bois Cotlette, Dominica in the Early Nineteenth Century. *Proceedings of the XXII Congress of the International Association for Caribbean Archaeology.* St. Johns, Antigua.

Haviser, J. B. (ed.)

1999 *African Sites: Archaeology in the Caribbean.* Princeton NJ, Markus Wiener Publishers.

Hicks, D.

2007 *"The Garden of the World:" An Historical Archaeology of Sugar Landscapes in the Eastern Caribbean.* Oxford, Archaeopress.

Higman, B.W.

1988 *Jamaica Surveyed: Plantation Maps and Plans of the Eighteenth and Nineteenth Centuries.* Kingston, Institute of Jamaica Publications, Jamaica.

Higman, B.W.

1998 *Montpelier, Jamaica: A Plantation Community in Slavery and Freedom, 1739-1912.* Kingston, Jamaica, The Press University of the West Indies.

Journot, F. and G. Bellan

2011 *Archéologie de la France monderne et contemporaine.* Paris, La Découverte.

Kelly, K.G.

2002 African Diaspora Archaeology in Guadeloupe, French West Indies. *Antiquity* 76: 333-334.

Kelly, K.G.

2004 Historical Archaeology in the French Caribbean: An Introduction to a Special Volume of the Journal of Caribbean Archaeology. *Journal of Caribbean Archaeology* Special Issue No. 1: 1-10.

Kelly, K.G.

2008 Plantation archaeology in the French West Indies. *Rêves d'Amériques: Regard sur l'archéologie de la Nouvelle-France / Dreams of the Americas: Overview of New France Archaeology, Archéologiques* Hors série 2: 55-69.

Kelly, K.G.

2009 Where is the Caribbean? French Colonial Archaeology in the English Lake. *International Journal of Historical Archaeology* 13(1):80-93.

Kelly, K.G.

2011 *La Vie Quotidienne*: Historical Archaeological Approaches to the Plantation Era in Guadeloupe, French West Indies. In *French Colonial Archaeology in the Southeast and Caribbean* edited by K. G. Kelly and M.D. Hardy, pp. 189-205, Gainesville, University Press of Florida.

Kelly, K.G.

2014 *Les Rues Cases Nègres*: archaeology of slave life in the French West Indies. *Archaeology of Colonial Slavery*. Paris, La Découverte.

Kipple, W.E.

2001 Sugar Monoculture, Bovid Skeletal Part Frequencies, and Stable Carbon Isotopes. *Journal of Archaeological Science* 28: 1191-1198.

La Rosa Corzo, G.

2005 Subsistence of *Cimarrones*: An Archaeological Study. In *Dialogues in Cuban Archaeology*, edited by L. Antonio Curet, S.L. Dawdy and G. La Rosa Corzo, pp. 163-180, Tuscaloosa, University of Alabama Press.

Le Roux, Y.

1994 L'Habitation guyanaise sous l'Ancien Régime, Etude de la culture matérielle. Unpublished Ph.D. dissertation, Department of History, Ecole des Hautes Etudes, Paris.

Le Roux, Y., R. Auger and N. Cazelles

2009 *Les jésuites de l'esclavage Loyola: l'habitation des jésuites de Rémire en Guyane française*. Québec, Presses de l'Université du Québec.

Lenik, S.

2011 A Jesuit Plantation and Church in the Caribbean Frontier: Grand Bay, Dominica (1748-1763). *Proceedings of the XXIII Congress of the International Association for Caribbean Archaeology* 147-159. English Harbor, Antigua.

Lenik, S.

2012 Mission Plantations, Space, and Social Control: Jesuits as Planters in French Caribbean Colonies and Frontiers. *Journal of Social Archaeology* 12(1): 41-61.

Mañon-Arredondo, M.

1978 Importancia arqueología de los ingenios indo-hispanicos de las Antillas. *Boletín del Museo del Hombre Dominicano* 7(10): 139-164.

Pulsipher, L.M. and C.M. Goodwin

2001 "Getting the Essence of It:" Galways Plantation, Montserrat, West Indies. In *Island Lives: Historical Archaeologies of the Caribbean,* edited by P. Farnsworth, pp. 165-203, Tuscaloosa, University of Alabama Press.

Régent, F.

2004 *Esclavage, métissage, liberté: La Révolution française en Guadeloupe, 1789-1802.* Paris, Bernard Grasset.

Richard, G.

1998 L'Habitation caféière "La Grivelière" à Vieux Habitants, Guadeloupe. Paper presented at the Congrés National des Sociétés Historiques et Scientifiques Antilles Guyane, Fort-de-France, Martinique.

Siegel, P.E. and E. Righter, (editors)

2011 *Protecting Heritage in the Caribbean.* Tuscaloosa, University of Alabama Press.

Singleton, Th.

2005 An archaeological study of slavery on a Cuban coffee plantation. In *Dialogues in Cuban Archaeology,* edited by A. Curet, S. L. Dawdy and G. La Rosa Corzo, pp.181-199, Tuscaloosa, University of Alabama Press.

Ursulet, L.-C.

2004 L'Habitation Beauséjour: une plantation martiniquaise remarquable et pérenne. *In Situ: Revue de Patrimoines* 5: 1-8.

Vega, B.

1979 Arqueologia de los Cimarrones del Maniel del Bahoruco. *Boletín del Museo del Hombre Dominicano* 12: 11-48.

Weik, T.M.

1997 The Archaeology of Maroon Societies in the Americas: Resistance, Cultural Continuity, and Transformation in the African Diaspora. *Historical Archaeology* 31(2): 81-92.

Weik, T.M.

2012 *The Archaeology of Antislavery Resistance.* Gainesville, University Press of Florida.

Wilkie, L.A. and P. Farnsworth

2005 *Sampling Many Pots: An Archaeology of Memory and Tradition at a Bahamian Plantation.* Gainesville, University Press of Florida.

Woodward, R.P.

2006 Medieval Legacies: The Industrial Archaeology of an Early Sixteenth Century Sugar Mill at Sevilla la Nueva, Jamaica. Unpublished Ph.D. dissertation, Archaeology. Burnaby, BC, Simon Fraser University.

Woodward, R.P.

2011 Feudalism or Agrarian Capitalism? The Archaeology of the Early Sixteenth-Century Spanish Sugar Industry. In *Out of Many, One People: The Historical Archaeology of Colonial Jamaica,* edited by J. A. Delle, M. Hauser and D. V. Armstrong, pp. 23-40, Tuscaloosa, University of Alabama Press.

Chapter 2

Archaeological Investigations at Betty's Hope Plantation, Antigua

Some preliminary thoughts on theory

Prof. Dr. Georgia L. Fox

Department of Anthropology
California State University
Chico
gfox@csuchico.edu

Abstract

This paper proposes two *preliminary* working models for historical archaeology and Caribbean plantation archaeology at Betty's Hope Plantation, Antigua: Niche Construction Theory, and a modification of World System's Theory, Hornby and Crumley's earth system/world system model, both which seek to understand the impact of human populations on their ecological and developmental environments. In this instance, the environment is the island plantation system of the Eastern Caribbean, with special emphasis on Betty's Hope, which serves as a work-in-progress case study.

Résumé

Cet article propose deux modèles préliminaires de travail pour l'archéologie historique et l'archéologie des plantations Caraïbes à la plantation Betty Hope, Antigua : La Théorie de la construction de niche, ainsi qu'une modification de la théorie du système monde, la théorie du système terre/système monde de Hornby et Crumley. Toutes deux cherchent à comprendre l'impact des populations humaines sur leur environnement écologique et de développement. Dans le cas présent, l'environnement est le système de la plantation insulaire dans la Caraïbe orientale, avec un accent particulier sur le site de Betty Hope, qui sert d'étude de cas.

Resumen

Este documento propone dos modelos de trabajo preliminar para la arqueología histórica y la arqueología del Caribe plantación en Hope Plantation Betty, Antigua: Teoría de la Construcción de nicho, y una modificación del sistema de análisis del mundo, Hornby y la tierra Crumley sistema / modelo del sistema mundial, tanto, que buscan comprender el impacto de las poblaciones humanas en sus ambientes ecológicos y de desarrollo. En este caso, el medio ambiente es el sistema de plantación isla del Caribe Oriental, con especial énfasis en la esperanza de Betty, que sirve como un caso de estudio con el trabajo en curso.

Keywords

Caribbean, Antigua, historical archaeology, plantation, Niche Construction Theory, World Systems Theory

Mots-clés

Caraïbes, Antigua, archéologie historique, plantation, théorie de la construction de niche, système d'analyse du monde

Palabras clave

Caribe, Antigua, arqueología histórica, plantación, Teoría de la Construcción de nicho, sistema de análisis del mundo

2.1 Introduction

The purpose of this paper is to provide a brief overview of recent investigations at Betty's Hope Plantation, Antigua, within the context of preliminary theoretical perspectives in which to frame our work. This paper is by no means a definitive account of the current work at Betty's Hope; rather, this is an attempt to develop alternative approaches to Caribbean plantation archaeology and historical archaeology, with Betty's Hope serving as a case study. The two theoretical perspectives we are exploring are Niche Construction Theory (NCT) and an environmental modification of Wallerstein's World's System Theory (WST). Both are mutually exclusive, but when combined, can offer a broad approach to understanding the Caribbean sugar plantation in all of its complexity.

The first model, Niche Construction Theory (NCT), provides a multifaceted palette in which to analyze the cumulative effects and impacts of human activities on the colonial Caribbean landscape. As Laland and O'Brien (2010: 315) observe, NCT, usually the domain of evolutionary biology, can be useful to archaeologists because "it encourages us to think beyond climate, instability, and an external environment as causes of evolutionary events and to quantify and incorporate human activities as active variables in driving both environmental change and human evolution."

Key among such considerations is the role of human-induced change on the landscape (Laland & O'Brien 2010: 314). Niche Construction Theory therefore allows for a "biologically and culturally informed conceptual framework suited to the human sciences—one that recognizes the active agency of humans as part causes of their own development, history, and evolution....[including] a rich material culture" (Laland & O'Brien 2010: 318).

The second theoretical framework, a modification of Wallerstein's model as proposed by Alf Hornberg and Carole Crumley (2007) in their edited volume, *The World System and the Earth System: Global Socioenvironmental Change and Sustainability since the Neolithic,* illustrates the web of far-reaching consequences resulting from human impacts on the landscape. A prime example of this can be seen in the human dependency on sugar. Once cane became the chief agricultural commodity in the Caribbean, the whole process of agricultural initiatives in the English Caribbean colonies—the sugar plantocracy, the importation of African slaves, and the maintenance of the whole industrial system, resulting from human engineering of the landscape—led to a series of developments that set in motion a wave of actions that had repercussions throughout the Atlantic World.

2.2 The site

Known for its fertile soils, Betty's Hope is situated in the Central Plain of Antigua. The plantation has existed since 1651, but became the property of Christopher Codrington I in 1674, and remained in the Codrington family until its sale in 1944. Under the aegis of the Betty's Hope Trust, the site still has extant buildings, such as two prominent windmills, part of the still house, cisterns, and a Visitor's Center. The starting point for excavations began with the Great House in 2007. Because the house had not survived, not much is known about it. This, along with the importance of the plantation to the island's history and its connection to the English sugar plantocracy of the Eastern Caribbean—of which the Codrington family figured prominently— provided further impetus to excavate the house, which served as the site's base of operations and functioned as the seat of English government in the Caribbean from 1688 to 1704.

Archaeological research at Betty's Hope has been further enhanced through the copious documentary record in the form of the Codrington Papers, housed in the Archives of Antigua and Barbuda, which contains almost 300 years' worth of correspondence, ledgers, and accounts, by the Codrington family. In the six field seasons of archaeological excavations, the size, extent, and complexity of the plantation is only beginning to reveal itself as extensive shovel tests, mapping and surveying and remote sensing have been conducted. Concentrated efforts in GPS and GIS mapping of the site has proved to be infinitely useful in determining the spatial outlay of the plantation, as this methodology has for other researchers working in the Caribbean (see Armstrong 2001). As with most long-term occupations, Betty's Hope experienced modifications in response to changes in technology, the vagaries and unpredictability of climate and weather, and availability of slave and free labor. This is partly evidenced by discernible changes in the form of repairs and upgrades throughout the site, as in the visible repair of a large crack in the main windmill, and an add-on to the recently excavated kitchen. Artifacts site-wide are predominantly eighteenth-century, with seventeenth-century and nineteenth and early twentieth-century cultural material occurring at both ends of the time spectrum. Most of the artifacts are comparable to other English colonial sites in the Caribbean comprising imported ceramics such as transferwares, Chinese porcelain, coarse earthenwares, German stonewares, as well as musket balls and gunflints, children's toys, buttons, sewing notions, iron implements, and an extensive collection of faunal remains that are in the early stages of analyses. Extensive archaeological remains have been found in the form of architectural elements such as hand-wrought nails, lead caulking, window glass, some painted wood, and large iron bolts, as well as window shutter pins, and painted plaster. One of the most rewarding aspects of archaeology at Betty's Hope has been the architecture of the Great House through the discovery of seventeenth-century foundational structural walls built from large, hand-carved limestone blocks imported from the British Isles, as well as locally carved limestone. Well-laid flooring in the form of imported brick and tile from Britain has also been recovered at the site. More architectural features in the form of walls and floors identified during shovel tests conducted in 2012 were located north of the Great House, and would have comprised part of the "Great House Complex" of support buildings, such as the servant's quarters, overseer's office, and blacksmith shop. The area of slave housing has not yet been located. However, tantalizing clues in the form of Afro-Antiguan wares, phosphate testing results, with GPS and GIS mapping are providing hints of the location.

2.3 Theoretical approaches to studying Betty's Hope

2.3.1 Niche Construction Theory

Although there is still much to be done at the site, what is evolving from our excavations is a greater appreciation of the plantation's impact on the landscape. Careful mapping of the known features at the site using GPS survey and GIS overlays to the original Codrington maps of 1710 and 1755 offer clues into the spatial dynamics of land use at Betty's Hope. What is emerging is a dialectic between three centuries of perceived ideas about agricultural production and how humans, as active agents of change, create unintended consequences on the landscape.

Archaeological evidence from a sugar plantation and its environs can contribute to our understanding of the consequences resulting from the actions and decisions made over almost three centuries of concentrated land use that created a host of new selective pressures caused by intensive agriculture. As O'Brien and Laland (2012: 436) observe, Niche Construction Theory (NCT) can provide a way of understanding how human trade-offs can transform and deeply affect the stability, and connectivity of ecosystems and the ways in which human activity can destroy such webs of connectivity. This is especially relevant, as "culturally derived selection pressures can be stronger than noncultural ones"

(O'Brien & Laland 2012: 437). This is especially apparent when a deliberate choice is made on one dominant crop, sugar, which can crowd out other species and organisms (see Eerkens & Lipo 2005; Laland & Brown 2002). Although NCT has been primarily used in recent research into the origins of agriculture and the domestication of plants and animals, agriculture during the colonial period offers an avenue to view the connections between the actions of the sugar planters and the ecological impacts on such islands as Antigua, which have finite resources (Shipman 2010; Smith 2007; Zeder 2008; Zeder et al. 2006). As Riede notes (Riede 2012: 87, 93), humans are "extraordinarily potent niche constructors" whose activities can be documented through the archaeological record, where "the interplay between the human physical, social and cognitive worlds... all happen within environmental contexts." In island contexts, ecosystems can be especially vulnerable, as "whole ecosystems can be transported from one locale to another," which Kirch refers to as "transported landscapes" (Kirch 1997: 217; Riede 2012: 92). In the mental template of the colonial sugar planter, notions of agricultural productivity were imposed on the surrounding, albeit alien landscape (Martin 1785; Blanton 2003: 190-191; Meltzer 2003: 223-224).

As an industrial complex located on a small island, a sugar plantation like Betty's Hope, was "an interrelated aggregate of human experience" that exceeded the boundaries of the tropical Americas (Curtain 1996: xii). Originally over 700 acres in size and with a labor force of 300-400 slaves at its peak, Betty's Hope was one of the largest plantations on Antigua (Dyde 2000: 30). Vast fields of sugar production, a host of buildings, slave quarters, domestic animal pens, and rainwater cisterns present a considerable array of influences affecting the health of the humans and other organisms who shared this space. The impact on the landscape is further intensified by the introduction of non-native species, prevailing agricultural practices, impacts on soil nutrients, deforestation, concentration on a singular crop, management of water and livestock, and the alteration of the landscape from roadways and shifts in population, all of which could adversely affect fragile island ecosystems on Antigua. Such impacts would undoubtedly create new selection pressures upon island ecosystems, and for the archaeologist, offer another way to view plantation life and material culture through the prisms of biology and social agency.

To determine which factors had specific impacts requires a deep-time study of the landscape at Betty's Hope through the careful study of the flora and fauna of both past and present. This will require a multidisciplinary approach, comparing the archaeological record with documentary evidence, and research in palynology, climatology, bioarchaeology, and other relevant disciplines. In our research at Betty's Hope, a multifaceted approach chronicling rainfall patterns, drought, and climate, as well as deforestation, soil erosion and depletion, and the enormous expenditure of both human and natural resources can only contribute to a much broader and holistic understanding of Antigua and Caribbean landscapes pre- and post-Contact. For example, in comparing the archaeological evidence to the archival record, concerns about drought were dramatically manifest in two ways at Betty's Hope: 1) through the existing extensive and impressive water catchment system; and 2) in the form of annual rainfall tabulations and numerous references to drought in the Codrington Papers. For instance, in an 1872 correspondence to Sir Gerald Codrington from George Holborow, the attorney for the Codrington estates, Holborow remarks "I am sorry to have again to report a dry fortnight, the Island looks drier even than when you left. There is hardly anything green to be seen."

Ironically, the wholesale destruction of island forests to clear the way for cane agriculture partially shaped the very drought conditions that caused so much anxiety for the planters. How much deforestation does it take to create such conditions and what were the biological repercussions? These are questions that archaeologists, along with colleagues in other disciplines, can begin to address for the colonial period within the NCT framework. Environmental reconstructions hold promise in addressing such questions. Although environmental reconstructions have predominated in prehistoric archaeology, historical archaeology is well suited for such types of investigations. Drawing upon the groundbreaking work of Pulsipher (1986), *Watts (1987), Fitzpatrick* & Keegan (2007), Kirch (2009), *and especially Dan Hicks' recent excellent monograph (2007: 1-9),* a solid basis for environmental archaeology and historical ecology for the colonial period can be established. Environmental reconstructions for parts of the Caribbean and Antigua and Barbuda are slowly emerging through careful data collection and analysis by archaeologists, paleobotanists, palynologists, and others, including a very exciting study on Barbuda by Sophia Perdikaris and her colleagues. In this regard, preliminary data from a 6-meter deep core sample taken by Peter Siegel and John Jones from Ayer's Creek, a drainage near Betty's Hope, indicates an extremely high rate of sedimentation over several hundred years, suggesting an overuse of terrestrial resources, deforestation, and erosion (Jones, pers. com. 2012).

In 2009, a mortar sample taken from Betty's Hope was analyzed by Jones, and found to include various taxons of invasive grasses, including cane, as well as other non-native species. Results for pre-Contact forest species from deep coring samples taken on Antigua will be forthcoming by Jones, Siegel, and their colleagues, so the final results are currently pending. Further coring is planned for the area around Betty's Hope, as well as more survey work, which will aid in determining changes to the land. Core samples and sedimentary analysis from Mercer's Creek, which lies just slightly northeast of Betty's Hope and is the main watershed/creek area for the plantation, hold promise as our research continues. Another facet of a multidisciplinary research entails the human costs from a sociobiological perspective. The enslaved Africans of Betty's Hope negotiated a world of diet and disease, as they coped with the plantation's environmental conditions. Betty's Hope was one of the key locations for the origins of Antigua's 1736 slave revolt "conspiracy", as discussed by Gaspar (1985). Although slavery itself was certainly cause enough for revolt, human suffering from nutritional deficiencies and related diseases may have partially contributed to the overall effort to slave resistance. As Corruccini et al. (1982) and Varney (2007, 2011) demonstrate, research in bioarchaeology holds great potential in helping to elucidate possible connections between colonial Caribbean natural and constructed environments and the health of the people who inhabited the region.

2.3.2 The World System/Earth System Model

Complementing the Niche Construction model is an ecological modification of Wallerstein's World System's Theory (Wallerstein 1974), which is also updated and enhanced by NCT. In this case, a modification of Wallerstein's model as proposed by Hornberg and Crumley (2007), known as the world system/earth system model, examines how humans, through social and economic actions, impact their environments in a much wider web. This is accomplished through a set of mechanisms that redistributes resources from the periphery to the core, the *core* being the developed center of power and the *periphery* being the underdeveloped area that is exploited for its raw materials. In this case, the core was London (and later Bristol), and the periphery consisted of the New World colonies such as Antigua, where Betty's Hope is located. Peripheral areas are divided into two zones, the semi-peripheral or middle zone, containing some of the attributes of both the core and the periphery, and the larger outlying periphery, characterized by its labor-intensive production and simple technologies (Eisenmenger & Giljum 2007: 293).

In the case of England and its colonies, the development of this commercial arrangement relied heavily on London's economic, social, and, political capital (Abel 2007: 56). In the drive toward wealth accumulation in the early modern period, the outward flow of goods from London to the colonies made London the central hub to the growing colonies, thus creating a relationship of dependency at both ends, usually eliminating a semi-periphery. Within this system, Wallerstein (1980) identifies four temporal features (stages). The first comprises *cyclical rhythms*, that is, short-term fluctuations of economy, while *secular trends* refer to the deep long-term trends, such as general economic growth or decline. Another temporal feature is the concept of *underconsumption*, whereby short-term profits can produce glut, which then undermines the health of an economy by reducing both wages and the demand for a product. The last temporal feature is *crisis*, which can severely impact the system, resulting in chaos to the point of collapse.

How the world system/earth system model informs the work at Betty's Hope and complements NCT is through understanding the wider implications of cane agriculture. With multiple trade routes connecting England with the Eastern seaboard colonies, Africa, and the Caribbean, a host of factors converged, linking "slavery, plantation agriculture, mining...[and] forestry" that would affect human societies and their ecosystems in this intricate web of relationships (Frank 2007: 315).

Here the world system meets the earth system, as marked by increasing socioenvironmental change on a broader scale. As spatial entities, ecosystems are not static. As natural open systems of energy, ecosystems exhibit fluctuations and are therefore subject to both mild and dramatic transformations (Abel 2007: 57-58). In relation to human societies and culture change, anthropologists have long recognized the interplay between humans and their environment as part of human ecology (Butzer 1982; Alvard 2003). These relationships can be cyclical in nature and are characterized by dynamic fluctuations and feedback loops (Hall & Turchin 2007: 74-75). In the integration of the world system's concept with the human-environmental connection through large-scale environmental change, the cyclical aspects of both systems can be traced through almost three centuries. Here, Wallerstein's *cyclical rhythms* and *secular trends* of a successful agricultural enterprise play out, sometimes resulting in a state of crisis. As Delle (1996: 48) argues, part of the problem in the core-periphery relationship is that even though parties at both ends aim for greater production and wealth accumulation in the system, their modes of strategy may vary and conflict, resulting in Wallenstein's predicted *crisis* phase, when competitive actors foreground their own objectives to the exclusion of others. In the developing capitalist world system, a crisis phase could be further exacerbated by environmental change and ecological devastation throughout the Caribbean region. The human desire for sugar took its toll. As an unsustainable institution, the sugar plantation system led to great human suffering of enslaved Africans, considerable pressures on island ecosystems, and the eventual decline and collapse of the plantation system itself. The question is, had beet sugar not replaced sugar cane on the world market, how much longer could cane agriculture be sustained on these Caribbean islands? It can be argued that because cane agriculture was unsustainable, collapse was inevitable, but the planters either did not see it coming, or maybe they did and cut their losses, particularly after emancipation, when they no longer had a labor force they could depend on and or control.

2.4 Conclusion

The legacy of sugar and its impact on the landscape is still felt today. With the collapse of the sugar plantation economy, many Caribbean nations have struggled with the post-colonial realities of transitioning from sugar to tourism and other industries. It can also be argued that weather patterns in the present-day Caribbean have been sufficiently impacted by earlier deforestation. Combined with global climate change, such long-term impacts have yet to be fully assessed. As archaeologists, we search for the linkages between dynamic systems and subsystems of human-environmental relationships and historical events that play out over time. Caribbean sugar plantations offer a wide spectrum and unique opportunity to investigate colonial landscapes from a holistic perspective. By proposing two work-in-progress frameworks, Niche Construction Theory, and the world system/ earth system model, investigations of a sugar plantation like Betty's Hope can helps us conceptualize and understand the sugar plantation in all of its manifestations and complexities, as well as the socioecological transformations that played out in the English Caribbean and in the wider Atlantic world beyond.

Acknowledgements

I would like to thank Dr. Reginald Murphy and Nicki Murphy for their generous and continued support to conduct research at Betty's Hope Plantation.

References

Abel, T.

2007 World-Systems as Complex Human Ecosystems. In *The World System and the Earth System*, edited by A. Hornborg and C. Crumley, pp. 56-73. Left Coast Press, Walnut Creek.

Alvard, M.S.

2003 The Adaptive Nature of Culture. *Evolutionary Anthropology* 12: 136-149.

Armstrong, D.V.

2001 A Venue for Autonomy: Archaeology of a Changing Cultural Landscape, the East End Community, St. John, Virgin Islands. In *Island Lives: Historical Archaeologies of the Caribbean*, edited by P. Farnsworth, pp.142-164. University of Alabama Press, Tuscaloosa.
Blanton, D.B.

2003 The Weather is Fine, Wish you Were Here, Because I'm the Last One Alive: "Learning" the Environment in the English New World Colonies. In *Colonization of Unfamiliar Landscapes: The Archaeology of Adaptation,* edited by J. Rockman and J. Steele, pp. 190-200. Routledge, London.

Butzer, K.W.

1982 *Archaeology as Human Ecology: Method and Theory for a Contextual Approach.* Cambridge University Press, Cambridge.

Codringon Papers

1872 Correspondence to Sir Gerald Codrington from George Holborow. June 11. Roll C-56, National Archives of Antigua and Barbuda.

Curtin, P.D.

1998 *The Rise and Fall of the Plantation Complex.* Cambridge University Press, New York.

Delle, J.A.

1996 An Archaeology of Crisis: The Manipulation of Social Spaces in the Blue Mountain Coffee Plantation Complex of Jamaica, 1790-1865. Ph.D. Dissertation, University of Amherst. University Microfilms, Ann Arbor.

Dyde, B.

2000 *A History of Antigua: The Unsuspected Isle.* MacMillan Education, Ltd., London.

Eisenmenger, N. and S. Giljum

2007 Evidence from Societal Metabolism Studies for Ecological Unequal Trade. In *The World System and the Earth System,* edited by A. Hornborg and C. Crumley, pp. 288-302. Left Coast Press, Walnut Creek.

Eerkens, J. W. and C. P. Lipo

2005 Cultural Transmission, Copying Errors, and the Generation of Variation in the Archaeological Record. *Journal of Anthropological Archaeology* 24: 316–334.

Fitzpatrick, S.M. and W.F. Keegan

2007 Human Impacts and Adaptations in the Caribbean Islands: an Historical Ecology Approach. *Earth and Environmental Science Transactions of the Royal Society of Edinburgh* 98: 29-45.

Frank, A.G.

1978 *World Accumulation, 1492-1789.* Monthly Review Press, New York.

2007 Entropy Generation and Displacement: the Nineteenth-Century Multilateral Network of World Trade. In *The World System and the Earth System,* edited by A. Hornborg and C. Crumley, pp. 303-316. Left Coast Press, Walnut Creek.

Gaspar, D.B.

1985 *Bondmen and Rebels: a Study of Master-Slave Relations in Antigua.* Duke University Press, Durham.

Hall, T.D. and P. Turchin

2007 Lessons from Population Ecology for World Systems Analyses of Long-Distance Synchrony. In *The World System and the Earth System,* edited by A. Hornborg and C. Crumley, pp. 74-90. Left Coast Press, Walnut Creek.

Corruccini, R., J.S. Handler, R.J. Mutaw and F.W. Lange

1982 Osteology of a Slave Burial Population from Barbados, West Indies. *American Journal of Physical Anthropology* 59: 443-459.

Hicks, D.

2007 *'The Garden of the World: 'An Historical Archaeology of Sugar Landscapes in the Eastern Caribbean.* British Archaeological Series 1632, Oxford.

Hornberg, A. and C. Crumley (editors)

2007 *The World System and the Earth System: Global Socioenvironmental Change and Sustainability since the Neolithic.* Left Coast Press, Walnut Creek.

Kirch, P.V.

2009 *Island Societies: Archaeological Approaches to Evolution and Transformation.* Cambridge University Press, Cambridge.

1997 *The Lapita Peoples. Ancestors of the Oceanic World.* Blackwell, Oxford.

Laland, K.N. and G.R. Brown

2002 *Sense and Nonsense: Evolutionary Perspectives on Human Behaviour.* Oxford University Press, Oxford.

Laland, K.N. and M.J. O'Brien

2010 Niche Construction Theory and Archaeology. *Journal of Archaeological Method Theory* 17: 303–322.

Martin, S.

1785 *An Essay on Plantership*. Printed by Robert Mearns, Antigua.

Meltzer, D.

2003 Lessons in Landscape Learning. In *Colonization of Unfamiliar Landscapes: The Archaeology of Adaptation,* edited by J. Rockman and J. Steele, pp. 222-241. Routledge, London.

O'Brien, M.J. and K.N. Laland

2012 Genes, Culture, and Agriculture: An Example of Human Niche Construction. *Current Anthropology* 53(4): 434-470.

Pulsipher, L.

1986 *Seventeenth-Century Montserrat: An Environmental Impact Statement.* Historical Geography Research Series 17: GeoBooks, Norwich, England.

Riede, F.

2012 Theory for the A-Theoretical: Niche Construction Theory and its Implications for Environmental Archaeology. In *N-TAG TEN, Proceedings of the 10th Nordic TAG Conference at Stiklestad, Norway 2009,* edited by R. Berge, M. E. Jasinski, and K. Sognnes, pp. 87-98. British Archaeological Reports 2399, Archaeopress, Oxford.

Shipman, P.

2010. The Animal Connection and Human Evolution. *Current Anthropology* 51: 1–20.

Smith, B.D.

2007 Niche Construction and the Behavioral Context of Plant and Animal Domestication. *Evolutionary Anthropology* 16:188–199.

Varney, T.L.

2011 The Royal Naval Hospital cemetery at English Harbour, Antigua: Not Just the "Grave of the Englishman," pp. 291-300. *Proceedings of the XXIII International Congress for Caribbean Archaeology*, Antigua.

2007 Does Diet Reflect Group Membership? A Stable Isotope Analysis of Human Remains from the Royal Naval Hospital emetery at English Harbour, Antigua, W.I., pp. 667-676. *Proceedings of the XXI International Congress for Caribbean Archaeology,* Trinidad, 2005.

Wallerstein, I.

1974 *The Modern World System.* Academic Press, New York.

1980 *The Modern World System II. Mercantilism and the Consolidation of the European World Economy, 1600-1750.* Academic Press, New York.

Watts, D.

1987 *The West Indies: Patterns of Development, Culture, and Environmental Change since 1492.* Cambridge University Press, Cambridge.

Zeder, M. A.

2008 Domestication and Early Agriculture in the Mediterranean Basin: Origins, Diffusion, and Impact. *Proceedings of the National Academy of Sciences* 105(33): 11597-11604.

Zeder, M. A., Bradley, D. G., Emshwiller, E. and B. D. Smith (editors)

2006 Documenting Domestication: New Genetic and Archaeological Paradigms. University of California Press, Berkeley.

Chapter 3

Slave Community Food ways on a French Colonial Plantation

Zooarchaeology at Habitation Crève Cœur, Martinique

Diane Wallman

Ph.D. Candidate
Department of Anthropology
University of South Carolina
Columbia
South Carolina
dianewallman@gmail.com

Abstract

This research explores how a slave community on a French colonial plantation learned, adjusted, formulated, and expressed a distinct conception of their material needs through everyday subsistence practices, despite the extreme constraints of slavery. To address this objective, I critically integrate archaeologically recovered faunal remains and historical data from 18th and 19th century slave and post-emancipation Afro-Caribbean household deposits on the plantation site of Habitation Crève Cœur. Crève Cœur is situated in the commune of St. Anne on the island of Martinique in the Lesser Antilles. Since 2005, Dr. Kenneth Kelly from the University of South Carolina and his team have completed four seasons of archaeological research at Crève Cœur to examine the material vestiges of slave life. This work has delineated discrete and largely undisturbed slave occupations on the terraced slopes of the hill located above and behind the maison de maître, including well-preserved faunal remains. My project relies on an environmental archaeology methodology, specifically zooarchaeology, coupled with historical data to investigate the system of food procurement, processing/preparation, distribution, preservation, consumption, and discard. Laboratory analyses included identification, age and size assessment, quantification and taphonomic evaluation of the assemblage of faunal remains recovered from sub-surface survey and excavation. These data reveal that through the everyday practice of food acquisition, production and consumption, the enslaved laborers at Crève Cœur improved the material conditions of life, despite the severe limitations of plantation slavery. Through these practices, the slaves formulated the skills, knowledge and social relations that contributed to the transformation of individuals with disparate histories into an intergenerational community with a shared heritage.

Résumé

Cette recherche explore la manière dont une communauté esclave sur une plantation coloniale française a appris, ajusté, formulé et exprimé une conception distincte de leurs besoins matériels par des pratiques de subsistance quotidienne, en dépit des contraintes extrêmes de l'esclavage. Pour atteindre cet objectif, j'intégre les restes fauniques et des données historiques concernant les esclaves au XVIIIe et XIXe siècles et les dépôts post-émancipation des ménages afro-antillais sur le site de plantation Habitation Crève Cœur. Crève Cœur est situé dans la commune de Sainte-Anne sur l'île de la Martinique dans les Petites Antilles. Depuis 2005, le Dr Kenneth Kelly de l'Université de Caroline du Sud et son équipe ont effectué quatre saisons de la recherche archéologique à Crève Cœur afin d'examiner les vestiges matériels de la vie des esclaves. Ce travail a permis de délimiter l'emplacement d'un village d'esclave relativement peu perturbé sur les pentes en terrasses de la colline située au-dessus et derrière la maison de maître, ce bon degré de conservation concerne entre autres les restes osseux. Mon projet repose sur l'archéozoologie, couplée à des données historiques pour enquêter sur le système d'approvisionnement, la transformation ou la préparation, la distribution, la conservation, la consommation, et le rejet des aliments. Les analyses de laboratoire comprennent l'identification des espèces, l'âge et l'évaluation de la taille des individus, la quantification et l'évaluation taphonomique de l'assemblage des restes de faune récupérés lors de la fouille. Ces données révèlent que par la pratique quotidienne d'acquisition des aliments, de production et de consommation, les travailleurs asservis à Crève Cœur on pu améliorer leur conditions matérielles de vie malgré les limitations liées à la nature du système de la plantation esclavagiste. Grâce à ces pratiques, les esclaves ont pu développer des compétences, des connaissances et des relations sociales qui ont contribué à la transformation d'individus ayant des antécédents disparates en une communauté intergénérationnelle liée par un patrimoine commun.

Resumen

Esta investigación explora cómo una comunidad de esclavos en una plantación colonial francesa aprendió, formularse, y expresó una concepción clara de sus necesidades materiales a través de prácticas de subsistencia cotidiana, a pesar de las limitaciones extremas de esclavitud. Para abordar este objetivo, he integrado restos arqueológicos de fauna y datos históricos de depósitos de los hogares afro-caribeños en el sitio de plantación de Vivienda Creve Coeur de los siglos 18 y 19. Creve Coeur está situado en la region de Santa Ana en la isla de Martinica en las Antillas Menores. Desde 2005, el Dr. Kenneth Kelly de la Universidad de Carolina del Sur y su equipo han completado cuatro temporadas de investigación arqueológica en Creve Coeur para examinar los vestigios materiales de la vida de esclavos. Este trabajo ha delineado las ocupaciones del esclavo discreto y tranquilo en gran medida de las laderas en terrazas de la colina situada por encima y por detrás de la maison de maître, incluyendo fauna bien conservados. Mi proyecto se basa en zooarqueología, junto con los datos históricos para investigar el sistema de adquisición de alimentos, elaboración / preparación, distribución, conservación, consumo y descarte. Los análisis de laboratorio incluyeron la identificación, edad y tamaño de la evaluación, cuantificación y evaluación tafonómica del conjunto de restos de fauna recuperados de estudio del subsuelo y excavaciones. Estos datos revelan que a través de la práctica cotidiana de la adquisición de alimentos, la producción y el consumo, los trabajadores esclavizados en Creve Coeur mejoraron sus condiciones materiales de vida, a pesar de las graves limitaciones de la esclavitud en las plantaciones. A través de estas prácticas, los esclavos desarollaron las habilidades, el conocimiento y las relaciones sociales que contribuyeron a la transformación de los individuos con historias dispares en una comunidad intergeneracional con un patrimonio compartido.

Keywords

slavery, zooarchaeology, foodways, plantation archaeology

Mots-clés

esclavage, zooarchéologie, les habitudes alimentaires, l'archéologie des plantations

Palabras clave

la esclavitud, zooarqueología, costumbres alimenticias, la arqueología de las plantaciones

3.1 Introduction

This research examines the everyday practice of food acquisition, production and consumption of the enslaved laborers on a French colonial plantation, to reveal how a community of slaves improved the material conditions of life, despite the severe constraints of plantation slavery. To address this objective I aim to identify the primary and interrelated factors influencing foodways within the slave community, as I integrate archaeologically recovered faunal remains and historical evidence from 18th and 19th century slave and post-emancipation Afro-Caribbean household deposits on the plantation site of *Habitation Crève Cœur* on Martinique. This study relies on zooarchaeological methodology, coupled with historical data. This methodology archaeologically investigates the system of food procurement, processing/preparation, distribution, preservation, consumption, and discard;

a series of practices defined in the anthropological literature as "foodways" or "cuisine" (Farb and Armelagos 1980; Douglas 1984; Goody 1982; Mintz and DuBois 2002).

In this chapter, I first address the research orientation of my dissertation project and then present preliminary findings from the project on zooarchaeological analyses completed at the *Muséum National d'Histoire Naturelle* (MNHN) in Paris, France. Data analyses and quantification of the faunal assemblage are in progress, but these initial results clearly indicate that the slave community at Crève Cœur developed a highly diverse system of foodways utilizing resources available on the landscape both within and beyond the plantation boundaries.

Crève Cœur is a critical resource for reconstructing the history of slavery, and the realities of slave life due to excellent preservation conditions at the site, and because it is one of the few French Caribbean sugar estates to be investigated by archaeologists. The plantation operated from the mid 18th through 19th centuries, primarily for the production of sugar and its byproducts for export to the *métropole* and the French colonies. The site contains standing ruins of industrial buildings, the *maison de maître* (the planter's house/great house), outbuildings associated with sugar production and storage, material deposits of slave occupations and is situated on public lands used by the local commune government as a site for heritage awareness and tourism (Kelly 2008: 396). Archival research to date has not yet located the exact founding date, but the plantation first appears on the Carte Moreau du Temple in 1770 (Figure 1), as a sugar estate, with extensive industrial

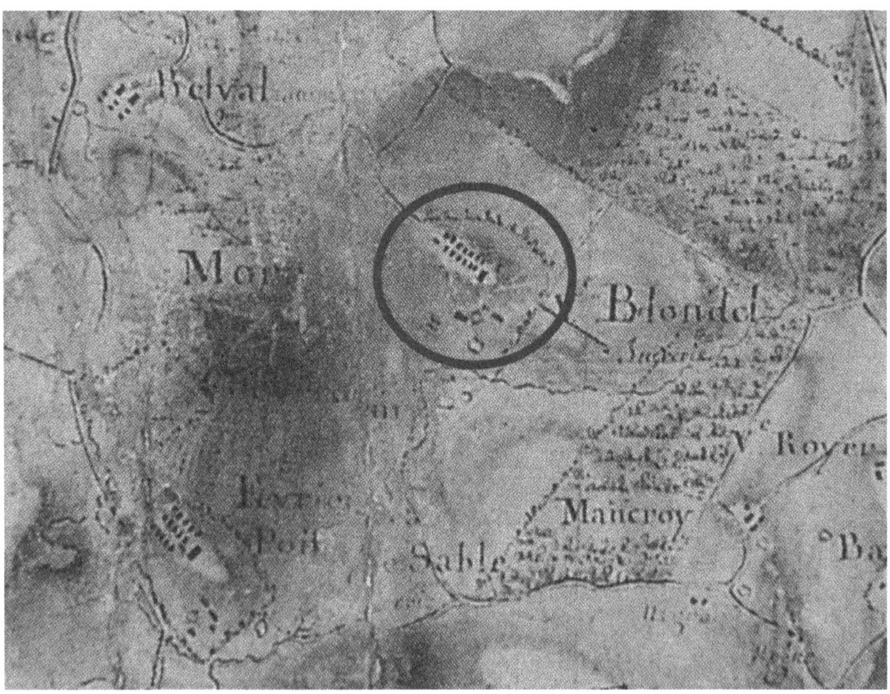

Figure 1. Crève Cœur, Carte Moreau du Temple in 1770 (Bousquet-Bressolier et al. 1998).

buildings, an animal mill, the *maison de maître*, and a row of at least fourteen slave houses (Bousquet-Bressolier et al. 1998). Beginning in 2005, Dr. Kenneth Kelly from the University of South Carolina directed four seasons of archaeological research at Habitation Crève Cœur to address the creation of Creole cultures in the French West Indies through an investigation of the material vestiges of everyday life, with a particular focus on reconstructing the lifeways of enslaved laborers (Kelly 2008: 392).

Excavations have delineated discrete and largely undisturbed slave household occupations on the terraced slopes of the hill located above and behind the *maison de maître*, including well-preserved faunal remains. The deposits date from the initial operation of the plantation in the late 18th century through the post-emancipation (1848) period on the island, allowing for a diachronic perspective of the community from slavery to freedom. Excellent preservation conditions at the site allowed for the recovery of over 10,000 specimens of fauna, which is comparable to or larger than other faunal assemblages recovered from Caribbean colonial slave contexts (Armstrong 1990; Higman 1998; Klippel 2001; Wilkie & Farnsworth 2005).

This research contributes to archaeological and anthropological investigations of colonialism and cultural transformations during slavery as it begins to deconstruct the local material expressions of larger historical processes. While most New World plantation archaeology focuses on British colonial sites (Armstrong & Hauser 2009; c.f. Delpeuch 2001 and Waselkov 2009), this project provides a novel context, focusing on the understudied historical period in the French West Indies. Archaeology at Crève Cœur builds on growing interest in comparative colonialism and slavery scholarship, particularly discussions of cultural transformation and community relations in colonial contexts. The broader impacts of this project articulate with local and global humanistic and scientific concerns. In particular, archaeological investigations at Crève Cœur have become an important resource for the commune of Sainte Anne in Martinique, and public outreach continues with the local community and government. The interest in the archaeology of slavery also transcends local communities, as postcolonial scholarship (Césaire 1972 [1955]; Fanon 1963) seeks to understand the role of enslaved communities in the production of modern 'Creole' Caribbean cultures and identities (Palmié 2006). Finally, the nature of this research situates the historical occupants of Crève Cœur within a particular social and physical landscape, providing valuable faunal data for reconstructing past human-environment relationships.

3.2 Ecological setting

Martinique is a volcanic island located in the Lesser Antilles chain in the Caribbean Sea. Crève Cœur is situated on the southern St. Anne Peninsula, a karst landscape with a series of small hills of dry forests composed of limestone and volcanic rock interspersed with small drainage systems (Kimber 1988:17). The plantation was established near the *Marin Cul-de-Sac*, an important economic and ecological harbor with extensive shoreline mangrove swamps. The island of Martinique provides various habitats for terrestrial and aquatic fauna, available as subsistence resources to the island's inhabitants. Based on modern ecological studies, 14 species of marine mammals (Jeremie 2003), and five species of sea turtles, (Chevalier & Lartiges 2001) have been reported on the coasts of Martinique. Over 40 species of decapod and 13 species of freshwater crustaceans (Maréchal 1998; Lim & Meunier 2002), 20 species of freshwater mollusks (Bouchet & Von Cosel 1991), 360 species of marine mollusks, and 40 species of echinoderms have been identified on the island (Lamy & Pointier 1984). An inventory of fish around the island of Martinique has documented 143 species of reef fish, 87 species living on the edge of mangroves (Bouchon & Laborel 1986; Bouchon & Bouchon 1992), 65 species in seagrass beds (Bouchon & Bouchon 1992) and 22 species of freshwater fish (Lim & Meunier 2002).

The ecological and geological setting of the island provided diverse resources on which settlers and plantations depended. Travelers' accounts from the colonial period provide some indications of the variety of fauna exploited by the Caribs, colonists and slaves on Martinique. Accounts document the consumption of manatee (*Trichechus manatus*) and several large turtles (*Chelonia mydas, Chelonia caretta, Chelonia Kempii,* and *Eretomochelys imbricata*) (Du Tertre 1667-71 v2: 216). In addition, these accounts indicate that land and sea crabs were important foods, as were conch (*Strombus gigas* and *Melongena melongena*), crayfish (*Panulinurus argus*) oysters (*Crastostrea rhizophorae*), and numerous fish species (Du Tertre 1667-71 v2: 223). Terrestrial wild fauna on the island noted in historical accounts include the iguana (*Iguana delicatissima*), the agouti (*Dasyprocta antillensis*), the rice rat (*Megalomys desmarestii*) and the opossum (*Didelphis marsupialis*); the last believed to have been introduced by colonists (Kimber 1988: 124). Mules, horses and oxen were brought to Martinique for use in sugar production, while chicken, sheep, goats and pigs were imported for subsistence (Kimber 1988: 172). Historical accounts indicate that beef was imported in the 17th and 18th centuries from Europe and the West Indies, and later from Puerto Rico, Brazil and North America, and that salted cod was a large part of slave subsistence (Kimber 1988: 179; Munford 1991: 631).

Archaeological investigations of prehistoric Caribbean sites corroborate early colonial accounts of the island's economic fauna. Wild terrestrial mammals typically recovered from prehistoric Lesser Antilles sites include extinct rice rats (tribe Oryzomyini) and agouti (Grouard 2001; Wing 2001: 114). Serrand's (2007) survey of invertebrate assemblages from four Ceramic sites in the southern Martinique identifies 17 economic molluscan species. These include various gastropods, such as conch, West Indian Topshell (*Cittarium pica*), chiton (*Acanthopleura granulata*), and numerous bivalves (Serrand 2007: 427). Additional archaeological investigations on the Lesser Antilles indicate prehistoric exploitation of various land and marine crabs, as well as inshore, pelagic and reef fish (Grouard 2001; Grouard & Berard 2005).

3.3 Historic context

The European colonization of Martinique began after Columbus' fourth voyage to the West Indies, during which he landed on the island in 1502. With the increasing European desire for commodities such as sugar, coffee, and indigo arose a vast demand for cheap labor resulting in the forced movement of over 14 million people from Africa to European colonies (Curtin 1969). Habitation Crève Cœur was in operation while Martinique was under French control during the major shift to sugar monoculture that occurred throughout the Caribbean in the 18th century. During this period, the world economy was evolving from mercantilism to capitalism, leading to "the creation of colonies, the establishment of experimental economic enterprises in various world areas, and the development of new forms of slave-based production in the New World, using imported slaves" (Mintz 1985: 55). While cane agriculture began in the colonies in the early 17th century, French plantation agriculture developed slowly compared to that of the Dutch and English, with few African slaves transported to the island until after 1665, when trading increased in Martinique and Guadeloupe (Watts 1987: 296). Colonial-era sugar plantations in the Caribbean were notorious for the substantial physical demands placed on the enslaved laborers. Sugar production required an "army of labor" to cut and haul cane, and to work the crushing and boiling machinery that was used during boiling season (Tadman 2000). Both bioarchaeological and historical demographic studies have demonstrated that slave populations on sugar estates in the Caribbean suffered from exceedingly high mortality rates and were faced with intensive health risks (Curtin 1968; Tadman 2000; Shuler 2009). Due to the focus on profit making by planters, slaves on plantations such as Crève Cœur were forced to produce substantial output, requiring exhaustive labor and placing the slaves in constant risk of malnutrition, illness and death.

Within the French Colonial system, from 1685 to the abolition of slavery in 1848, slavery was regulated by the *Code Noir*, or Black Code, a charter drafted to protect slaves. This code ostensibly mandated a uniform dietary minimum for slaves in all the French colonies (Tomich 1991: 305), and Articles 22–25 dictated that each week, planters would provide: "two pots and a half, Paris measure, cassava flour, or three cassava, each weighing 2 and 1/2 pounds at least, or the equivalent, with 2 pounds of corned beef, 3 pounds of fish or other things in proportion" (*Édit du Roi* 1685*)*. The regulations stipulated by the Code Noir indicate an extremely controlled setting on French plantations, but archaeological evidence and historical accounts provide a more nuanced interpretation of the slave landscape.

In reality, the manner in which slaves obtained subsistence within French Caribbean colonies differed from plantation to plantation as regulations were difficult to enforce (Debien 1964; Tomich 2004: 146). Historical and archaeological research demonstrates that while some planters provided rations for enslaved populations, other planters encouraged slaves to garden, procure, and prepare their own food to relieve themselves of the 'burden' of having to feed the slaves (Debien 1964; McKee 1999: 43; Mintz & Price 1976; Pulsipher 1990; Pulsipher & Goodwin 1999; Scott 2001; Tomich 1991, 2004). In the French West Indies, the scale of self-provisioning by enslaved laborers reportedly increased over time, and by emancipation in 1848, slaves were encouraged to grow and raise their own food, and work-free Saturdays were almost universally substituted for rations (Debien 1964; Price 1966; Tomich 2004: 146). Slaves likely exploited any such 'freedoms' gained within the system, manipulating their free time on their own terms to improve their welfare and conditions of life. Scholars suggest that the subsistence practices used by enslaved laborers such as gardening, raising livestock, hunting and gathering during this free time were the central feature of slave communities on Caribbean plantations (Benoit 2007; Heath and Bennett 2000). Further, traveler's accounts from the 18th and 19th centuries (e.g. Bouton in 1640; Labat in 1722; Soleau in 1835) indicate a lively internal Afro-Caribbean market system in Martinique, with slaves actively engaging in the marketing of produce and livestock (Tomich 1991). Historians also suggest that French planters encouraged the formation of families within slave communities (Thornton 1998: 173), which would have fostered inter-generational transmission of cultural practices. The analysis of faunal remains from Crève Cœur examines the responses, adjustments and negotiations of slaves within this unbalanced and uncertain social and natural environment, allowing for an evaluation of how daily subsistence practices contributed to the economic and social organization of the slave community.

3.4 Slave Community Foodways

The enslaved laborers at Crève Cœur thus grew food, raised livestock, ate, slept and interacted within the planter-designated provision grounds (*places a nègres*) and slave quarters (Figure 2) (Kimber 1988; Tomich 1991b). These provision grounds and yard gardens constituted a central focus of slave community social relations (Beckles 1991; Berlin & Morgan 1991; Benoit 2007; Heath & Bennet 2000; Marshall 1991; Mintz & Price 1976; Price 1991; Pulsipher 1990; Tomich 1991, 1994, 2001). In this instance, I identify the slave 'community' as an "ever-emergent social institution that generates and is generated" by household, intra-household, and suprahousehold interactions, structured and synthesized by daily practices over a period of time (Canuto and Yaeger 2000: 5). Such suprahousehold relations would have included participation in island Afro-Caribbean markets, which allowed for social and economic interactions with people and landscapes beyond individual plantation boundaries (Price 1966; Tomich 1991a, 1991b, 2004). My dissertation research at Crève Cœur investigates the material traces of these daily practices and interactions through the integration of anthropological theory and environmental archaeology, contextualized by previous research in the African Diaspora. I argue that the slave population secured relative control over their economic conditions through the development of daily subsistence practices, negotiating the physical and social constraints of the plantation and the natural environment. An increased reliance on community-based provisioning led to economic and social interactions beyond the boundaries of the plantation, with participation in informal island market systems and the exploitation of diverse

Figure 2. Slave Quarters, Sugar Plantation, Martinique, 1826. (Image Reference NW0309, as shown on www.slaveryimages.org, sponsored by the Virginia Foundation for the Humanities and the University of Virginia Library.)

habitats. The practices and interactions associated with subsistence contributed to the formulation and transformation of economic and social organization within the slave and later free community at Crève Cœur.

The analysis of faunal remains from Crève Cœur examines the responses and adjustments of enslaved Africans and their descendants to a novel social and natural landscape, investigating the negotiation of the plantation structure by the slave community. Colonial Martinique was the site of extensive interaction between groups of mostly French Europeans, Africans and Caribs. This research connects to broader questions of the social, cultural and economic consequences of these interactions that occurred within a specific setting, structured by French colonial institution of plantation slavery that perpetuated inequality and the subjugation of certain groups. Specifically, the faunal and historical data collected allow for an assessment of the ecological and social variables influencing the daily subsistence practices among the enslaved population at Crève Cœur on the island landscape. Using a multiscalar and diachronic approach, the end goal of this research is to examine processes of slave community organization and social dynamics over time, while also exploring community participation in broader economic and ecological systems on the island through subsistence practices. Through the zooarchaeological analysis of the faunal remains from the site, we can evaluate the subsistence strategies used by the enslaved laborers at Crève Cœur to survive and maintain some level of control over their daily lives and needs despite these extreme circumstances. The faunal data can also illuminate the movement and mobility of slaves across the plantation and island landscape through the identification of resource exploitation and technology.

3.5 Archaeology at Crève Cœur

Excavations at the site were concluded in 2010 after four field seasons. While the compilation and analysis of data remain in preliminary stages, the material record sampled from the site yields significant insight into the lifeways of the enslaved laborers at Crève Cœur, which represents a unique archaeological dataset from the understudied French Caribbean historic period. The long-term project explores the transformation of lifeways and culture examining the daily strategies used by enslaved laborers, contributing to comparative slavery scholarship in the Caribbean (e.g. Armstrong 1990, 2000; Farnsworth 1996, 2001; Handler & Lange 1997; Haviser 1999; Hicks 2007; Klipple 2001; Pulsipher 1991; Schroedl & Ahlman 2002; Singleton 1995, 1999; Wilkie 2000).

Excavations focused on the location and sampling of slave occupations on the site and this research delineated discrete and largely undisturbed slave house occupations on the terraced slopes of the hill located above and behind the *maison de maître*, including well-preserved faunal remains (Figure 3). Excavations in 2007, 2008 and 2010 focused on 6 slave house terraces, and a single locus associated with the *maison de maître,* identified through shovel test surveys completed in 2005 (Figure 4). Test units and trenches were set within each of the six discrete occupation areas, resulting in the recovery of over 45,000 artifacts including ceramics, metal, glass, bone, daub, charcoal and lithics (e.g. gun flints). Soil samples were consistently collected for flotation from all sealed contexts in the excavation, aiding in the recovery of botanical remains in addition to small faunal specimens, e.g., fish, bird, small mammals, absent from other datasets in the region. Samples were collected volumetrically, and on a per case basis (Popper and Hastrof 1988:6). Either 5 L (2007) or 10 L (2008, 2010) of soil was collected and floated, using a manual device constructed on site, from all units starting at the post-humus level of excavation and continuing to the close of the unit. All unsampled soil was screened on-site using 4 mm excavation screens. In the instance of discreet features identified during excavation, the entire sample was collected and floated.

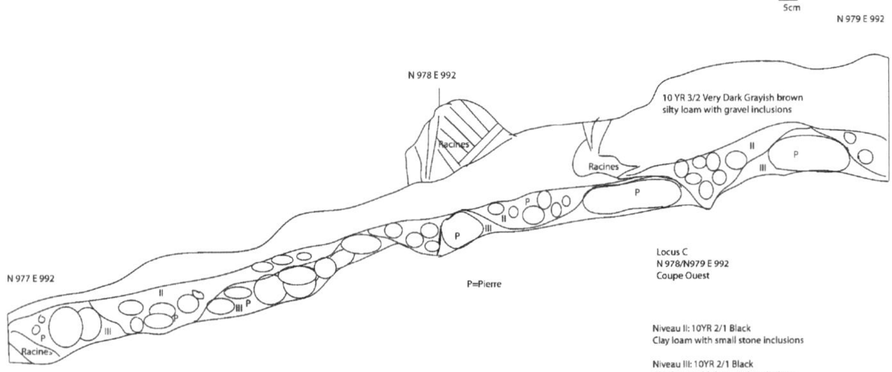

Figure 3. Profile of excavated slave occupation (Locus C) on terraced slope of hill.

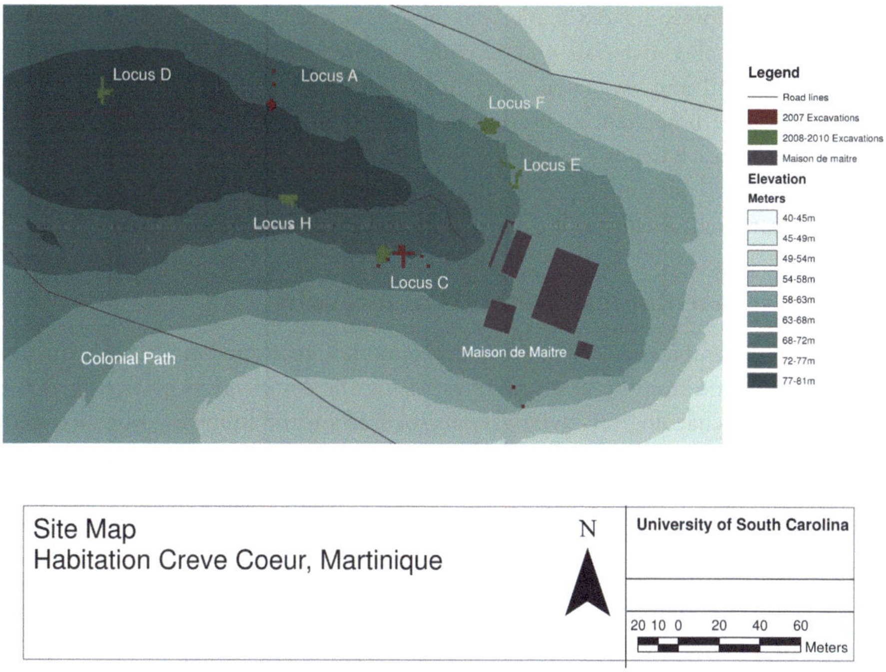

Figure 4. Crève Cœur Site Map.

Locus	Context	18th Century	Early 19th Century	Mid 19th Century	Late 19th Century
A	Slave Row		X		
C	Slave Row	X	X		
D	Slave Row			X	
H	Slave Row			X	X
E	Domestic dependancy[1]	X	X	X	X
F	Domestic dependancy[1]	X	X		
M	Planter's House		X	X	

Table 1. Context and chronology of discrete deposits identified through excavation. 1: Deposits associated with slave dwellings adjacent to the kitchen at the maison de maître.

Although archival research and data analysis continue, initial observations of the recovered materials suggest that deposits sampled from the 7 loci investigated at the site range from the late 18th century through the late 19th century. Further assessment will allow for a detailed spatial and diachronic examination of materials at the site, elucidating daily practices within the enslaved community at various points throughout the plantation's operation. Preliminary evaluations of the deposits suggest that there are at least 14 temporally distinct occupations (Table 1). Some of these represent non-continuous reuse of platforms, while others are deposits from continuous occupations. Temporal designations are based on preliminary artifact and stratigraphic analyses, with attention to ceramic types along with any datable materials (e.g. coins, maker's marks, dated objects, etc.). Future in-depth analyses of stratigraphy and materials will provide a more refined chronology when the data is compiled and evaluated. Specifically, mean ceramic dates (South 1977) and kaolin pipe bore stem analysis dating (e.g. Harrington 1978) will establish date ranges for each deposit identified through examination of stratigraphy. These analyses will provide more precise dates for each distinct deposit, providing a tighter chronological control for diachronic and intra-community comparisons.

3.6 Zooarchaeological methods and results

The faunal assemblage analyzed includes materials recovered from both on-site dry screening and from flotation samples. Using the comparative collection at the MNHN, zooarchaeological investigations focused on the following objectives: 1) Identification of the species consumed, and the production or acquisition methods and sites; 2) Determination of the contribution of species to the diet; 3) Evaluation of the distribution of faunal resources across the community; 4) Identification of the suite of factors that influence the formation of the deposit, including human taphonomic and post-depositional processes; and 5) Assessment of the potential changes to faunal populations affecting assemblage composition, such as reduction in size or age due to overfishing or overharvesting of shellfish.

Taxon	NISP
Mammalia	
Sus scrofa (Pig)	220
Bos taurus (Cattle)	152
Ovis/Capra (Sheep/Goat)	186
Ovis aries (Sheep)	67
Capra hircus (Goat)	44
Equus sp. (Horse)	3
Canis familiaris (Dog)	18
Felis cattus (Cat)	3
Wild (Terrestrial)	
Didelphis marsupialus (Opossum)	30
Herpestes sp. (Mongoose)	9
Dasyprocta antillensis (Agouti)	15
Rattus sp. (Rat)	43
Mus musculus (Mouse)	37
Total	824

Table 2. Identified mammal remains (NISP).

Although compilation, analysis and quantification of the data is ongoing, initial results of faunal analyses indicate that the slave community at Crève Cœur formulated a complex system of foodways, which included a diversity of wild and domestic taxa. Quantification continues, but to date, the evaluation of the data collected has identified approximately 10,000 specimens. Of these, approximately 40% were identifiable to the level of Family, Genus or species. Based on he identifications completed, domestic mammals were an important part of the diet of the slave community at the plantation, and households also actively exploited a varied array of natural resources available on the island for subsistence (Table 2). Cattle, pig, sheep, and goat remains recovered from house deposits suggest that a large part of the diet consisted of domestic livestock. Observed preliminary skeletal part representation indicates that pig, goat and sheep were locally raised, possibly on-site, as those elements identified to these taxa came from the entire animal. The observable greater relative abundance of lower limb and distal rib beef cuts, on the other hand, which comprise approximately 95% of the 152 cattle remains identified, indicate that most of the beef consumed originated from barreled imports. A small amount of Equid remains were identified (a single molar and a fragmented tarsal bone) suggesting that the slaves consumed old or deceased horse or mules, but only rarely.

In addition to the domestic mammals consumed, the enslaved laborers at Crève Cœur raised poultry and also exploited resources available in the landscape within and surrounding the plantation, including the trapping of small mammals, such as opossum, agouti and the exotic mongoose (introduced in the second half of the 19th century). Commensal animals such as dogs, cats, and rats were also recovered in the samples, but there is no evidence so far that these taxa were consumed by the site occupants.

Based on the preliminary analysis of bird remains from the site, chicken was principal avian species consumed, with the additional identification of Guinea fowl (*Numida sp.*), and pigeon or dove (Family Columbidae). Interestingly, however, despite the good preservation conditions, few bird remains (N=126) were identified in the overall assemblage, although eggshells are present throughout the deposits. Based on historical accounts and other faunal assemblages from

Phylum/Class	Taxon	Common Name
Phylum Mollusca		
Class Gastropoda	*Cittarium pica*	West-Indian Topshell
	Strombus gigas	Queen Conch
	Strombus pugilis	Milk Conch
Class Bivalvia	*Anadara notabilis*	Eared Ark Clam
	Codakia orbicularis	Tiger Lucine
	Lucina pectinata	Thick Lucine
	Crassostrea rhizophorae	Mangrove Oyster
Class Polyplacophora	*Acanthopleura granulata*	Fuzzy Chiton
	Chiton marmoratus	Chiton
Class Malacostraca	*Ucides cordatus*	Mangrove Crab
Class Echinoidea	*Lytechinus variegatus*	Green Sea Urchin
Class Amphibia and Reptilia		
Order Testudines	Family Cheloniidae	Marine turtle
Suborder Serpentes	*Bothrops lanceolatus*	Martinican pit viper
Suborder Lacertalia	*Anolis sp.*	Anole Lizard
	Family Gekkonidae	Gekko Lizard
Order Anora	Family Bufonidae	Toad
	Eleutherodactylus sp.	Frog

Table 3. Identified fauna.

Taxa (Family)	Common Name	Inshore	Coral Reefs	Offshore
		Shallow waters between shoreline and reef; sandy, muddy, rocky, & vegetated substrates	All coral reefs and adjacent coral and rock banks	Offshore waters beyond coral reefs; deep waters
Chondrichthyes				
Dasyatidae	Stingray	X	X	X
Ginglymostomatidae	Nurse Shark	X	X	
Carcharhinidae	Reef Shark	X	X	
Osteichthyes				
Albulidae	Bonefish	X	X	
Elopidae	Ladyfish	X		
Megalopidae	Tarpon	X	X	
Clupeidae	Herrings, sardines	X	X	
Mugilidae	Mullets	X		
Muraenidae	Moray Eel	X		
Belonidae	Garfish/Needlefish		X	X
Hemiramphidae	Balao (halfbeaks)	X	X	
Holocentridae	Squirrelfish		X	
Centropomidae	Snooks		X	
Serranidae	Groupers		X	X
Malacanthidae	Tilefishes		X	
Carangidae	Jacks, Scads	X	X	X
Lutjanidae	Snappers	X	X	
Gerreidae	Mojarros	X	X	
Haemulidae	Grunts	X	X	
Sparidae	Sea Breams, Porgies	X	X	
Labridae	Wrasses	X	X	
Scaridae	Parrotfishes		X	
Acanthuridae	Surgeonfish	X	X	
Sphyraenidae	Barracudas	X	X	X
Scombridae	Mackarel, Tuna	X	X	X
Trichiuridae	Cutlassfish			X
Balistidae	Triggerfish	X	X	X
Diodontidae	Porcupine fish	X	X	

Table 4. Habitat ranges of identified fish taxa.

Caribbean plantation sites, this is unexpected. The sparcity of avian remains could suggest that chickens were raised mainly for egg-production, and possibly traded or sold in the Afro-Caribbean markets on the island.

Further, the slave and later free community at Crève Cœur harvested a diverse range of terrestrial and aquatic species, including sea turtle (N=7), land crab (N=4), sea urchin (N=205) and a variety of marine and mangrove shellfish (N=2389) (Table 3). Common shellfish identified within the deposits include the West-

Figure 5. Modified bone artifacts (Clockwise from left: Button; Die; Pendant; Pin Case).

Indian Topshell (*Cittarium pica*), Chitons (*Acanthopleura granulata* and *Chiton marmoratus*), and mangrove oysters (*Crassostrea rhizophorae*).

An evaluation of the procurement sites used by the enslaved laborers provides an understanding of the movement of slaves beyond the plantation and throughout the island landscape and also allows for an evaluation of the methods used to obtain subsistence resources. Based on the families and species of fish identified thus far, the sample includes considerable diversity of locally procured taxa exploited by the enslaved laborers at Crève Cœur. To identify the primary procurement sites exploited by the slave community, three general habitat types are delineated and the fish families are classified by their primary habitat association (Table 4).

The first general habitat area is referred to as inshore, and includes mangroves, salines, estuaries and the littoral zone. This category includes the shallow waters between shoreline and coral reef, and also sandy, muddy, rocky, and vegetated substrates. These sites provide habitats for an extensive variety of vertebrate and invertebrate species, and these resources were available along the coasts of the island, accessible by foot. The second habitat is coral reefs, which provide the foundation for significant faunal and floral biodiversity, and would be accessible just off the coast. The final is pelagic or offshore habitats, which would require the use of boats to access.

Based on the taxa identified to at least the level of Family (N=1,597), the slaves at Crève Cœur focused extensively on the exploitation of inshore and reef habitats, which is corroborated by the mangrove and shoreline habitats of the identified shellfish. Initial observations of the results of faunal analysis allow for estimates of the relative frequency of exploitation of each particular habitat by the site inhabitants. The particular species identified within the families indicate that approximately 80% come from inshore habitats, 20% from reef and only about 1% from open or pelagic waters.

3.7 Discussion

The faunal data, combined with artifactual evidence indicate that the slaves were likely fishing in mangroves and along coasts with small nets, a practice known as seining. The numerous species of shellfish identified within the assemblage also indicate a preference for these procurement sites (see Table 3). Despite the 4mm screen used during excavation, and the numerous flotation samples processed, no fishhooks were recovered from the site. In contrast, however, excavations have located a preponderance of lead fishing weights from within slave occupation deposits. While sampling bias is always a possibility, the faunal and artifactual evidence suggest that inshore net fishing or seining, a practice that continues today, was the preferred method for procuring fish, as opposed to traveling on boats to acquire pelagic species. The plantation is located 1.25k from the Marin cul-de-sac. The cul-de-sac is lined with mangrove swamps, habitats to various species of shellfish, crustaceans and juveniles of numerous marine fish species. Further, this cul-de-sac contains various small coral reef formations, habitats for hundreds of species of fish, shellfish and crustacea. The identification of locally-available wild fauna, the recovery of fishing tools, along with the considerable diversity of fish and shellfish taxa identified indicate that the slave community at Crève Cœur were procuring at least some of their own subsistence resources.

Analysis continues using standard zooarchaeological methods including taxonomic identification, skeletal part representation, estimates of dietary contribution and diversity, allometric scaling of fish to calculate fish size to determine technology and changes in faunal populations, and the evaluation of human and natural taphonomic processes. Once analyses are complete and chronology is established for the site, these data will allow for an assessment of the variation of procurement sites and methods among households within slave community, and any change over time.

Finally, it is important to note that while animal resources provided subsistence for the enslaved community at Crève Cœur, bone provided a raw material for various materials. Specifically, modified bone artifacts recovered from excavations include bone dice likely used for gaming, numerous types and styles of bone buttons and a possible needle case for clothing and tailoring needs, and also bone modified and polished for personal adornment (Figure 5).

The faunal remains indicate that the slaves at Crève Cœur were somewhat reliant on community self-provisioning, allowing for physical, economic and social interactions beyond the boundaries of the plantation. This mobility provided opportunities for interaction with slaves from other plantations, in addition to free African-Caribbean city-dwellers, merchants and fisherman living along the coasts of the island, as noted in historical documents. Based on ethnohistorical and ethnographic accounts, the acquisition of wild fauna, fish in particular, reportedly had a profound impact on slave community relations (Price 1966). These preliminary results clearly indicate that the slave community at Crève Cœur negotiated their survival and coped with the cruelties of slavery by creating a system of foodways that involved self-sufficiency, creativity, and careful strategizing within a constrained social and ecological setting. Sidney Mintz (1996: 36) argues that with the freedom to choose one's food, and the ability to choose what to produce or catch to eat, slave communities were able to create a cuisine of their own, thus forming a solid foundation for the formation of Afro-Caribbean cultures. By manipulating their physical and ecological surroundings, the enslaved laborers at Crève Cœur learned, adjusted, and developed unique community strategies through everyday subsistence practices, despite the extreme constraints of plantation slavery.

Acknowledgements

I thank IACA and the Université des Antilles and de la Guyane for the opportunity to contribute to this edition. This material is based upon work supported by the National Science Foundation under Grant No. 1117214. Fieldwork and analysis for this project was funded in part by grants from the University of South Carolina Richard L. Walker Institute Of International Studies, and the Department of Anthropology at the University of South Carolina. I thank the director of the Habitation Creve Coeur field project, Kenneth Kelly. I thank Sandrine Grouard and the laboratory UMR 7209 du CNRS, *Muséum National d'Histoire Naturelle*, Paris, France for guidance and training during analysis. I would also like to thank the Service Regional d'Archeologie, Fort-de-France, Martinique for access to the collection and continued assistance with the project.

References

Armstrong, D.

1985 Afro-Jamaican slave settlement: archaeological investigations at Drax Hall. In *The archaeology of slavery and plantation life*, edited by Th. A. Singleton, pp. 261-287. New York, Academic.

1990 *The Old Village at Drax Hall Plantation: An Archaeological Study of Afro-Jamaican Settlement.* Chicago, University of Illinois Press.

Armstrong, D. and M. Hauser

2009 A Sea of Diversity: Historical Archaeology in the Caribbean. In *The International Handbook of Historical Archaeology.*, edited by T. Majewski and D. Gaimster, pp. 583-612. New York, Springer

Beckles, H.

1991 An Economic Life of Their Own: Slaves as Commodity Producers and Distributors. In *Barbados/ Slavery and Abolition: A Journal of Comparative Studies* 12 (special issue): 31-47.

Benoit, C.

2007 Gardens in the African Diaspora: Forging a Creole Identity in the Caribbean and the U.S. In *Gardens and Cultural Change: a Pan-American Perspective,* edited by M. Conan and J. Quilter, pp. 29-46. Washington DC, Dumbarton Oaks.

Berlin, I. and P. Morgan

1991 Introduction. *Slavery and Abolition: A Journal of Comparative Studies* 12 (special issue):1-30.

Bouchet, P. and B. Von Cosel

1991 Les mollusques terrestres et fluviatiles des Départements d'Outre-Mer. *Rapport d'étude bibliographique. Paris, Muséum d'Histoire Naturelle*: 109.

Bouchon, C. and J. Laborel

1986 Les peuplements coralliens des côtes de la Martinique. *Ann. Inst. Océanogr.* 62(2): 199-237.

Bouchon-Navarro, Y., C. Bouchon, et al.

1992 "L'ichtyofaune des herbiers de phanérogames marines de la baie de Fort de France (Martinique, Antilles françaises)." *Cybium* 16(4): 307-330.

Bousquet-Bressolier, C., M. Pelletier, and D. Bégot

1998 *La Martinique de Moreau du Temple, 1770.* Paris, Comité des travaux historiques et scientifiques.

Bouton, J.

1640 *Relation de l'establissement des Francois depuis l'an 1635, en isle de la Martinique, l'une des Antilles de l'Amerique, des moeurs des sauvages de la situations et des autres singularitez de l'isle.* Paris, S. Cramoisy.

Césaire, A.

1972 [1955] *Discourse On Colonialism.* Translated by Joan Pinkham. New York, Monthly Review Press.

Chevalier, J. and A. Lartiges

2001 Les tortues marines des Antilles. *ONCFS*: 59.

Curtin, P. D.

1968 *The Atlantic Slave Trade: A Census.* Madison, University of Wisconsin Press.

Debien, G.

1964 La Nourriture des Esclaves sur les Plantations des Antilles Françaises aux XVIIè et XVIIIè Siècles. *Caribbean Studies.* 4(2): 3-27.

Delpuech, A.

2001 Historical Archaeology in the French West Indies: Recent Research in Guadeloupe. In *Island Lives: Historical Archaeology of the Caribbean.* Paul Farnsworth, editor. Tuscaloosa, University of Alabama Press.

Du Tertre, Father J.B.

1667-71 *Histoire generale des Antilles Habites par les Francais.* 4 vols.

Fanon, F.

1963 *The Wretched of the Earth.* Translated into English by Richard Philcox. New York, Grove Press.

Farb, P. and G. Armelagos.

1980 Consuming Passions: The Anthropology of Eating. Boston, Houghton Mifflin Co.

Farnsworth, P.

1996 The Influence of Trade on Bahamian Slave Culture. *Historical Archaeology* 30(4): 1-23.

Farnsworth, P. (editor)

2001 *Island Lives: Historical Archaeologies of the Caribbean.* Tuscaloosa, University of Alabama Press.

Franklin M.

2001 The archaeological and symbolic dimensions of soul food: race, culture, and Afro-Virginian identity. In *Race and the Archaeology of Identity*, edited by Ch. E. Orser, pp 88-107. Salt Lake City, University of Utah Press

Goody J

1982 *Cooking, Cuisine and Class.* Cambridge University Press

Grouard, S.

2001 *Subsistance, Systemes Techniques et Gestion Territoriale en Milieu Insulaire Antillais Precolombien : Exploitation des Vertebres et des Crustaces aux epoques Saladoides et Troumassoides de Guadeloupe (400 av. J.C. a 1500 ap. J. C.).* These en Sciences humaines et sociales, lettres et langues (Nouveau Doctorat). U.F.R. Sciences Sociales et Administration Ecole doctorale Environnement et Archeologie.

Grouard S. and B. Berard,

2005 Les resources animales en Vertébrés et en Crustacés d'une population Saladoïde au Diamant – Plage de Dizac (Martinique, FWI). *20th International Congress for Caribbean Archaeology*, Santo Domingo, 29 June-06 July 2003 : 169-180.

Gumerman, G.

1997 Food and Complex Societies. *Journal of Arhcaeological Method and Theory.* 4(2): 105-139.

Handler, J.S. and F.W. Lange

1997 An African-Type Healer/Diviner and His Grave Goods: A Burial from a Plantation Slave Cemetery in Barbados, West Indies. *International Journal of Historical Archaeology.* 1: 91-130.

Harrington, J. C.

1978 Dating stem fragments of seventeenth- and eighteenth-century clay tobacco pipes. In *Historical Archaeology: A Guide to Substantive Contributions*, edited by R. L. Schuyler, pp. 63–65. Farmingdale, NY, Baywood.

Hauser, M.

2008 *An Archaeology of Black Markets: Local Ceramics and Economies in Eighteenth-Century Jamaica.* Gainesville, University Press of Florida.

Haviser, J.B. (editor)

1999 *African Sites Archaeology in the Caribbean.* Kingston Jamaica, Ian Randle, and Princeton, New Jersey, Markus Weiner.

Heath, B. and A. Bennett

2000 "The little Spots allow'd them": The Archaeological Study of African-American Yards. *Historical Archaeology* 34(2): 38-55.

Hicks, D.

2007 *The Garden of the World': An Historical Archaeology of Sugar Landscapes in the Eastern Caribbean.* Volume 3 Studies in Contemporary and Historical Archaeology. Archaeopress.

Higman, B. W.

1998 *Montpelier Jamaica: A Plantation Community in Slavery and Freedom 1739-1912.* Bridgetown, Barbados, The Press University of the West Indies.

Jeremie, S.

2003 Abondance, distribution et comportement des cétacés dans les eaux territoriales à la Martinique en début de printemps, mars-avril 2003. *Mémoire de DEA en Océanologie, Laboratoire d'Océanologie-Sart Tilman-B6 Chimie, Université de Liège*: 80.

Kelly, K. G.

2008 Creole Cultures of the Caribbean: Historical Archaeology in the French West Indies. *International Journal of Historical Archaeology.* 12: 388-402.

Kimber, C. T

1988 *Martinique Revisited: The Changing Plant Geographies of a West Indian Island.* College Station, Texas A&M University Press.

Klippel, W.E.

2001 Sugar Monoculture, Bovid Skeletal Part Frequencies, and Stable Carbon Isotopes: Interpreting Enslaved African Diet at Brimstone Hill, St. Kitts, West Indies. *Journal of Archaeological Science* 28: 1191-1198.

Labat, J.B.

1722 *Nouveau voyage aux isles de l'Amerique.* 6 volumes. Paris (New edition 1724, The Hague; new edition 1742 (8 volumes), Paris, new edition 1972, Fort-de-France).

Lamy, D. and J. P. Pointier

1984 La faune malacologique marine de la Martinique. *Xenophora. A. F. d. Conchyliologie.*: 9-17.

Lim, P. and F. J. Meunier

2002 Atlas des poissons et des crustacés d'eau douce de la Martinique." *Patrimoines Naturels.* 51: 120

Loftfield, T.C.

2001 Creolization in Seventeenth-Century Barbados. In *Archaeology of Atlantic Africa and the African Diaspora*, edited by A. Ogundiran and T. Falola. Bloomington, Indiana University Press.

Maréchal, J.P.

1998 Guide de la faune et de la flore sous-marines. *Littoral de la Martinique.*

McKee, L.

1999 Food Supply and Plantation Social Order: An Archaeological Perspective. In *"I, Too, Am America": Archaeological Studies of African-American Life,* edited by T. A. Singleton, pp. 218-239. Charlottesville, University of Virginia Press.

Mintz, S. W.

1985 *Sweetness and Power: The Place of Sugar in Modern History.* New York, Penguin Books.

Mintz S.W. and C.M. Dubois

2002 The Anthropology of Food and Eating. *Annual Review of Anthropology.* 31: 99-119.

Mintz, S. W. and R. Price

1976 *An Anthropological Approach to the Afro-American Past: A Caribbean Perspective.* Philadelphia, Pennsylvania, Institute for the Study of Human Issues.

Munford, C. J.

1991 *The Black Ordeal of Slavery and Slave Trading in the French West Indies, 1625-1715.* Lewiston: The Edwin Mellen Press.

Palmie, S.

2006 Creolization and its Discontents. *Annual Review of Anthropology.* 35: 433-56.

Popper, V. S. and C. A. Hastrof

1988 Introduction. In *Current Paleoethnobotony: Analytical Methods of Cultural Interpretations of Archaeological Plant Remains,* edited by C. A. Hastorf and V. S. Popper, pp. 1-16. Chicago, University of Chicago Press.

Price, R.

1966 Caribbean Fishing and Fisherman: A Historical Sketch. *American Anthropologist.* 68(6): 1363-1383.

1991 Subsistence on the Plantation Periphery: Crops, Cooking, and Labour among Eighteenth-Century Suriname Maroons. *Slavery and Abolition: A Journal of Comparative Studies* 12 (special issue):107-12.

Pulsipher, L.M.

1990 They Have Saturdays and Sundays to Feed Themselves. *Expedition 32(2)*

1991 Galways Plantation, Montserrat. In *Seeds of Change,* edited by H.J. Viola and C. Margolis, pp. 139-159. Washington D.C., Smithsonian Institution Press.

Pulsipher, L.M. and C.M. Goodwin

1999 Here where the old time people be: reconstructing the landscapes of the slavery and post-slavery era on Montserrat, West Indies. In *African sites archaeology in the Caribbean,* edited by J. B. Haviser, pp. 9–37. Kingston, Jamaica, Ian Randle.

Schroedl, G.F. and Ahlman, T.M.

2002 The Maintenance of Cultural and Personal Identities of Enslaved Africans and British Soldiers at the Brimstone Hill Fortress, St. Kitts, West Indies. *Historical Archaeology.* 36(4): 38-49.

Scott, E. M.

2001 Food and Social Relations at Nina Plantation. *American Anthropologist.* 103(3): 671-691.

Serrand, N.

2007 L'exploitation des invertebres durant l'occupation ceramique tardive du sud de la Martinique: Apercu diachronique au travers des sites de Dizac, Salines, Trabaud et Macabou. *Proceedings of the Twenty-First Congress of the International Association for Caribbean Archaeology,* Trinidad and Tobago. July 25-July 30, 2005.

Shuler, K.A.

2010 Life and Death on a Barbadian sugar plantation: Historic and bioarchaeological views of infection and mortality at Newton Plantation. *International Journal of Osteoarchaeology.* 20:2.

Silver, I. A.

1963 The Ageing of Domestic Animals. In *Science in Archaeology,* 1st ed., edited by D. Brothwell and E. Hias, pp. 283-302. Thames and Hudson, London.

Singleton, T.A.

1995 Archaeology of slavery in North America. *Annual Review of Anthropology* 24:119– 40.

Singleton, T.A. (editor)

1999 "I Too am America": Archaeological Studies of African-American Life Charlottesville, University of Virginia Press.

Soleau, A.

1835 *Notes sur les Guyanes frangaise, hollandaise, anglaise, et sur les Antilles fraincaises (Cayenne, Surinam, Demerary, la Martinique, la Guadeloupe)* Paris, France, Ministere de la Marine des Colonies.

South, S.

1977 *Method and Theory in Historical Archaeology.* New York, Academic Press

Tadman, M.

2000 The Demographic Cost of Sugar: Debates on Slave Societies and Natural Increase in the Americas. *The American Historical Review.* 105(5).

Tomich, D.

1991 The Other Face of Slave Labor: Provision Grounds and Internal Marketing in Martinique. In *Caribbean Slave Society and Economy,* edited by H. Beckles and V. Shepard, pp. 304-318. New York, The New Press.

1991b Une Petite Guinee: Provision Ground and Plantation in Martinique: 1830-1848. *Slavery and Abolition: A Journal of Comparative Studies* 12 (special issue):68-91.

2004 *Through the prism of slavery: labor, capital, and world economy.* Lantham. Bowman & Littlefield Publishers.

Thornton, J.

1998 *Africa and Africans in the making of the Atlantic world, 1400-1800*, New York, Cambridge University Press.

Waselkov, G.A.

2009 French Colonial Archaeology. In *The International Handbook of Historical Archaeology,* edited by Terisita Majewski and David Gaimster, pp.613-628. New York, Springer.

Watts, D.

1987 *The West Indies: Patterns of Development, Culture and Environmental Change Since 1492.* London, Cambridge.

Wilkie, L.

2000 Culture Bought: Evidence of Creolization in the Consumer Goods of an Enslaved Bahamian Family. *Historical Archaeology* 34(3): 10-26.

Wilkie, L. and P. Farnsworth

2005 *Sampling Many Pots. An Archaeology of Memory and Tradition at a Bahamian Plantation.* Gainesville, University Press of Florida.

Wing, E. S.

2001 The Sustainability of Resource Use by Native Americans on four Caribbean islands. *International Journal of Osteoarchaeology* 11: 112-126.

Yaeger, J. and M.A.Canuto

2000 Introducing an Archaeology of Communities. In *The Archaeology of Communities: A New World Perspective*, edited by M.A. Canuto and J. Yaeger, pp. 1-15. London, Routledge.

Chapter 4

L'Alimentation dans une plantation Guadeloupéenne du XVIIIe siècle

Le cas de l'habitation Macaille (Anse Betrand)

Noémie Tomadini, Sandrine Grouard et Yann Henry

Noémie Tomadini
Archéozoologie, Archéobotanique, Sociétés Pratiques, Environnements
Muséum National d'Histoire Naturelle
Paris
noemie.tomadini@gmail.com

Sandrine Grouard
Archéozoologie, Archéobotanique, Sociétés Pratiques, Environnements
Muséum National d'Histoire Naturelle
Paris
grouard@mnhn.fr

Yann Henry
HADES
Balma
yann.henry@hades-archeologie.com

Abstract

The first results of archaeozoological study of Macaille's plantation (Anse-Bertrand, Guadeloupe), dated from end of seventies century to 1780, are discussed in this paper. Excavation carried under the direction of Y. Henry in 2007 revealed two dump areas associated with two structures and one fire place, which are located in three areas distinct. The aim of this present work is to specify the population's diet and the subsistence choices from the settlers and the slaves. Faunal remains show that marines resources, available in the vicinity of the site, were exploited by settlers in supplement to their own diet coming from the Old World. Furthermore, our study specially focuses on the two dump areas, in order to check homogeneity or heterogeneity of both samples. Drawing a parallel between our results and historical source about the slave plantation's diet in the French Indies, we tried to specify what kind of people (settlers or slaves) had made these dump areas, and assign a function to the structures. These results will be completed by the whole remains study.

Résumé

Cet article décrit les premiers résultats de l'étude archéozoologique réalisée suite aux fouilles de l'habitation Macaille (Anse Bertrand, Guadeloupe), occupée entre la fin du XVIIè et les années 1780. La fouille réalisée en 2007 sous la direction de Y. Henry ont mis au jour deux fosses dépotoirs associées à deux structures d'habitats et un foyer situés dans trois zones bien distinctes de l'emprise de fouille. Le but principal de cette étude est de définir l'alimentation et les stratégies de subsistance des populations de cette habitation sucrerie, colons et esclaves confondus. Le spectre de faune global indique que les colons se sont appropriés les ressources marines présentes à proximité du site, afin d'agrémenter l'alimentation de mise sur le « Vieux-Continent ». En outre, notre étude s'est plus particulièrement concentrée sur les deux fosses dépotoirs de ce site, afin de déterminer l'homogénéité ou l'hétérogénéité entre ces deux assemblages. En mettant ces résultats en parallèle avec les textes historiques portant sur l'alimentation des esclaves des plantations aux Antilles françaises, nous avons essayé de définir les acteurs de ces dits rejets et ainsi, attribuer une fonction aux bâtiments présents à proximité de celles-ci. Ces premières hypothèses seront ou non confortées par l'étude du reste du mobilier.

Resumen

Este articolo describe los primeros resultados del estudio arqueozoológico realizado en respuesta a las excavaciones de la hacienda de Macaille (Anse Bertrand, Guadalupe), ocupada desde el fin del siglo XVII y hasta los años 1780. La excavacion realizada en 2007 bajo la dirección de Y. Henry muestraron dos zonas de residuos asociadas con diferentes estructuras de habitationes y un hogar situado en tres zonas distintas de l'excavación. El objetivo principal de este estudio es definir la alimentación y las estrategias de subsistencia de las poblaciones de esta vivienda azucarera, colonos y esclavos confundidos. Muestras de fauna global indica que los colonos se apropiaron los recursos marinos presentes cerca de ese lugar, para adornar su costumbre alimentaria del " Viejo - Continente ". Además/ Hademás, nuestro estudio se concentró más particularmente sobre ambos zonas de residuos de este sitio, para determinar la homogeneidad o la heterogeneidad de ambos conjuntos. Comparando estos resultados con los textos históricos sobre la alimentación de los esclavos en las plantaciones de las Antillas francesas, tratamos de definir a los actores de estos dichos retoños y así, atribuir una función a los edificios presentes cerca de éstas. Estas primeras hipótesis serán o no confirmadas con el estudio del resto del mobiliario.

Key words

French Antilles, plantation, alimentation, subsistence, diet's dichotomy

Mots-clés

Antilles françaises, habitation, alimentation, stratégie de subsistance, dichotomie alimentaire

Palabras clave

Antillas francesas, hacienda, alimentación, estrategias de subsistencia, dicotomià alimentar

4.1 Introduction

«*Dis-moi ce que tu manges, je te dirai ce que tu es* » écrivait Jean Anthelme Brillat-Savarin en 1825 dans son ouvrage sur la Physiologie du goût. En effet, l'alimentation étant un fait marqueur de l'identité culturelle d'une population et les « choix » alimentaires un témoignage des différences socioculturelles au sein d'un groupe d'individus, il semble possible de discriminer deux populations entre elles.

Suite à la découverte de nombreux restes de vertébrés et d'invertébrés lors de la fouille de l'Habitation Macaille (Anse-Bertrand, Guadeloupe ; Henry et al. 2009), une étude archéozoologique a été réalisée en 2009 afin de définir l'alimentation et les stratégies de subsistance des populations de cette habitation datée du XVIIIe siècle, colons et esclaves confondus. Cette étude s'est plus particulièrement concentrée sur les deux fosses dépotoirs de ce site, afin d'en déterminer l'homogénéité ou l'hétérogénéité.

En effet, les fosses dépotoirs FOS 01 et FOS 20 ne se trouvant pas dans la même zone du site et se trouvant associées à des structures différentes, la première à différentes unités d'occupations liés à la vie domestique et agricole et la seconde à un espace résidentiel, elles pourraient résulter de deux modalités distinctes de rejets des déchets. Ainsi ces fosses pourraient indiquer une différence de classe sociale et permettraient de percevoir les régimes alimentaires d'une part des colons et d'autre part des esclaves.

4.2 Site et matériel

Situé sur la commune d'Anse-Bertrand, à l'extrémité septentrionale de l'île de Grande-Terre, le site de Macaille a été découvert en 2006 lors d'une opération de diagnostic entreprise dans le cadre de la construction d'un lotissement *rue des Pommes cannelles* (Figure 1). La fouille, réalisée en novembre et décembre 2007 sous la direction de Y. Henry (Hadès), a occasionné la découverte et l'étude d'une modeste habitation occupée assez brièvement, probablement entre les années 1720 et 1770.

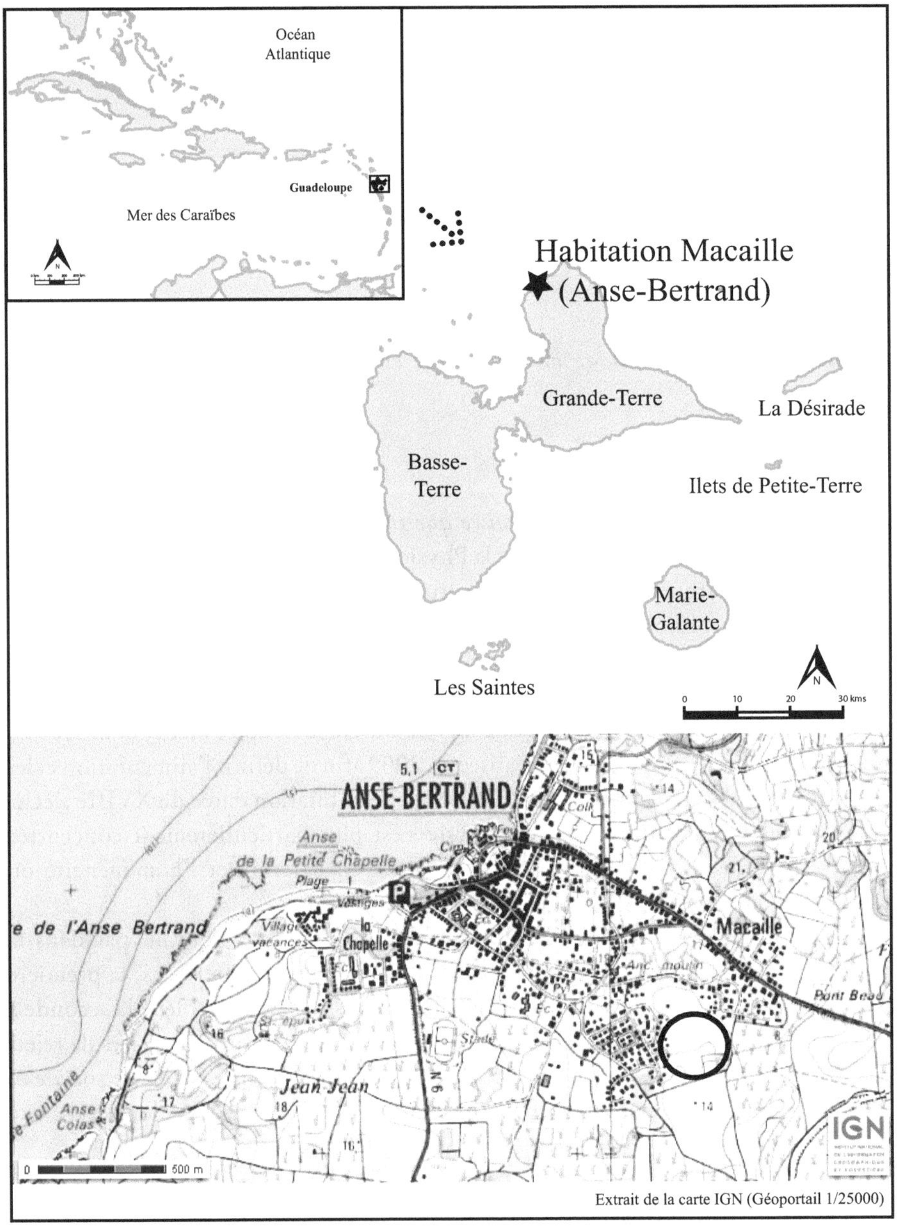

Figure 1. Localisation du site de Macaille, rue des Pommes cannelles (Anse-Bertrand, Guadeloupe ; modifié d'après IGN et Géoatlas).

Délimité au sud par une palissade rectiligne en bois, le site comprend quinze bâtiments à ossature de poteaux en bois orientés selon un axe nord-sud plus ou moins bien respecté (Henry et al. 2009; Figure 2). Au sud-ouest, on retrouve un espace résidentiel comprenant trois bâtiments, trois ensembles de structures sans organisation perceptible et un foyer isolé, qui est d'ailleurs le seul foyer ayant été identifié sur le site. Au nord, on distingue un second espace résidentiel comprenant

Figure 2. Plan général du site de Macaille - hypothèses d'organisation spatiale et fonctionnelle (Relevé de Y. Henry, I. Rougier ; dessin de Y. Henry, Hadès, 2009).

cinq bâtiments et une fosse dépotoir dont la limite nord déborde de l'emprise de fouille. Enfin à l'est, sont installés sept unités d'occupations, un groupe de creusements quadrangulaires interprétés comme des aménagements liés à des activités de culture et une deuxième fosse dépotoir, que délimitent au sud une longue palissade en bois.

Au regard du plan général du site, l'ensemble de ces bâtiments et structures semblent obéir à une organisation concertée. En effet, leurs emplacements ménagent des espaces vierges, interprétés comme des couloirs de circulation. L'un chemine depuis l'accès aménagé dans la palissade au sud, et se dirigent d'une part vers le nord (le long des bâtiments UO8 et UO12) et d'autre part vers le nord-ouest, séparant ainsi les bâtiments UO 01 et UO 02 des bâtiments UO 08, 09 et 10 (Figure 2). A la croisée de ces couloirs de circulations, la fosse dépotoir 01 constitue vraisemblablement un aménagement essentiel sur le site de Macaille par sa position centrale et la quantité de matériel ayant été découvert en son sein.

L'emprise de fouille, d'une superficie de 3600 m², n'a probablement pas circonscrit l'ensemble de l'habitation originelle. Sur la frange nord notamment, la présence de la fosse 20 signale peut-être, à l'image du dépotoir central (FOS 01),

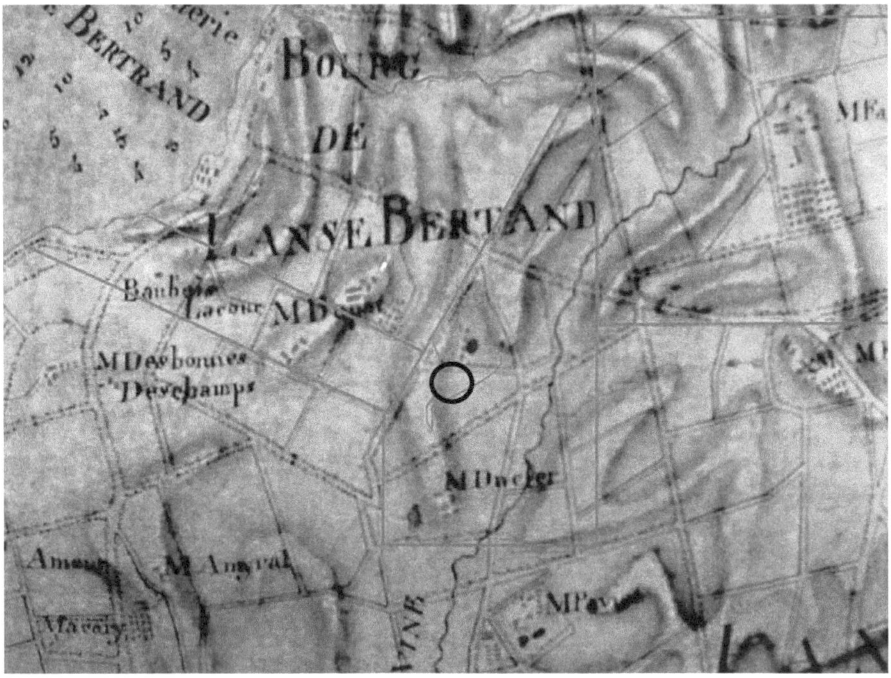

Figure 3. Extrait de la carte des Ingénieurs du Roi (1764-1768) ; en noir, l'emprise de la fouille (Van den Bel, 2006).

quelques bâtiments à proximité. Cette hypothèse se fonde aussi sur la présence d'une grotte et d'une mare artificielle à 70 m au nord (étudiés également lors de fouille de 2007), dont on soupçonne l'utilisation simultanée, celles-ci étant déjà figurées sur une carte des ingénieurs du roi daté entre 1764 à 1768 (Figure 3). Selon toute vraisemblance, la grotte aurait été fréquentée et aménagée (découverte d'un fragment de bord de forme à sucre), et la mare très vraisemblablement utilisée comme point d'eau pour les bêtes durant l'occupation du site. En outre, le prolongement de la palissade vers l'est indiquerait peut-être la présence d'autres bâtiments au-delà des constructions UO 14 et UO 15 (Figure 2).

Selon la carte de Saint-Maure de 1732, l'emprise de fouille se situerait à l'extrémité nord de la parcelle 639 détenue par petit Frères, parcelle vraisemblablement consacrée à la culture de la canne puisqu'une sucrerie y est mentionnée. La seconde carte, réalisée par les Ingénieurs du Roi entre 1764 et 1768, mentionne un dénommé M. Ducler comme propriétaire de la parcelle 639 et semble-t-il, d'une habitation sucrerie sans cases à nègres. Enfin, une carte marine de 1875 signale la présence de deux habitations (Grandfon et Lemercier) de part et d'autre de l'emprise de fouille. A cette époque, la parcelle ne comporte plus de bâtiment et semble être mise en culture (Gabriel 2009 ; In Henry et al. 2009).

L'acte notarial le plus ancien concernant l'habitation Macaille date de 1863 et fait référence à une habitation anciennement établie en sucrerie, appartenant à la famille Douillard-Grandfond. La parcelle d'environ cent dix-sept hectares comportait alors divers bâtiments, dont certains en très mauvais état, parmi lesquels se trouvait ceux qui était anciennement dévolus à la sucrerie. Un second acte, plus ancien (1899), évoque quant à lui plusieurs bâtiments à vocation domestique d'une part et manufacturière d'autre part. Aussi apprend-on qu'une chaudière à manioc, une sucrerie et un moulin à cannes étaient visibles sur la parcelle. La famille Douillard-Grandfond est toujours propriétaire des lieux. Pour l'habitation Ducler (encore appelée Habitation Mahaudière ou Lemercier-Ducler), les documents ont permis de remonter jusqu'au 16 mars 1838. Cet acte fait référence à la vente de la moitié de l'habitation Ducler à M. Lemercier qui, il faut le préciser, était déjà le « propriétaire » de l'autre moitié de l'habitation, ayant épousé la fille Ducler, Reine Perrine Sidonie, descendante des Douillard-Grandfond. Les habitations Macaille et Mahaudière étaient donc liées par le jeu des mariages, leur permettant ainsi de conserver le plus longtemps possible les terres dans le même giron familial (Gabriel 2009 ; In Henry et al. 2009).

A l'heure actuelle, le doute subsiste quant à la vocation manufacturière de cette habitation. En effet, malgré la découverte d'un nombre important de poteries dites «industrielles » (274 formes à sucres et 214 pots à mélasse) et de quelques ustensiles en métal que l'on pourrait éventuellement attribuer à une activité sucrière (plaque en cuivre percée de nombreux trous ressemblant aux « caisses à passer le sucre »), il est hasardeux de statuer sur la présence de cette activité sur le site de Macaille. L'absence de bâtiments industriels, de type moulin ou bien sucrerie (*etc.*), clairement identifiés lors de la fouille et le mutisme des documents d'archives du XVIIIè siècle à ce sujet laissent perplexe, surtout quand on sait l'essor du coton dans cette région de Grande-Terre à cette époque. Somme toute, au regard des documents cartographiques à notre disposition, le site de Macaille serait très probablement lié à l'habitation Petit Frères. Les bâtiments et structures découverts pourraient soit coïncider avec un lieu annexe à la véritable manufacture, soit à la « proto-habitation » sucrerie Petit Frère qui fut par la suite absorbée par une habitation voisine (Macaille-Grandfond au nord ou Ducler au sud).

A contrario, l'occupation domestique du site est bien documentée, que ce soit grâce aux artéfacts liés à l'installation des colons sur le site (outils en rapport avec le déboisement, la charpenterie et la menuiserie) ou ceux relatifs à la vie quotidienne sur cette habitation. En effet, la vaisselle -mobilier en céramique et faïence (NMI=212), ainsi qu'en verre (NMI=118)- a été trouvée en très grande quantité au sein des fosses dépotoirs et de manière plus succincte lors de la fouille de trous de poteaux. L'étude de la vaisselle réalisée par I. Gabriel (in Henry et al. 2009) a mis en exergue la primauté des productions importées européennes au détriment des productions locales sur le site, attestant des relations commerciales entre le Vieux Continent et l'île de Grande-Terre et, du statut social « assez » privilégié d'une partie des habitants du site de Macaille. Enfin, la découverte de nombreux restes de faune vertébrée et invertébrée au sein des deux fosses dépotoirs, du foyer et de onze trous de poteaux répartis sur l'ensemble du site, nous ont permis d'appréhender les pratiques alimentaires des habitants de cette plantation. C'est à cette dernière catégorie de vestiges que les pages qui suivent vont être consacrées.

4.3 Méthodes

L'identification des mollusques, crustacés, poissons, chéloniens, oiseaux et mammifères a été réalisée grâce à la collection constituée par Sandrine Grouard (UMR 7209) et des collections patrimoniales du Muséum national d'Histoire naturelle de Paris. Les déterminations ont été menées au plus bas niveau taxinomique possible (genre ou espèce).

L'analyse quantitative a été réalisée grâce à des décomptes bruts : en NRd (Nombre de Restes déterminés ; Poplin 1976 ; Grouard 2001). Seuls les fragments de nacre dus à la détérioration de la microstructure des burgos *Cittarium pica* lors de leur transport, n'ont pas été pris en compte pour le décompte du NRd, étant issus de cassures fraîches. Le Nombre Minimal d'Individus a été calculé en employant le NMI de fréquence (NMIf ; Poplin 1976) consistant à décompter, après la latéralisation de chaque élément, ceux qui sont les mieux représentés. Une attention particulière a été observée pour l'étude du *Cittarium pica*, pour qui le NMI a été décompté en tenant compte non seulement des coquilles complètes mais également des éléments complémentaires non répétitifs permettant une estimation maximale de ce type de taxon, par exemple, les ouvertures ou les apex (Serrand 2002). En outre le NMI de combinaison (NMIc), qui en prend en compte les âges, les tailles et les sexes des animaux, a été utilisé pour les taxons présentant un faible nombre de restes, afin d'estimer le nombre d'individus le plus exact.

L'étude concernant les modalités de consommation et le traitement des carcasses a été réalisée grâce au calcul du Pourcentage de Représentation des Parties Squelettiques, où le nombre de restes archéologiques par partie squelettique est pondéré par le nombre attendu de cette même partie squelettique pour un individu théorique et multiplié par le NMI estimé, selon la méthode mise au point par Dodson et Wexlar en 1979. Seul le boeuf (Bovinae), taxon domestique le mieux représenté, a fait l'objet de cette analyse.

Enfin, afin de mieux apprécier les modalités d'approvisionnement du burgo *Cittarium pica*, une série de mesures a été effectuée sur les spécimens complets, voire sub-complets, de cette population à partir de quatre variables (longueur, hauteur, longueur de la base et hauteur de l'ouverture ; d'après Serrand 2006). Néanmoins, chaque individu n'ayant pas le même état de conservation, l'enregistrement de toutes les mesures sur chaque individu n'a parfois pas été possible.

4.4 Résultats

Au total un peu plus de 8 kg de vertébrés et près de 51 kg de mollusques et crustacés ont pu être étudiés. Nous avons pu identifier 716 individus et 61 taxons (53 taxons natifs et 7 taxons domestiques importés ; Figure 4). Le chien domestique (*Canis familiaris*) déjà présent sur l'île au moment de l'arrivée des colons et ce depuis deux millénaires, n'a pas été inclus dans l'une ou l'autre de ces catégories. Celui-ci a été introduit par les Précolombiens céramistes Saladoïdes en Guadeloupe vers 500 av. J.-C. Il a ensuite été réintroduit lors de la colonisation européenne, aboutissant à un mélange des différentes origines et morphotypes (Grouard 2001). Les études sur la description anatomique de ces morphotypes sont en cours par ailleurs.

Les gastéropodes dominent le spectre de faune global, tant au niveau du nombre de taxons recensés (27), qu'au niveau du Nombre Minimal d'Individu (633). Le *Cittarium pica,* dont nous reparlerons plus en détail par la suite est sans conteste le taxon phare de notre assemblage avec 431 individus. En seconde position, les 13 taxons de poissons (15 individus) sont tous natifs des Antilles. Puis les bivalves avec 8 taxons et 37 individus décomptés sont suivis des mammifères domestiques avec 7

Espèces déterminées	NR	NR%	NMI	NMI%	PdR	PdR%
Gastropoda						
Fissurella nimbosa	10	0,5	10	1,4	7,5	
Cittarium pica	657	31,6	431	59,7	42304,1	71,0
Gaza fischeri	1		1	0,1	0,8	
Astraea caelata	34	1,6	32	4,4	785,7	1,3
Astraea tecta	1		1	0,1	1,1	
Astraea tuber	45	2,2	39	5,4	1005,8	1,7
Synaptocochlea picta	1		1	0,1	0,4	
Nerita peloronta	1		1	0,1	3,2	
Nerita tesselatta	2	0,1	2	0,3	0,8	
Nerita versicolor	8	0,4	6	0,8	7,6	
Tectarius muricatus	2	0,1	2	0,3	2,1	
Cerithium eburneum	1		1	0,1	1,4	
Strombus gallus	20	1,0	11	1,5	1716,4	2,9
Strombus gigas	25	1,2	17	2,4	3588,9	6,0
Talparia cinerea	3	0,1	3	0,4	65	0,1
Cassis flammea	1		1	0,1	40,4	0,1
Tonna maculosa	1		1	0,1	2	
Charonia variegata	6	0,3	4	0,6	618,5	1,0
Purpura patula	6	0,3	6	0,8	30,6	0,1
Thais haemastoma	1		1	0,1	714	1,2
Thais deltoidea	3	0,1	3	0,4	39,4	0,1
Conus cf. *daucus*	1		1	0,1	3	
Drepanotrema sp.	1		1	0,1	0,1	
Bulimulus guadalupensis	84	4,0	58	8,0	12,1	
Marisa cornuarietis	1		1	0,1	0,1	
Truncatella caribaeensis	1		1	0,1	0,1	
Truncatella pulchella	1		1	0,1	0,2	

Espèces déterminées	NR	NR%	NMI	NMI%	PdR	PdR%
Bivalvia						
Pinctada imbricata	1		1	0,1	4	
Lima lima	1		1	0,1	5,1	
Lucina pectinata	74	3,6	29	4,0	214,7	0,4
Codakia orbiculata	2	0,1	2	0,3	13,4	
Chama cf. *congregata*	1		1	0,1	35,7	0,1
Chama cf. *florida*	1		1	0,1	48,3	0,1
Americardia media	1		1	0,1	3,3	
Congeria leucophaeata	1		1	0,1	1,9	
Polyplacophora						
Chiton sp.	13	0,6	2	0,3	9,6	
Crustacea						
Gecarcinus sp.	66	3,2	7	1,0	36,97	0,1
Coenobita clypeatus	1		1	0,1	1,12	
Teleostei						
Tylosurus crocodilus	4	0,2	1	0,1	2,3	
Epinephelus sp.	2	0,1	1	0,1	1,82	
Caranx sp.	1		1	0,1	0,13	
Lutjanus cf. *vivanus*	8	0,4	3	0,4	1,03	
Lutjanus sp.	1		1	0,1	0,12	
Rhomboplites aurorubens	1		1	0,1	0,007	
Haemulidae	1		1	0,1	0,11	
Haemulon sp.	2	0,1	1	0,1	0,16	
Sparidae	1		1	0,1	0,08	
Sparisoma sp.	1		1	0,1	0,09	
Balistes sp.	1		1	0,1	0,2	
Melichtys sp.	1		1	0,1	0,04	
Diodon hystrix	1		1	0,1	8	
Chelonii						
Cheloniidae	1		1	0,1	175,41	0,3
Aves						
Anatidae	1		1	0,1	0,56	
Gallus domesticus	8	0,4	3	0,4	9,08	

Espèces déterminées	NR	NR%	NMI	NMI%	PdR	PdR%
Mammalia						
Canis familiaris	9	0,4	2	0,3	40,61	0,1
Bos taurus	330	15,9	8	1,1	6745,93	11,3
Caprinae	8	0,4	1	0,1	30,04	0,1
Ovis aries	6	0,3	1	0,1	90	0,2
Capra hircus	2	0,1	2	0,3	18,11	
Sus scrofa domesticus	48	2,3	2	0,3	109,43	0,2
Equus caballus	2	0,1	1	0,1	82,9	0,1
Hominidae	1		1	0,1	19	
Total déterminés	**1521**		**722**		**58660,5**	

Indéterminés	NR	NR%	NMI	NMI%	PDR	PdR%
Mollusca	8*	0,4			26,3	
Teleostei	10	0,5			4,4	
Aves	1	0,0			0,25	
"Grands Mammifères"	20	1,0			250,8	0,4
"Petits Mammifères"	21	1,0			29,32	
Mammalia	503	24,2			631,23	1,1
Total indéterminés	**555**				**942,29**	
TOTAL	**2076**				**59602,8**	

Figure 4. Fréquences brutes et relatives du spectre global en Nombre de Restes déterminés (NRd et NRd%), Nombre Minimal d'Individus (NMI et NMI%) et Poids de Restes (PdR et PdR%), sur le site de Macaille.

taxons pour 16 individus, dominés par le bœuf domestique (*Bos taurus*). Viennent ensuite les crustacés et les oiseaux comprenant 2 taxons l'un et l'autre. En ce qui concerne les oiseaux, nous avons pu identifier un taxon natif (Anatidae) et un gallinacé, taxon domestique importé (*Gallus gallus domesticus*). Enfin, représentés par un taxon chacun, 2 polyplacophores et une tortue marine (Cheloniidae) ont été décomptés.

4.4.1 Taxons domestiques introduits

En ce qui concerne les espèces domestiques introduites et même si nous n'avons pas d'informations écrites sur le mode d'abattage de ces animaux, certains fragments illustrent bien les premières étapes de la découpe des carcasses.

Ainsi, deux vertèbres thoraciques de boeuf domestique (*Bos taurus*) trouvées au sein de la fosse dépotoir 01 présentent l'ablation de leur processus transverse et la section de leur processus épineux, indiquant une découpe du rachis et un débitage en tronçons de la carcasse. Les squelettes, complets, indiquent quant à eux l'abattage et la découpe bouchère de l'animal sur le site. De ces squelettes complets, il ne manque que les métapodes, qui ont probablement été extraits pour l'artisanat.

4.4.2 Appropriation des ressources guadeloupéennes

L'importance des taxons natifs sur le site de Macaille est indéniable. En effet, les mollusques dominent largement cet assemblage, quel que soit le type de décompte : nombre de taxons, Nombre Minimal d'Individus ou bien Nombre de Restes déterminés. En outre, les mollusques, poissons et crustacés regroupent alors à eux seuls plus de 97% du Nombre Minimal d'Individus décomptés lors de notre étude.

Toutefois si l'on extrait la part de mollusques dans l'assemblage, le spectre se révèle tout autre, les mammifères domestiques importés représentant à eux seuls 45,5 % du spectre total (Figure 5). Or, si l'on rapporte au nombre de coquilles la masse de chair, cela constitue en réalité une valeur nutritionnelle assez négligeable face à celle d'un mammifère domestique, à l'égal des poissons et des crustacés, de l'ordre de quelques grammes pour plusieurs dizaines de kilos de viande.

Par conséquent, malgré la grande quantité d'espèces natives dans l'alimentation des populations du site Macaille, celles-ci ne peuvent donc constituer qu'un complément alimentaire occasionnel ou symbolique, en appoint d'une alimentation essentiellement fondée sur l'apport carné des mammifères domestiques du Vieux continent. Toutefois, les taxons natifs sont essentiellement d'origine marine, ce qui est peut être la marque d'un choix culturel ou de classe sociale.

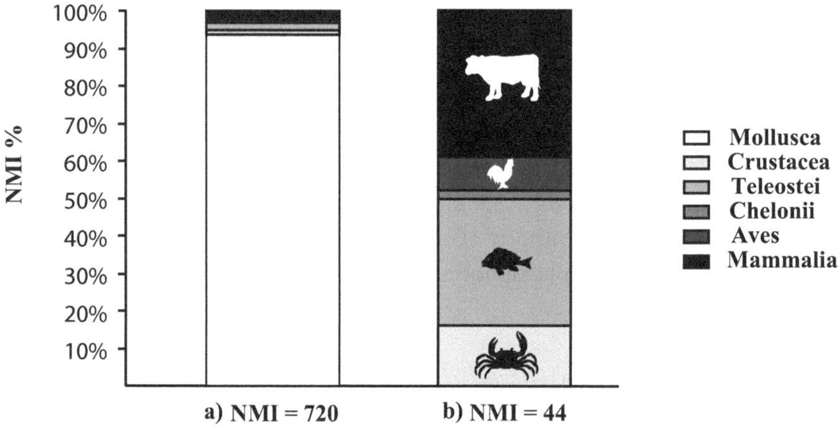

Figure 5. Proportion de chaque groupe zoologique (NMI%) au sein du spectre de faune global du site de Macaille ; a) en prenant en compte les mollusques, b) en excluant les mollusques.

4.4.3 *Spectre faunique des fosses dépotoirs FOS 01 et FOS 20*

L'étude taphonomique révèle que la fosse dépotoir 01 ne semble pas avoir été rebouchée immédiatement et qu'elle a très probablement servie pendant plusieurs saisons. En effet, plusieurs fragments osseux ainsi que 25 restes de lambi (*Strombus* sp.) issus de cette fosse dépotoir, présentent une altération de la surface indiquant des traces d'intempérisation (Behrensmeyer & Hill 1989). Ce n'est pas le cas de la fosse 20, qui semble avoir fonctionné et été rebouchée plus rapidement.

Au regard de leur spectre faunique respectif, certaines divergences apparaissent rapidement entre les deux fosses dépotoirs. En effet, à la différence de la fosse dépotoir 01, qui rassemble tous les groupes zoologiques recensés au sein du spectre de faune global, le matériel recensé au sein de la fosse dépotoir 20 rassemble seulement les gastéropodes, les mammifères domestiques importés et un gallinacé (Figure 6).

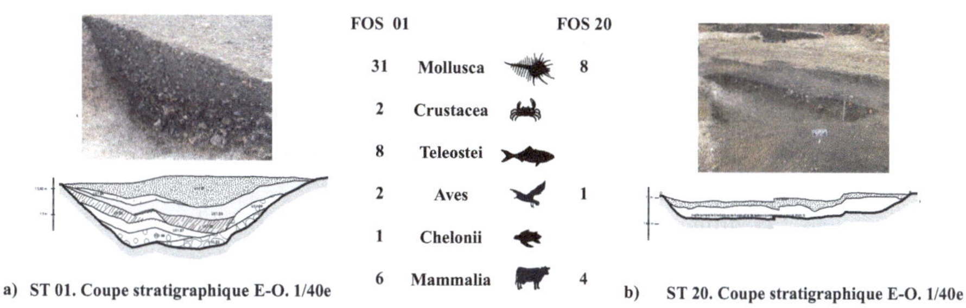

Figure 6. Proportion de chaque classe zoologique au sein des fosses dépotoirs, a) FOS 01, b) FOS 20 (Dessins et clichés Yann Henry, 2009).

Afin de confirmer ou non ces premiers résultats, nous avons effectué un test statistique (test de rang de Spearman) sur les Nombres de Restes déterminés par taxons pour chaque fosse. Les résultats obtenus ont montrés que bien que la fosse 01 présente une plus large diversité de taxons que la fosse 20, ces deux fosses ne sont pas significativement différentes. Ceci pourrait très certainement s'expliquer par le fait que 27 espèces recensées au sein de la fosse 01, et absentes de la fosse 20, ne sont représentées que par un seul individu.

4.4.4 *Le cas des burgos Cittarium pica*

Intéressons-nous maintenant au cas des burgos *Cittarium pica*, animaux gouteux et de bonne taille, qui, avec 431 individus décomptés pour l'ensemble du site, dominent largement l'assemblage total.

Nous avons décompté 265 individus au sein de la fosse dépotoir 01 et, 149 au sein de la fosse dépotoir 20. L'étude des tailles des individus recensés sur le site a permis de mettre en exergue un double approvisionnement, l'un sur les individus de classe moyenne (de 40 à 64 mm) et l'autre sur les grands spécimens (de 65 à 99 mm). Toutefois, nous avons pu constater que la fosse dépotoir 01 se caractérisait

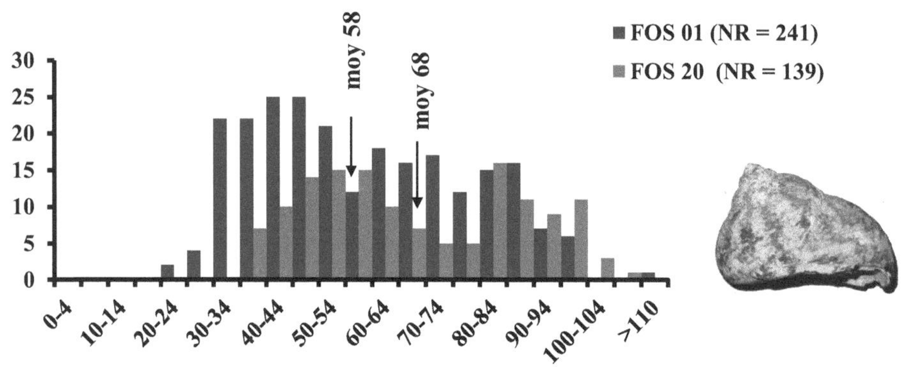

Figure 7. Distribution des individus de burgos, Cittarium pica, par classe de taille (longueur de la base Lb, mm) au sein de la fosse dépotoir FOS 01 et de la fosse dépotoir FOS 20.

plus particulièrement par des spécimens de taille moyenne et qu'*a contrario* la fosse dépotoir 20 se composait d'individus de plus grande taille (Figure 7).

Il faudrait à présent établir la contemporanéité (par une série de de datations 14C) des deux fosses pour confirmer ce double approvisionnement, ce qui permettrait peut-être de révéler une différence chronologique du prélèvement des individus.

Le site de Macaille étant situé à environ deux kilomètres des côtes les plus proches, le choix de collecte des burgos de toutes tailles était donc probablement intentionnel, les fruits de cette collecte pouvant être ensuite redistribués sur le site. Cette différence de taille peut également être liée soit à une collecte à des moments différents de l'année, soit parce que celle-ci a été réalisée par différentes personnes (*etc.*).

4.5 Hypothèses d'organisation spatiale du site

Les premières interprétations de l'habitation Macaille indiquaient une différenciation de chaque zone du site (Henry et al. 2009).

Au sud-ouest, un premier espace résidentiel composé de plusieurs bâtiments (UO 01 à UO 03). Au nord, un espace résidentiel qui correspondrait peut être au quartier d'habitation des esclaves (UO 08 à UO 12). En effet au début de l'esclavage sur les plantations, les quartiers d'esclaves étaient composés de cases individuelles contiguës à un jardin case. Ce qui semble être encore le cas à Macaille, bien qu'au XVIIIe siècle, la collectivisation de ces cases devient le modèle sur bon nombre d'habitation (Debien 1974). On parle alors de rues cases-nègres.

Et enfin à l'est, une zone regroupant plusieurs types d'activités : agropastorale d'une part, avec la présence de greniers aériens de plans carrés et de possibles enclos, et résidentielle d'autre part, avec deux bâtiments plus vastes que d'ordinaire sur le site et de plan régulier, UO19 et UO20. Bien que ces structures aient été le plus souvent interprétées comme étant des structures de stockage, le doute subsiste encore à propos du bâtiment 19. En effet, la régularité de son plan et ses dimensions importantes laissent ouverte l'hypothèse de la « grande case », bâtiment présent sur la plupart des plantations. Toutefois il convient également de noter le strict alignement entre ce bâtiment et l'accès aménagé dans la palissade qui ferme le site au sud, ce qui peut donc suggérer un bâtiment de remisage, entrepôt *etc.* L'une et l'autre hypothèse ne s'opposent pas nécessairement car celle-ci pouvait avoir différentes fonctions : habitation du maître, espace de stockage, ou encore, distribution des rations quotidiennes des esclaves sur certaines plantations, selon G. Debien (1974).

Si l'on suit ces premières observations, et à conditions que ces fosses soient contemporaines, alors le matériel retrouvé au sein de la fosse dépotoir 20 correspondrait au rejet alimentaire des esclaves. Quant à la fosse dépotoir 01, elle pourrait tout aussi bien correspondre aux rejets domestiques des colons qu'aux rejets des esclaves.

4.6 Dichotomie alimentaire entre colons et esclaves ?

En prenant l'hypothèse que la fosse 01 correspondrait aux rejets domestiques des colons et que la fosse 20 correspondrait aux rejets des esclaves, l'alimentation des colons sur cette habitation serait simplement plus diversifiée que celle des esclaves, essentiellement axée sur des espèces domestiques issues de l'Ancien Continent associé à quelques gastéropodes. Les rejets d'animaux domestiques de la fosse 20 seraient alors issus des reliefs des repas des maîtres utilisés en soupe. En effet, le rendement des esclaves dépendait avant tout de la manière dont ils étaient nourris. Les protéines issues de l'apport carné étaient donc nécessaires à ce rendement. Néanmoins d'après les propos de G. Debien (1964) au XVIIIe siècle, l'apport carné n'a plus aucune place dans l'alimentation des esclaves aux Antilles françaises et ce, malgré les prérogatives du Code Noir. Comment expliquer de ce fait la présence à la fois d'animaux domestiques et natifs au sein de la fosse dépotoir 20 ?

Il se peut donc que les textes historiques soient dogmatiques et non fondés sur une observation réelle des disparités existant entre habitations (que ce soit intra ou inter îles), de la chronologie, ou bien encore sans prendre en considération les ressources locales.

Enfin, dans le cas où les esclaves n'auraient pas reçu de ration carnée, ces deux fosses dépotoirs correspondraient aux rejets domestiques des colons uniquement. Les différences constatées au sein de ces deux fosses pourraient alors correspondre à l'élargissement de l'alimentation de base et à l'optimisation des territoires de chasse et de pêche présents à proximité du site de Macaille ; anticipant les disettes dont ils auraient pu souffrir.

4.7 Conclusions et perspectives

Un certain nombre de textes de chroniqueurs et d'archives coloniales offrent des témoignages sur l'alimentation des premiers colons qui se sont implantés dans ces nouveaux territoires : ils transportaient avec eux leurs habitudes culinaires (fruits et légumes, animaux). Mais, étant tributaires de l'arrivée des bateaux en provenance de métropole, les colons ont dû s'approprier les ressources disponibles autour d'eux au fil du temps et, de ce fait, élargir leur alimentation. De même, l'inventaire des vivres inclus dans les journaux de bords des navires négriers témoigne d'une nourriture principalement composée de bas morceaux d'animaux européens, complétés par des ressources locales. Ce que les fosses étudiées à Macaille semblent confirmer.

Les hypothèses que nous venons de développer, concernant une possible dichotomie alimentaire entre colons et esclaves semblent toutes, tout à fait plausible, et nous ne pouvons pas pour l'instant statuer sur la validité de l'une ou de l'autre. Bien que, selon les propos de Tardo-Dino (1985), l'alimentation des colons « *était à peu près semblable à celle des esclaves* ». Nous ne nous pourrons vraiment y répondre que lorsqu'on pourra comparer une poubelle d'habitation coloniale certifiée à une poubelle d'habitation d'esclave, à un instant défini.

La seconde moitié de la fosse 01 a été prélevée afin d'être tamisée et étudiée ultérieurement. Cette étude, ainsi que les futures études des poubelles des autres sites coloniaux découverts en Guadeloupe, et plus largement dans l'ensemble des Petites Antilles françaises, permettront de mieux cerner l'évolution du régime alimentaire des colons et celui des esclaves tant d'un point de vue régional que d'un point de vue chronologique.

Références bibliographiques

Behrensmeyer, A. K., et A.P. Hill

1980 *Fossils in the Making. Vertebrate Taphonomy and Paleoecology*. Chicago and London : The Chicago University Press.

Debien, G.

1964 La nourriture des esclaves sur les plantations des Antilles françaises aux XVIIe et XVIIIe siècles. *Caribbean Studies* 4(2):3-27.

1974 *Les esclaves aux Antilles françaises : XVIIe -XIXe siècle*. Société d'Histoire de la Guadeloupe et Société d'Histoire de la Martinique, Basse-Terre/Fort-de-France.

Dodson, P. et D. Wexlar

1979 Taphonomic investigations of owl pellets. *Paleobiology* 5:275–284.

Grouard, S.

2001 *Subsistance, systèmes techniques et gestion territoriale en milieu insulaire antillais précolombien. Exploitation des Vertébrés et des Crustacés aux époques Saladoïdes et Troumassoïdes de Guadeloupe (400 av. J.-C. à 1500 ap. J.-C.)*. Thèse de l'Université de Paris X- Nanterre, « Environnement et Archéologie ».

Henry, Y., F. Bigot, I. Gabriel, S. Grouard et N. Tomadini

2009 *Site de MACAILLE – Rue des Pommes Cannelles, Anse -Bertrand (Guadeloupe)*. Rapport final de fouille, Hadès.

Poplin, F.

1976a Remarques théoriques et pratiques sur les unités utilisées dans les études d'ostéologie quantitative, particulièrement en archéologie préhistorique. In *IXe Congrès de l'Union Internationale des Sciences Préhistoriques et Protohistoriques*, edited by L. Barral, pp. 124-141.

Serrand, N.

2002 *Exploitation des invertébrés marins et terrestres par les populations Saladoïdes et Post-Saladoïdes du Nord des Petites Antilles (500 B.C. – 1200 A.D.). Etude de cas et comparaisons.* Thèse de l'Université Paris I Panthéon-Sorbonne, Préhistoire-Ethnologie-Anthropologie.

2006 La Malacofaune. In *Fouille préventive de la Gare Maritime de Basse Terre (Guadeloupe).* Rapport final de fouille, Inrap GSO, pp. 126-184.

Tardo-Dino, F.

1985 *Le collier de la servitude. La condition sanitaire des esclaves aux Antilles françaises.* Editions caribéennes, Paris.

Chapter 5

Archaeological mitigation of a plantation family burying ground in Antigua

Tamara L. Varney

Lakehead University
Department of Anthropology
Thunder Bay
Canada
tvarney@lakeheadu.ca

Abstract

A site located on land leased by the US Air Force was initially thought to have only 3 relocated tombstones on it. Initial investigation revealed the presence of an actual historic cemetery that its usage was bounded from circa AD 1746 to 1820 based on dates inscribed on two of tombstones. Consultation with all stakeholders resulted in a decision to mitigate the cemetery to avoid any future disturbance. Archaeological, historical and osteological investigation of the site represents the first mitigation of an entire historic cemetery site on the island, and revealed some interesting contrasts with a previous project that focused on the burials of lower ranking naval personnel and enslaved Afro–Caribbeans. This project also represented investigation of a relatively unstudied burial population, that of members of the elite of colonial society. As such, the investigation provides a new window into life during the early historic period of the island that can be extrapolated to the entire region.

Résumé

Sur un terrain loué par l'armée de l'air des Etats Unis nous supposions la présence uniquement de trois pierres tombales déplacées. L'enquête initiale a en fait révélé la présence d'un véritable cimetière historique dont la période d'activité a pu être située entre 1746 et 1820 grâce aux dates inscrites sur les pierres tombales. La consultation de l'ensemble des parties prenantes a entraîné la mise en place d'une opération archéologique préventive afin d'éviter toute perturbation future. L'enquête archéologique, historique et ostéologique du site représente la toute première opération de ce type concernant un cimetière historique complet sur l'île et elle a révélé certains contrastes intéressants avec un projet précédent qui mettait l'accent sur les sépultures de membres de rang inférieurs du personnel de la marine et d'esclaves Afro–Caribéens. Ce projet a également représenté une enquête sur une population de sépulture relativement mal connu, celle des membres de l'élite de la société coloniale. Ainsi, l'enquête offre une nouvelle fenêtre dans la vie au cours des débuts de la période historique de l'île qui peut être extrapolée à toute la région.

Resumen

En un inicio, se pensó que un sitio localizado en terrenos arrendados por la Fuerza Naval de los Estados Unidos de América solamente existían 3 tumbas relocalizadas. Una investigación inicial reveló la presencia de un cementerio histórico cuyo uso data de 1746 hacia 1820 D.C. acorde a las fechas que aparecen inscritas en dos de las tumbas. Se realizó una consulta con todas las partes pertinentes la cual resultó en la decisión de mitigar completamente el cementerio para evitar molestias en el futuro. La investigación arqueológica, histórica y osteológica en este sitio representa la primera mitigación completa de un cementerio histórico en la isla. Éstas han revelado algunos contrates interesantes con un proyecto anterior que se enfocó en el entierro de personal naval de bajo nivel y esclavos afrocaribeños. Este proyecto también representó la investigación de una población relativamente poco estudiada: aquella de los miembros de la élite de la sociedad colonial. De tal modo que la investigación provee una nueva ventana a la vida durante un período primitivo histórico de la isla el cual puede ser extrapolado a la región completa.

Keywords

Historic archaeology, cemetery, plantation, Antigua

Mots-clés

Archéologie historique, cimetière, plantation, Antigua

Palabras clave

Arqueología histórica, cementerio, plantación, Antigua

Over the past decade, several historic cemeteries on Antigua have been exposed due to inclement weather, or discovered due to land development. Archaeological mitigation of these cemeteries has revealed burials ranging from British military personnel, including Navy–owned enslaved labourers, to members of the plantocracy (e.g., Varney & Nicholson 2001; Varney 2011). While these sorts of excavations typically begin as salvage activities, the potential for interesting research questions develops naturally as the project progresses. Bioarchaeological data from these sites provides a broad understanding of colonial life in Antigua and the greater region, as it allows access to the remains of the people themselves rather than relying solely on indirect evidence of human behaviour.

The skeletons of these people reflect biological accommodations to life on Antigua. Evidence from these skeletons, when combined with archaeological and historical evidence, allow a comprehensive understanding of the patterns of lifestyle and health of Antiguan colonial populations of the 18th and 19th centuries. Until recently, excavation and study of historic cemeteries has been uncommon not only in Antigua, but throughout the entire Caribbean. This is especially true of investigations of the burial grounds of non–enslaved colonists. The importance of these sites containing individuals of European origins cannot be overstated; it is only through analysis of all individuals from historic Antigua that a comprehensive picture of colonial life in the region can be reconstructed.

The focus of this chapter is on a plantation family burying ground that was excavated during the summer field seasons of 2007 and 2008. Each year a portion of the excavation was carried out in conjunction with a University of Calgary archaeological field school. Although the field seasons were short, this allowed a maximum of work to be done while providing exceptional training for students. This site was only the second such cemetery to be explored on Antigua, the Warner family cemetery being partially excavated in 2004–06 (Rebovich & Varney 2012). Together these two plantation family cemeteries have provided some interesting contrasts with the few other previously excavated historic period cemeteries.

The site is located in the northeast of Antigua near the present day airport, on land leased by the US Air Force for their Centralized Instrumentation Facility.

Figure 1. View of the site before mitigation.

Initial inspection of the site found a chain–link fence surrounding three tombstones, with a modern sign indicating that this was the Nibbs family burying ground. We had been told that the three tombstones on the site had probably been relocated there from nearby, placed upon a bed of gravel, with a fence then erected around them. Indeed, a superficial view of the site was consistent with such a scenario.

Inside the fence we found one small stone marker present on top of a gravel bed, with two larger markers nearby. At first glance neither of the two larger stones appeared to be original to the site. One of the two larger markers was fixed in place with modern concrete, and the other had been placed upon plywood resting on some cut blocks of historic vintage. Investigation revealed that those cut blocks had not been placed there recently, but rather were the top layer of a buried structure that appeared to be typical of the original bases of these types of large horizontal tombstones. This finding led us to suspect that there was at least one grave at the site and possibly more. It was clear to all stakeholders that the best course of action would be to determine the extent of the site and if any burials were found, to relocate them, pending potential development plans for the site. Heavy earthmoving equipment was brought in and the fence and tombstones

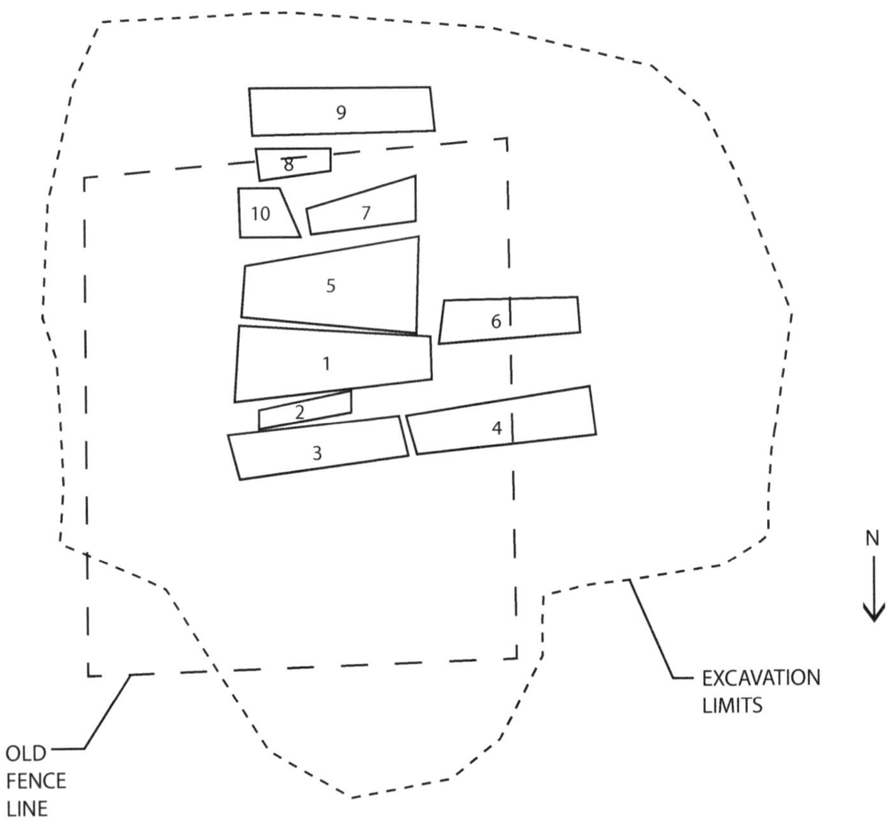

Figure 2. Map of the site showing the grave shaft features after the topsoil had been removed.

removed, with the latter being relocated for curation. Topsoil was scraped off using a backhoe equipped with an appropriately modified bucket. The area was then shovel cleaned, revealing 10 potential grave shaft features. Most of the features had already been identified in the course of excavation by the backhoe operator, who could feel the difference in resistance as the bucket passed over them. As predicted, there was not one grave at the site but rather an entire cemetery. After the mitigation was complete, the site was re–landscaped so that no visible traces of it remain.

Investigation into the history of the site began with the inscriptions on the tombstones. The first discovery was that the two larger stones were not made of locally found material, unlike the smallest stone which was of local origin. The large stones were carefully engraved with uniform and sophisticated script and images, with one of the stones bearing the name of an engraver in Bristol, England – again, unlike the small stone which was crudely carved. In contrast to the fine engraving on the other two stones, the small stone had been relatively roughly inscribed with a name now obscured, that had 'departed life on '1st of Oct' in a year and at an age that are now illegible. All of these facts indicated that the larger

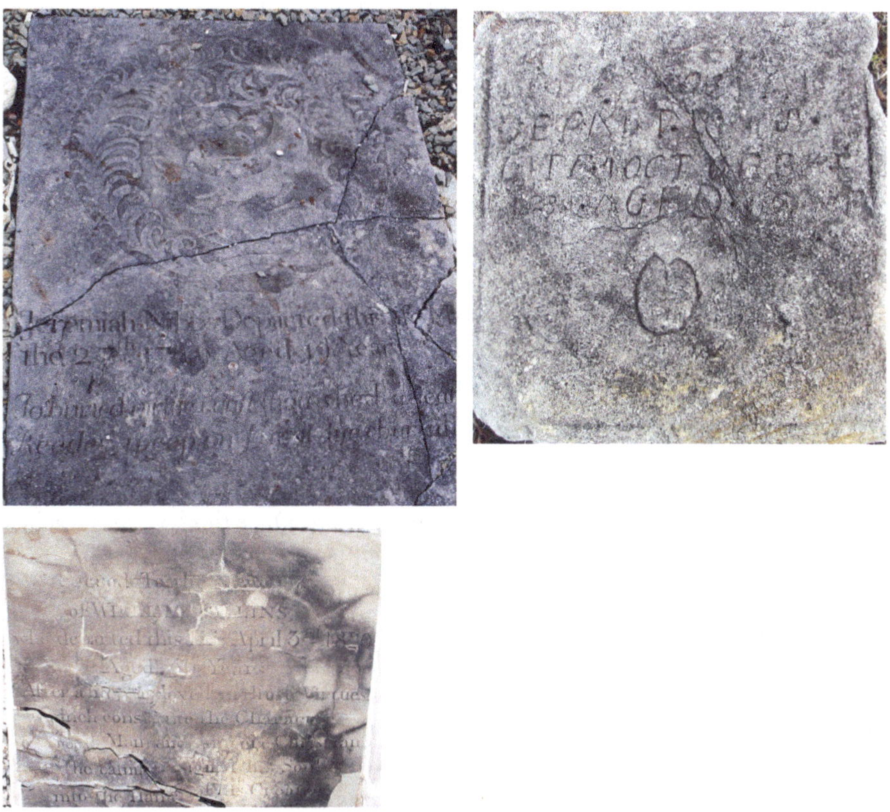

Figure 3. Tombstone inscriptions. Top left Jeremiah Nibbs; lower left William and Mary Hall Collins; upper right is the smaller marker made from local stone (note – not to scale).

two of the three tombstones at the site were of foreign manufacture and had been imported from England. These tombstones provided much valuable information about the site.

One of the tombstones was inscribed with the name 'Jeremiah Nibbs,' providing us with a starting point for our initial investigations that focused on that family name. Oliver's *History of Antigua* (1894) includes a listing of Nibbs family members that were interred in a family burying ground at Barnacle Point during the period from 1746 to 1808. Inspection of a 1775 map (Bowen 1747) revealed several plantations very close to Barnacle Point in the area of our site. We felt safe in the assumption that it was indeed the Nibbs family burying ground.

Jeremiah Nibbs died in 1746, giving us a potential start date. As a point of interest, a James Langford Nibbs, who was a third generation member of the family in Antigua, was an associate of George Austen – the father of the famous novelist Jane Austen – whom he appointed as trustee for some of his Antigua estates (Park and Rajan 2000). It has been speculated that the Antiguan plantation referred to in Jane Austen's novel *Mansfield Park* was modeled on the Nibbs estates.

The second large stone was inscribed with two names: William Collins, who died in 1820, and his daughter Mary Hall Collins, who predeceased him in 1815. Therefore, we can assume that this burying ground was in use until at least 1820. The appearance of the Collins name may indicate a change in control of the estate sometime between 1808 and 1820. Further to that point, the list of deceased Nibbs family members in Oliver's *History of Antigua* concludes with the last Nibbs to have been buried in the burying ground at Barnacle Point in August of 1808. According to Oliver, William Collins' death in 1820 was followed by his interment at the family burying ground (Oliver 1894). This presumably refers to the Collin's family cemetery, which may have then been that formerly in possession of the Nibbs family at Barnacle Point.

The third and smallest marker was made from locally available material. In contrast to the fine engraving on the other two stones, this one had been relatively roughly inscribed with a name since obscured, that had 'departed life on '1st of Oct' in a year and at an age that are also no longer legible.

Once the grave shaft features were revealed in the topsoil scrape, the sterile overburden was removed in thin layers with the backhoe to within a few centimeters of the top of the coffin in each grave shaft. Once this level was reached, a trench of greater depth was always maintained beside each grave shaft as it was excavated to facilitate easy access to the excavation. All further excavation was done by hand until each burial was fully removed. At the end of the mitigation, 10 burial features had been excavated yielding the remains of 12 individuals. Two of the features (Burials 2 and 8) were much smaller in all dimensions than the other graves. Excavation revealed small coffin outlines that clearly confirmed them to have been the burial places of infants. Two of the larger features contained multiple individuals, not from purposeful contemporaneous multiple interment but rather sequential burials. In one such instance (Burial 1), the act of burying the most recent individual had disturbed the remains of prior interments. The intact skeleton of the last interred individual was in a typical extended, supine position inside a coffin, with the partial remains of three adults and a juvenile packed relatively tightly around the head end of the coffin. As discussed below, another instance (Burial 5) was the sequentially–stacked double burial that contained the remains of William Collins and his daughter.

Preservation of all the excavated materials, including the coffins and skeletal remains, was very poor. In the infant burials, no skeletal material was found at all; however, undisturbed remnants of small coffins confirmed that the small grave shaft features had been used for burial. The poor preservation can be attributed to the soft marl, well known locally for its corrosive properties, which makes up the soil at the site. Such lime–based clay is known to hasten decomposition of bone in the burial environment (Collins et al. 2002). In the adult burials, it was the skull and teeth that were most often present and in the best condition, most of the post–cranial skeleton having completely disintegrated. When long bones were present, it was often only the anterior cortex that remained. A darkened colour and fibrous, loose texture to the soil marked where bony elements had previously been. Termites were abundant in the graves on the south side of the site and although they were found in great numbers around the skulls, they had caused no apparent damage to the bone. The buried plywood laid down atop the site between field seasons did not fare as well however, and after a year it was only present as a thin shell. A large canvas tarp that had covered the plywood entirely disappeared presumably due to the corrosive nature of the soil. The relatively well–preserved portions of some skeletons, such as four fused cervical vertebrae in Burial 10, stood in sharp contrast to the general state of the bone in the graves. There did not appear to be any spatial or temporal pattern to the preservation over the site.

The generally poor preservation of the skeletal material rendered any comprehensive analysis impossible, although some data were recovered. It was quite fortunate that sex determinations could be obtained for most of the adult individuals, and reasonably precise age estimates were derived for three individuals: one young adult, and two juveniles. These determinations had to be done *in situ* rather than risk the loss of information as the fragile elements were recovered. Based on cranial morphology and the scant remains of the few os coxae, there were seven adult males, one adult female, and two adults of indeterminate sex. There were also two juvenile individuals of indeterminate sex, one aged four and the other 10–14 years of age.

Preservation of the coffins and associated hardware was also generally poor. Although the marl soil at the site might have had an influence on this poor preservation, similarly poor preservation has been identified at other historic cemetery sites that have been excavated on Antigua (Varney & Nicholson 2001). The shape of the coffins was only discernible from the pattern of hardware remnants, most of which was in fragments. All interments were in hexagonal wooden coffins that were similar in basic size and construction to those found in roughly contemporaneous sites elsewhere on the island. The coffins of adults and the older juvenile had eight swing bail handles, while the smaller coffins for the infants had four fixed handles. Another similarity with the other excavated sites in Antigua was the almost complete lack of personal effects. Such items that were found are similar to those identified at the other sites, and were limited to a few copper alloy straight pins and a couple of one–holed bone buttons found in the torso area of many of the adult burials (Varney and Nicholson 2001).

The unique feature at this site was the presence of ornamentation upon the coffins. As mentioned above, the poor preservation rendered detailed reconstruction impossible. The simplest remains of coffin decoration were rows of brass tacks along the sides of the coffin. As most remnants of the wooden coffin body itself had long decayed away, it was often these tacks, some of which still had small fragments of wood adhering to them, that revealed the shape of the coffins. The brass and iron nails used in the construction of the coffins were also present but more widely spaced. The context and orientation of the head and shank of the *in situ* brass alloy tacks made determination of some coffin details easier to discern. Small fragments of textile were sometimes found adhered to the brass tacks, reflecting their role in securing the fabric that would have covered both the outside and inside of the coffin. Fragments of white metal strips and sheeting that had been impressed with various designs were also plentiful.

Conjectural reconstruction based on the positioning of the fragments indicates banding of white metal both along the sides and across the breadth of the coffins. Designs on these strips consisted of embossed ovals bordered on both sides by a braided cord motif. White metal sheeting impressed with designs of swirling vines, florets and leaves could be discerned from fragments that once adorned the coffin lid. Similarly patterned fragments were also found on the coffin handle lugs, which at one time had been ornate, but due to the ferrous metal content of the handles had been distorted by corrosion to the extent that the patterns were no longer discernible. The sketch of the coffin ornamentation that could be discerned was consistent with funerary practices contemporaneous with the burying ground (Litten 1991).

Coffin plates of white and/or copper metal overlying ferrous metal were evident in all but the grave of Jeremiah Nibbs (Burial 3) and one of the infants. Since the actual coffin lids had long ago disappeared to decay, these plates were found above or upon any surviving skeletal remains. Most of the coffin plates had disintegrated to very small fragments or dust, and any imagery or inscriptions had been long lost. An exception is the coffin plate found in Burial 4 which has some discernible text and imagery. A partial inscription in white painted text underlies three flying cherub heads, and is framed by two trumpet–blowing angels. The word 'daily' can be read, likely part of an epitaph to the deceased who died at age 39 in the year 1816. The name of the deceased is no longer discernible. Given the previous assumptions made about changes in the control of the property over time, the date in the inscription suggests that this may have been a member of the Collins family.

The Nibbs family members interred in the family burying ground from 1746 to 1808 that are listed in Oliver (1894) consist of four males and two females, presumably all adults, as well as one infant, for a total of seven recorded burials. If we exclude the three Collins burials, there is fairly good, although not perfect,

Figure 4. Coffin plate Burial 4 – it was very fragmentary but careful examination yielded some detail (see text).

Figure 5. Lettering on the coffin top of Burial 3.

correspondence between Oliver's list and the remains excavated. Three excavated individuals including one adult, one juvenile and one infant are not accounted for in the published list. This discrepancy may be due to omissions due to lack of data for all burials in the historic record. This may not be surprising considering that Oliver's list was published in 1894, almost 90 years after the last listed burial in 1808.

The only grave that is easily matched to one of the names on Oliver's list is Burial 3, the interment place of Jeremiah Nibbs, who died in 1746. One of the large tombstones was a marker for his grave and indicates that he was 19 years of age at the time of his death. This grave did, indeed, contain skeletal remains consistent with a very young adult male. The coffin was decorated with multiple rows of brass tacks along its lid and sides that were in excess of the amount that would be needed to fasten fabric coffin lining or covers. The lid also bore wooden alpha–numeric characters outlined with brass tacks. The copper content of the tacks were in all likelihood responsible for the remarkable preservation of these items. Only one of the letters had been damaged so that its identity was initially unclear upon its discovery. Although the lid had long collapsed, the positioning of the many letters and numbers provided the clues necessary to decipherment. After they were all uncovered, they were revealed to be the initials of the deceased, his year of death and his age at time of death.

The second of the two large tombstones was inscribed for two members of the Collins family and lay above Burial 5, which, indeed did contain the remains of two individuals, one buried atop the other. The upper burial had the only completely legible coffin plate, which was inscribed with the name of William Collins, his age and date of death. The sex and rough age estimation of the remains associated with this coffin plate were consistent with an older adult male, providing good correspondence between the remains, the associated coffin plate and the tombstone. The lower burial contained a skeleton that had ambiguous sex traits and an associated coffin plate in very poor condition. Only the position of this burial beneath both William Collins and the tombstone provided evidence to its probable identity as his daughter Mary Hall Collins.

The sole other planter family cemetery to be the subject of an archaeological investigation on Antigua was the Warner family burying ground, where only three grave shaft features were completely excavated (Rebovich & Varney 2012). The feature designated Burial 1 at that site was shallow and had not actually been used for interment. Burial 4 was the interment of a 5 month old child buried in a coffin whose handle grip remnants were similar to those found in the Nibbs site. Burial 2 was the grave of an adult male who had been interred in a coffin with metal strapping, which although relatively plain, was similar in its placement on the coffin to those found at the Nibbs family burying ground.

Two distinct dissimilarities were noted between the interments at the Nibbs family burying ground and those from the naval hospital cemetery excavated on the island from 1998–2001 (Varney & Nicholson 2001). These contrasts are perhaps attributable to the socioeconomic background and residency of the interred. The military cemetery associated with the Royal Naval Hospital contained individuals that were of lower rank not only in the Navy, but also likely in overall society as well. Individuals who were very likely enslaved were also interred in this cemetery. Inclusion of members of the enslaved underclass was a notable characteristic of the naval site that reflects a division of military and civilian practice. Civilian cemeteries were always segregated, with the families of the plantocracy representing the upper echelons of Antiguan society, a contrast with the populations serving in the Navy.

The second contrast was in the plainness or complete lack of coffins at the naval hospital cemetery site (Varney 2011; Varney & Nicholson 2001). Again this underscores the social divide between the military stationed on Antigua and civilian residents of the island. A naval hospital obviously had a more frequent need for expedient burial than a family. The lack of close familial and other support networks of military personnel ensured swift, unceremonial interment. The disparities in resources, both economic and social, are apparent when compared to the attention paid to the burial of deceased in this planter family burying ground.

One common feature all of the cemeteries excavated on the island is the paucity of personal effects found with the human remains. This suggests that inclusion of such items were not part of any of the burial rituals regardless of residency or station of life.

Further comparison of the cemeteries is currently being done via gross osteological analysis, stable isotope analysis and trace element analysis. These promise to further the insight into colonial life that began with the mitigation of these cemetery sites. Sites such as the one that is the focus of this chapter are particularly interesting as most cemetery sites that have been excavated on Antigua and elsewhere in the region have been the burial grounds of the enslaved or other underclass people. Investigation and dissemination of work on sites such as the Nibbs family burying ground allows a unique look at the plantocracy, and permits a comparative, and more integrative approach, to our understanding of colonial life on Antigua and the surrounding region. The importance of mobilizing the information cannot be stressed enough. Not only is such work on any segment of colonial populations relatively uncommon and therefore important, it is often only known to limited audiences due to its publication being limited to specialist reports to and by government departments. It is only through the sharing of such information that these data can then be coupled with other lines of evidence to better inform our understanding of the colonial past of not only Antigua, but the entire region.

References

Bowen, E.

1747 *A new and accurate map of the island of Antigua or Antego, taken from surveys, and adjusted by astronl. observations. Containing all the towns, parish churches, forts, castles, windmills, roads &c.* Printed for William Innys, R.Ware, A. Ward, J. and P. Knapton, J. Clarke, T. Longman and T. Shewell, T. Osborne, H.Whitridge, London.

Collins, M.J., C. M. Nielsen–Marsh, J. Hiller, C. I. Smith, J. P. Roberts, R. V. Prigodich, T. J. Wess, J. Csapò, A. R. Millard and G. Turner–Walker

2002 The Survival of Organic Matter in Bone: a review. *Archaeometry* 44(3):383–394.

Litton, J.

1991 *The English Way of Death: the common funeral since 1450*. Robert Hale, London.

Oliver, V. Langford

1894 *The History of the Island of Antigua, one of the Leeward Caribbees in the West Indies, from the first settlement in 1635 to the present time.* Mitchel and Huges, London.

Park, Y.M. and S.R. Rajeswari

2000 *The Postcolonial Jane Austen.* Routledge, NY.

Rebovich, S. and T. Varney

2012 *A summary report on 2004 & 2006 mitigations at Warner's Estate (PAH–001). Report on file at the Dockyard Museum, English Harbour, Antigua, W.I.*

Varney, T. L.

2011 The Royal Naval Hospital cemetery at English Harbour, Antigua: not just the "Grave of the Englishman". *Proceedings of the XXIII International Congress for Caribbean Archaeology, Antigua, 2009*. pp. 447–459. Antigua.

Varney, T. L. and D. V. Nicholson

2001 Digging the "Grave of the Englishman": a preliminary report on excavations at a former British Navy Hospital cemetery, English Harbour, Antigua. *Proceedings of the XVIII International Congress for Caribbean Archaeology, Grenada, WI*, 1999. Tome I, pp. 329–335. Grenada.

Chapter 6

Administering Diversity

Comparison of Everyday Life and Trade on Two Plantations in Early Colonial Dominica (1763-1807)

Mark Hauser

Department of Anthropology
Northwestern University
Evanston
Illinois
mark-hauser@northwestern.edu

Abstract

In 1763 Dominica was the last island to be formally colonized in the Caribbean basin. Located between Guadeloupe and Martinique, two islands colonized by France in the mid seventeenth century, Dominica was declared Neutral and a homeland for the exiled Kalinago. Estates like Bois Cotlette represent a particular kind of settlement during the colonial period. Though poorly documented, and beyond the watchful eye of colonial structures and rules, these phenomenon were central to the economic and social transformations of the region. I make two arguments here. First, that slavery and markets were constituent elements for the British Empire. Second, slavery in these instances cannot be defined solely through the idioms of property or chattel- rather it was mechanism of governance through which the empire administered diversity.

Résumé

En 1763 la Dominique fut la dernière île du bassin caraïbe a être officiellement colonisée. Située entre la Guadeloupe et la Martinique, deux îles colonisées par la France au milieu du XVIIe siècle, la Dominique fut déclarée neutre et son occupation réservée aux Kalinago durant la période coloniale. Les habitations comme celle de Bois Cotlette représentent ainsi une forme particulière d'installations coloniales. Bien que faiblement documentés et se déroulant en dehors des règles et des structures coloniales, ses phénomènes furent centraux dans les changements sociaux qu'a connu la région ainsi qu'à son économie. Nous souhaitons ici développer deux points. Premièrement, l'esclavage et l'économie de marché furent des éléments constitutifs pour l'empire britannique. Deuxièmement, l'esclavage dans ces conditions ne peut être seulement définie en termes de propriétés (chattel slavery), il fut aussi un mécanisme de gouvernance qui servit à l'empire britannique a administrer la diversité.

Resumen

Esultados preliminares obtenidos en Bois Cotlette, Dominica y limitados a finales del siglo XVIII indican un conjunto complejo de redes económicas anidadas en la producción del paisaje. Hoy día, en Dominica los registros de historias orales, documentales y arqueológicos son limitados. Los patrones de estas fuentes en el siglo XIX apuntan a un comercio fluido de productos y a veces de personas - un comercio cuya naturaleza ilícita continua hoy día. Extendiéndonos al siglo XVIII, donde le registro documental es muy fragmentado y la historia oral es de poca resolución, nuestra única opción como una de nuestras herramientas principales para entender el comercio normalizado pero poco documentado es el registro arqueológico. Propiedades como Bois Coltlette pueden ser interpretadas como parte de un movimiento fronterizo, extendiendo la modernidad europea a través de regímenes de control y tecnologías de espacio. Estas fronteras representan historias completamente distintas. La explotación de los límites fronterizos no sólo consolidan el control sino que también se aprovechan de las relaciones sociales variegadas que se llevaron acabo en múltiples niveles sociales.

6.1 Introduction

In this chapter I make the argument that empires governed their diverse land-holding subjects in the Caribbean through slavery. I utilize archaeological and historical evidence from two enclaves in Dominica: Portsmouth and Soufriere and compare two plantations (Figure 1). These communities were occupied during the height and eventual demise of plantation slavery (1763-1834), were settled by Europeans of multiple national backgrounds, enslaved Africans, and Kalinago (or indigenous) inhabitants. While the exact contours of these settlements differ, variation in size, density and context are predictable given the environmental, legal, economic constraints that freeholders and leaseholders found themselves. The material dispositions of their inhabitants, however, were not predictable.

This chapter is part of a larger a project that seeks to compare these two community histories and the social lives of enslaved laborers in them. Before writing this history I realized it was important to describe the histories and social lives of the people who owned the estates. In general plantation slavery in the Caribbean has been examined as a way to describe an emergent world system in which a plantation serves as one locus in a world system composed of imperial metropoles such as London, and colonial peripheries such as Dominica; or as a site of cultural continuity and inventiveness despite asymmetrical relationships of power. While

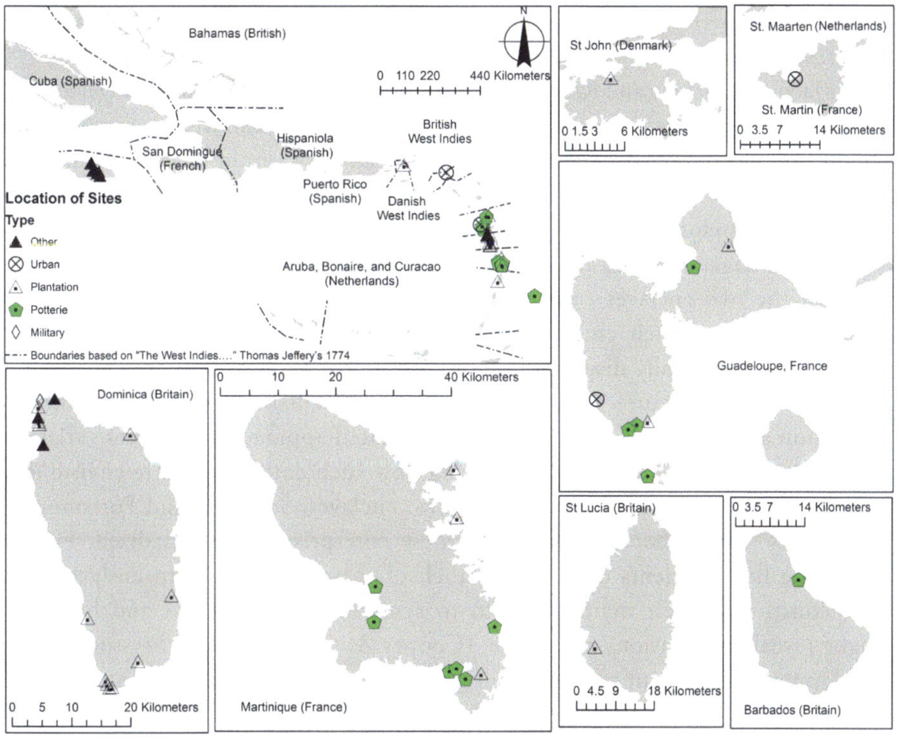

Figure 1. The Caribbean in 1763. Recreated from Jeffries 1768. Location of Dominica.

these two approaches are not mutually exclusive, they have presented somewhat of a dichotomy in the historiography and archaeology of the Caribbean: that of structure versus agency; slavery versus slave life; mercantile regime versus everyday life in the colonial world. In both perspectives the plantation is a function of predatory capitalism where the ambitions of merchants, planters, and political elites worked more or less together in lockstep with metropolitan ambitions. In contrast, diversity and agency is located in the actions of enslaved Africans. In this chapter I argue that our understanding of Caribbean colonial society is greatly improved if we also consider the agency of estate owners and their different ambitions in historical context. Here slavery is not only an economic relationship of labor, but also a way to govern. It was a strategy through which empires, like Great Britain, involved new and existing subjects into their colonial administrators.

The Eastern Caribbean in the eighteenth century is an ideal place to explore these questions for a number of reasons. First, the documentary record, including land lists, slave registers and accounts produce, provides details about material practice and governing policies that aid in archaeological interpretation. This provides a great resource to describe the potential differences between measures taken by imperial administrators and the practices of colonial settlers and slaves, especially in relation to the administering of diversity. Second, as a region it was a terrain of enormous territorial dispute over colonies that produced considerable wealth in comparison to their population and size within the respective managing empires. It was, therefore, of intense interest to the Atlantic empires.

As Jacques Mathieu and Reginald Auger have noted (Mathieu 2008; Auger 2008), in mercantile enterprises, such as establishing a sugar plantation, entrepreneurs would first have to envision their enterprise, then they would have to acquire the means through which to actualize that enterprise, and only then would they create monumental architecture to symbolically display their success. A comparison of two estates, Sugar Loaf and Bois Cotlette, shows that some of the differences found between the two enclaves can be largely explained by the decisions of planters as they envisioned their enterprise, acquired the means including buildings and slaves, and symbolically displayed their wealth in the form of imported goods and monumental architecture. Specifically I begin by discussing general approaches to plantation archaeology and show how a multi-sited approach introduces variation that must be considered when considering how such enterprises were envisioned. I then turn to a comparative analysis of two enclaves, Soufriere and Portsmouth, and estates within them to show how these enterprises were actualized. Finally I examine how residents of estates in each of these enclaves, both enslaved and free, constituted their material world to symbolize their success and how this might reveal the 'tensions of empire' (Cooper & Stoler 1998). The story of the development and layout of plantation settlements and things found in the house yards of enslaved laborers tells a story that makes sense when we put aside historical narratives that were the product of the times in which these people lived.

6.2 Sugar estates in the Caribbean colony

In 1763 Britain assumed control of the formerly neutral island of Dominica and with it approximately eight hundred French subjects and enslaved people that labored in their informal industries[1]. Before 1763 the last island colonized by England was Jamaica in 1655. While the Western Design which prompted the take-over of Jamaica could best be described as England stumbling into empire, by 1763 stipendry magistrates, colonial administrators, and Parliamentarians thought they knew what they were doing. On Dominica four interrelated issues with settlement of the island were: 1) securing the political and economic integrity of the island through the building of fortifications to monitor enemy (in this case French) navies and contraband trade generating wealth for the metropole through immediate sugar production (Sheridan 1963); 3) mitigating the power of a politically active planter class (Ragatz 1963; Atwood 1791); and 4) integrating French settlers and their enslaved laborers who occupied land, grew coffee and purportedly had continued economic and social ties through trade with the French colonies of Martinique and Guadeloupe (Honychurch 1995; Atwood 1791; Edwards 1793).

Two properties, one outside of Portsmouth and the other near Soufriere, began to be retasked to sugar manufacture. Sugar Loaf Estate (Figure 2) is located in a wide alluvial plain along the Indian River directly to the south of Portsmouth.

1 Only one enterprise experimented with sugar- a mission/estate owned and operated by Perre la Violet a Grandbay in southeastern Dominica and this was ultimately unsuccessful (Lenik 2010).

While the property was initially purchased through a partnership in 1763, by 1768 it had passed into the hands of a London-based merchant, Richard Neave, who had aspirations for social advancement. During the course of the last quarter of the eighteenth century Neave would become a governor of the Bank of England and obtain the barrontage of Dangam Park. Bois Cotlette (Figure 2) lies in a saddle between Morne Vert and Morne Patate in the southwest of Dominica. It was named after the Bois Cotlette tree (*Citharexylum spinosum*). A French family, Louis and Adrien la Ferrier Constance settled this land in the late 1740's. By the mid 1770's it was acquired, through marriage, by Joseph Bellot. Unlike Neave, the Constances and the Bellots were long-term residents whose aspirations for social advancement would have been more immediately realized in colonial Dominica. Both estates were part of a larger constellation of imperial interests.

The Caribbean basin was the focus of European imperial design and contention in the seventeenth and eighteenth centuries. Laws passed by crowns and parliaments of Europe, wars fought and concluded with massive land transfers in the Caribbean Basin, and the flow of wealth, things, and people to and from the region highlight the centrality of the Caribbean in Atlantic empires. The boundaries of territorial holdings by European powers were not generally recognized until 1713 and remained contested throughout the eighteenth century. Legislative acts and imperial practices such as the *Asiento,* the *Exclusif* and the Navigation Acts codified these relationships to make imperial control more complete (Sheridan 1974). There

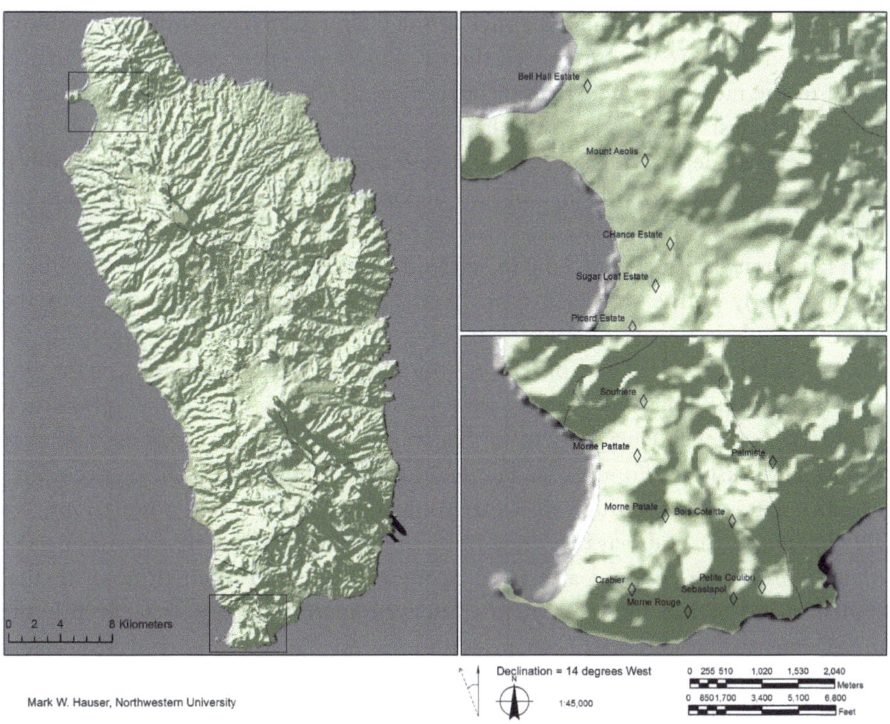

Figure 2. Location of Portsmouth (Top) and Soufriere (Bottom) enclaves. Location of is indicated with the blue dot. Sugar Loaf (Top) and Bois Cotlette (Bottom) Estates.

were, however, numerous colonial strategies of settlements, economic endeavors, military ventures and kinds of habitations that composed the mosaic of social and cultural practices in the Caribbean.

The most ubiquitous and economically important loci of human settlement and interaction were the ports and plantations. As such plantations and ports could be seen as both passive and active agents of imperial strategies of colonial settlement, the establishment of boundaries, and the policing of those boundaries. In general, between the seventeenth and nineteenth centuries, imperial agents typically viewed the Caribbean colony as both a source of harvested commodities and a market for mass produced goods (Sheridan 1994). Plantation settlements can be helpful in understanding the diverse strategies of colonial administrations in that they present a unit of observation that evokes both global and local relationships of power and exchange (Pulsipher 1995; Handler & Lange 1978; Armstrong 1983, 1990; Howson 1995; Reeves 1998; Delle 1994, 1998; Higman 1998; Wilkie & Farnsworth 2001). Intra-site comparisons of domestic contexts associated with elites and slaves have been particularly useful in understanding the institution of slavery and mechanisms of identity formation (Delle 1998, 1994). While some elements such as plantation layout tend to be circumscribed to particular plantations, the archaeological assemblages in house-yards, in plantation villages, and tenements and servants quarters in the city, tend to be constituted of a similar combination of goods made in Europe, North America, and locally (Kelly 2002, 2003; Kelly & Gibson 2005). Such goods can constitute idioms of material expression that were refashioned either through alteration or assemblage into ways unexpected by those who organized their production. These assemblages can also speak to the more local networks of reciprocity, exchange, and market activity in which both enslaved laborers and planters partook (Hauser et al. 2007). As such these data provide a wonderful comparative framework through which to establish a chronological framework for cultural deposits and to understand the material habits of planters and slaves.

Plantations as a focus of human settlement and interaction in the Caribbean begin as early as the sixteenth century in Hispaniola and continue up to the present. A plantation was typically an agricultural complex including fields (in use and fallow), gardens and provision grounds, residences of laborers, managers, and owners, buildings and features devoted to the processing of the agricultural products, and dependency structures that were tasked with everyday maintenance including workshops, store houses, laborer hospitals, and wharves. Different empires had different regimes through which they managed their enslaved populations. We are challenged to find ways to draw both similarities and differences among the island lives of the enslaved and freed peoples of the Caribbean through textual evidence and archaeological remains. Such comparisons allow a view into the management of colonies in both prescription and practice. Locating reasonably compact regions in which competing empires like Great Britain and France had subjects establishing plantations at the same time, become useful for determining the range of variation in the internal layout of plantations, the nature of economic interaction of the inhabitants of those plantations, and the degree to which spatial proximity brought about change over time.

The material conditions on which these empires were based were slavery and markets. In what is referred to as the middle passage, approximately 42 percent of the almost 12 million people abducted from West Africa were intended for the Caribbean. In theory, mercantilism was well suited for colonial empires. In British colonies, the English Navigation Acts privileged royal monopolies and metropolitan manufacturing interests. Envisioned as part of an imperial economy, Jamaica and Dominica were sources for sugar, coffee, and indigo as well as markets for goods manufactured in England, Ireland, and Scotland (Best 1998; Dunn 1972; Williams 1961). By 1770, the West Indies accounted for 25 percent of all British imports and 15 percent of all British exports (Deane 1965: 56). The Navigation Acts maintained this relationship, and although they saw numerous alterations through the course of the 18th century, they remained officially in effect until 1849.

Growing and processing materials like sugar, coffee, and indigo dye required enormous amounts of labor. According to the most recent estimates, of the 11.8 million Africans brought to the Americas, nearly 42 percent were brought to the Caribbean to work in the sugar, coffee, and indigo agroindustries. In 18th-century Dominica, this created a highly uneven slave society, in which enslaved laborers comprised 85 percent of Dominica's population. This majority was unevenly distributed on plantations in fertile valleys and coastlines, producing an effect whereby estate managers and resident owners were isolated from one another. Colonial assemblies promulgated codes designed to control slave populations (Goveia 1970) and ensure their care. Estate owners paid special attention to placement and organization of estates with two principle concerns: efficiency of movement (Higman 1987) and power (Delle 1998: 115; Singleton 2001). Certainly technologies of race and racialization were realized in such spaces (Delle 2001), but these landscapes also led to opportunities for the enslaved to circumvent observation and control (Hauser 2008: 35).

The distances between colony and empire were vast, and the territorial boundaries of the holdings were not contiguous. Sir William Young wrote about governing diverse populations of enslaved laborers, foreign nationals, free people of color, poor whites, and a plantocracy that often worked at cross-purposes to the colonial enterprise (Young 1807). Colonies needed to be provisioned despite vulnerabilities of merchant shipping to attack (Pares 1936), close proximity of competing mercantile interests (Perotin-Dumon 1991:58), and failures by merchant backers to anticipate island contingencies resulting from natural disasters (i.e., hurricanes and earthquakes; see Sheridan 1976:638). In addition, the asymmetrical power relations of slave society generated a constant threat of violence for all sectors of society (Burnard 2004: 104, 171).

Despite these difficulties, the profits and prestige that derived from owning estates would have to be powerful motivation for long term residents and new investors from the England. In popular culture, the Caribbean plantation owner became synonymous with material excess and wealth. Certainly in the world described by Jane Austen, the wealth generated to set the scene for so many intrigues in the circulation of daughters and surplus sons of London had a proximate origin in the Caribbean. Austen locates the provenance of such wealth in *Mansfield Park* in the form of Sir Thomas Bertram. Indeed, the phrase "so rich as a Jamaican Planter" continued to be used well after the demise of slavery in the mid-nineteenth century (Trollope 1859: 26). Neave was trying to profit off the recent acquisition of the Island by Britain. For Neave, a son of an English merchant who would have been considered 'new money', this property was part of increasingly large portfolio of overseas investment and way to display his status at home in London.

For the French who had lived in Dominica since the 1750's, the British takeover of the island represented two things. First, under informal French control, the Constances were most likely considered *petit blanc*- poor white settlers eking out a living on the margins of colonial Martinique. Sugar cultivation was kept to a minimum for several reasons. First, the informal and tenuous nature of settlements in disputed territory led to an ever-present fear of evacuation that prevented much in the way of formal investment. Second, British annexation enabled official foreign investment to build the machinery necessary to process sugar cane. Until this point, patrons in Martinique and Guadeloupe did not want competition and thus restricted investment in some enterprises such as sugar. In Dominica, most of the agricultural activities took the form of cotton [261,000 pied], cacao [952,000 pieds], plantains [253,000 pieds] and coffee [1585 pieds] (Boromé 1972:68). Along with British colonization came the first real opportunity to take advantage of the high demand for sugar in the world market.

In what follows I compare two enclaves (Portsmouth and Soufriere) and the estates found within them. Michelle Rolph Trouillot (1988: 27-32) described Dominica as a 'patchwork of enclaves' where until recently, different communities in the northern, southern and eastern parishes were relatively isolated from each other, each producing separate cultural trajectories. Focused around coastal villages, including Portsmouth and Soufriere, that acted as ports for inter-coastal trade, people inhabiting these enclaves developed economic and social ties, for which it was more expedient to travel to ports in nearby Martinique or Guadeloupe than the political capital of Roseau (Honychurch 1995a: 67-68). It should be noted that the Portsmouth Enclave is much larger than the Soufriere Enclave. Importantly, these enclaves are close to inter-coastal trade ports of various sizes that connect settlements within the enclaves to international and regional trade networks including Portsmouth and Roseau. In short, rough terrain on Dominica created independent communities that lacked substantial communication with each other. They were independent producers that competed with each other for foreign markets. Thus, we would expect differences in their production strategies. This is an excellent opportunity to address production from the perspective of plantation-owner agency, and to highlight contrasting agency on the part of plantation slaves.

6.3 Enclaves in Dominica

> *"A distant province of empire can only be wisely and well governed, in proportion as the interests and condition of the people, and the resources of the country, are known and understood. "* (Sir William Young 2nd barronett 1807)

In the opening passage, Sir William Young, son of the then President of the Commission for the Sale of Lands in the Ceded Islands and Lieutenant Governor for the Island of Dominica (1725-1788), hints at some of the difficulties in managing a diverse population and recognizing the diverse agendas of the inhabitants. While the rest of his monograph documents the varied successes of the British in the Windward Islands, it also documents the uneasy transition that inhabitants of the ceded islands had into the British realm. It is true that the acquisition of Dominica at the end of the Seven Years' War was in part an economic calculation. At the time the sugar colonies of Barbados and Jamaica, and Saint Domingue and Martinique were Britain and France's most economically important overseas territories. But the colonization was also important for developing solidarities and incorporating the interests of imperial subjects who might possibly act at cross-purposes. What follows is a comparison of two enclaves, Portsmouth and Soufriere, and the plantations that were established within them (Figure 2). Two estates are crucial to this analysis, Sugar Loaf and Bois Cotlette. The owners of these estates were potentially dissonant subjects in the British Empire.

In 1763 Britain was a polity slightly older than 50 years in which an English parliament subsumed a diverse population of Irish, Scots and Welsh subjects under a Hanoverian monarch. As historian Jack Greene describes the situation, England 'was, for much of the two centuries after 1560 and more especially after the union with Scotland, a composite state characterized by indirect governance, fragmented authority, an inchoate theory of national sovereignty, and limited fiscal, administrative, and coercive resources' (2000: 93; see also Greene, 2001). In 1708 the Act of Union imposed a single monarchy in England, Scotland and Wales and in 1714 the house of Hanover was placed on the throne. Add to that in 1715 and 1745 the Jacobite uprisings that attempted to restore the Stuart line on the throne. Ultimately by 1763 the government had developed considerable debt in its prosecution of the Seven Years' War (1757-1762), a significant portion of which was to merchants. In other words merchants became an increasingly important economic and political force in a metropolitan Britain where there was little history of political solidarity.

The conclusion of the Seven Years' War also saw the incorporation of francophone subjects, many of whom might have viewed the new political structures, mercantile regimes, and legal codes that accompanied formal colonization as an imposition to work around. Between the 1690s and the 1740s, various European squatters, coffee planters, lumbermen, and fishermen settled Dominica in the hope of finding a stake in an increasingly crowded and profitable Caribbean. By 1699, the English attempted to establish a fort just south of Roseau (in an area called Castle Comfort today) and by 1727, the Governor of Martinique appointed a commander to oversee the French subjects on the island. After 1763 colonial administrators were suspicious of the French and their allegiance to foreign powers. In 1798 Bryan Edwards remarked “To this day, however, the French inhabitants constitute the more numerous people in the island. These receive their manners and religion principally from Martinique, on which the island is looked upon as an appendage” (Edward 1794: 109).

When Britain absorbed Dominica, administrators promoted the establishment of sugar plantations. In 1763, 94,345 acres were apportioned, mapped and sold (Byres, 1776). This apportionment was documented in what has been referred to as the Byres Map, a document published by John Byres under the commission of Sir William Young (1725–1788), the President of the Commission for the Sale of Lands in the Ceded Islands (known hereafter as the Commission). It was linked to an index of ownership that detailed who the freeholders of the land were and who the leaseholders of the land were (Byres, 1777). This was not an outright land grab. Potential British owners were allowed to purchase property, however they were restricted to a relatively small 300 acres per purchaser. This was an attempt on the part of the commission to mitigate the growing planter interest. The remaining French subjects were also not allowed to own land and required to lease their property from the British crown until they were able to demonstrate their loyalty. Loyalty was demonstrated through an oath of allegiance to the sovereign, an oath of supremacy- no other power or religious authority was superior to the king, an oath that King George the III was the rightful king, and an oath rejecting trans-substantiation (Honychurch 1994).

We find both documentary and archaeological evidence that these prescriptions did result in a transformation of the landscape of Dominica. When Britain took over Dominica in 1763 the crown instituted several policies designed to administer the colony and create a profitable economy. Whereas between 1766 and 1769 the island produced an average of 186 tons of sugar per year, between 1775 and 1779 that number increased to 1872 tons per year demonstrating the success of these policies.

Labor had to be imported to meet the needs of the burgeoning sugar industry. Joseph Boromé estimates that by the time Britain took control of Dominica there were 7892 non-Kalinago inhabitants, of whom 5872 were enslaved Africans, 300 were free people of color and 1718 were white. Between 1771 and 1780, 36,930 slaves disembarked into Dominica (Transatlantic Database). In 1788 there were 14,967 enslaved laborers. These numbers represent a rapid increase in the intensity of slave trafficking to the island that mirrors other islands like Jamaica where in between 1751 and 1760 102,041 slaves disembarked and between 1771 and 1780 125,983 slaves disembarked. There is also a marked difference in the number of slaves disembarking and the resident slave population in 1788.

This is in part due to the high mortality rate of slaves working on sugar fields in the West Indies. It also was the result of Dominica’s status as a Freeport. In 1766, the British Parliament passed the Freeports Act, making four ports in Jamaica open to trade with the Spanish and two ports in Dominica open to trade with the French. The goal was to aggravate Spanish and French colonial interests and increase the markets for British produced industrial wares like ceramics, glass, and textiles and traded commodities such as humans (Christelow 1942: 311). Under this act, agricultural produce from Martinique and Guadeloupe was supposed to be transshipped through these ports and then sold to Britain. Similarly, British manufactured goods including textiles, glass, spirits, and ceramics were supposed to be transshipped to French merchants for use in Guadeloupe and Martinique.

We see a similar transformation if we focus on two enclaves. One enclave, Portsmouth, was dominated by English settlers and recent immigrant enslaved laborers, both new to Dominica. The other enclave, Soufriere, was composed of French speaking whites and island-born enslaved laborers of African descent. The Byres Map shows a higher density of properties in the Soufriere enclave than in the Portsmouth enclave. For example only two properties approached the limit of 300 acres: Soufriere Estate and Morne Patate Estate. The majority of the estates were less than 100 acres including Petit Coulibri, Morne Rouge, Crabier, and Bois Cotlette. On the other hand the Portsmouth enclave was dominated by large estates including Point Round, Picard, Sugar Loaf and Chance Hall estates. Small properties are indicated as the property of 'poor settlers' or small piece holds.

Despite this variation in property size, results from archaeological survey show an intensity of building projects dating to the last half of the eighteenth century and the first half of the nineteenth century. These included the construction of monumental architecture in the form of estate houses and the construction of industrial buildings. The vast majority of standing and ruined structures identified in the survey were directly or indirectly related to the processing of sugar cane. These structures included 2 water mills, 7 cattle mills, 2 steam mills and one windmill. The survey also identified 10 boiling houses- 3 in the Portsmouth enclave and 7 in the Soufriere enclave. In the Soufriere survey region there were thirty-one features described in the pedestrian survey that were potential house areas, 22 of which were located at Bois Cotlette (n=15). Numerous field walls, terraces, and fruit trees were identified and mapped. Surface scatters of ceramics indicate occupations for Bois Cotlette as early as the 1720s-1740s. The pedestrian survey identified two plantation settlements within the Portsmouth enclave survey region including Sugar Loaf Estate. Eleven platforms were identified and mapped due east of the estate house at Sugarloaf. These platforms could have contained as many as 11 laborer houses. Surface scatter for these areas indicate a late eighteenth and early nineteenth century occupation of the village (ca. 1760s-1830s). Both archaeological and documentary evidence show that with British colonization there was a reshaping of the built landscape in both enclaves. This built landscape indicates, to a certain extent, the success of British ambitions to attract people into a sugar industry on an island where it was previously nonexistent[2].

The survey does leave us with an interesting observation. In the area dominated by French settlers in 1763 there was a greater density of structures related to sugar production. The higher density of estates in the smaller enclave, Soufriere, can in part

2 Only one enterprise experimented with sugar- a mission/estate owned and operated by Perre la Violet a Grandbay in southeastern Dominica and this was ultimately unsuccessful (Lenik 2010).

be attributed to the shape of the terrain. This is certainly the case with at least one estate, Ravine Crabier. But, it is not as if land patents could not have consolidated contiguous properties such as Morne Rouge, Petit Couilbri and Bois Cotlette to make a single estate approximating 300 acres. It is also unlikely that the French did not take advantage of land surrounding Portsmouth that would ultimately become sugar estates after 1763. It is more likely that the density of estates in Soufriere is a result of the Commission's inclination to recognize the right for French subjects to continue to hold these properties in lease and own slaves to work the fields of those properties. The lower density of estates in Portsmouth is probably the result of the Commission's desire to attract British settlers and investors to this new colony. For wealthy merchants and bankers, Dominica represented the first real estate opened up to sale for the development of sugar estates in the Caribbean since the acquisition of Jamaica in 1655. A 300 acre parcel of land near a deep water harbor with flat alluvial plains would have been more appealing as an investment than a 78 acre parcel of land high in the hills in southern Dominica.

Archaeological survey and documentary records show an increase in building activities associated with sugar production after 1763. If we were to just rely on this survey data, the recovered archaeological landscape would tell a story in which both enclaves invested in sugar after colonization. Sugar's success led to an expansion of the scale of processing in order to maximize the money returned from the planter's initial investment. This led to some material practices which are variations on a theme. Villages of enslaved laborers are located downwind from the estate houses and industrial buildings are in close proximity to the fields on which those people labored. However saying that both enclaves were variations on a theme does not sufficiently explain significant differences. Parcels of land are smaller in Soufriere. Soufriere also contained evidence of processing coffee on five estates: Bois Cotlette, Petit Coulibri, Morne Rouge, Ravine Crabier and Morne Patate. These constitute different material practices on the part of the estates' owners. Soufriere probably could not compete with the larger estates in Portsmouth, requiring different strategies. There are at least two reasons why these differences existed: Because of the small sizes of estates in the south, they could not compete in scale or productivity with estates in the north. Differences could also be due to the different backgrounds of people who owned the properties and the slaves that worked on them. With either option, the diverse agendas and goals of investors, owners and leaseholders, needs to be taken into consideration when trying to explain slavery's material record in island colonies such as Dominica.

6.3.1 Sugar Loaf Estate

Eponymously named after a small hillock in the shape of a Sugar Loaf located on the property, the estate has functioned since 1763 (Figure 3). While this estate grew bananas and limes in the twentieth century, for the majority of its productive life owners grew and processed sugar cane. Today the former sugar fields are used for multiple purposes including a pen for horses. As a settlement for human habitation its life was much more abbreviated. The plantation settlement began as early as 1763 and continued until the 1830s. Two Irishmen, John Blackall and Nicholas

Comyn, were the original owners of the property that would later be identified as Sugar Loaf Estate (DLL 1763). The tenure of ownership was short lived and by 1768, Richard Neave, petitioned to purchase the property including 15 'negro' houses and 78 acres of cleared land.

Richard Neave, who resided in London, commissioned the assistance of Roseau based attorneys to acquire the means to turn this property into a functioning sugar estate. If we estimate that each house contained between five and six laborers per house, the village in the 1768 indenture would have housed 60 to 75 laborers. According to the 1817 Triennial Slave Register (DNA- SL1817) 137 enslaved

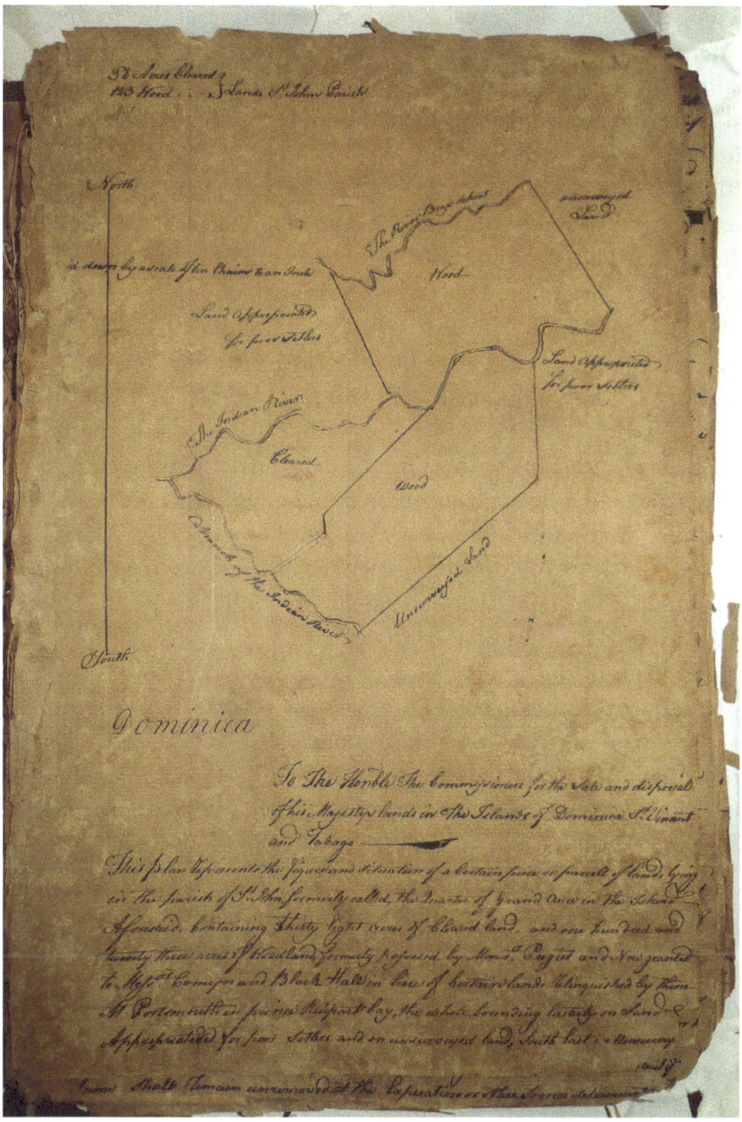

Figure 3. Indenture transferring the property of Nicholas Comyn and James Blackall to Richard Neave (1768). Courtesy of the Dominica National Archives.

laborers processed cane from 134 acres. The vast majority of enslaved laborers were born in Africa (85%), and half of the enslaved African population was born in Africa after 1795. All creole (born outside of Africa) enslaved laborers were born either on St John, Nevis or Montserrat between 1740 and 1780. The 1817 slave register does not list any Dominican born slaves over 6 years old. This indicates that there was either a high mortality of second generation slaves requiring a constant purchasing of laborers even 10 years after the official end of the slave trade or that the slaves were also being sold to other plantations. The majority of this population labored as field laborers with a few specialized tasks allocated to a more senior and experienced population.

Standing structures also reveal a quick accumulation of the means for this new sugar enterprise. In 1768, Neave instructed his attorney to purchase an additional 230 additional acres of contiguous lands (DLL 1768). Much of the land was wooded. This land needed to be cleared to be put into cane production. In addition an estate house was constructed and sugar works improved. According to Neave's instructions one water mill was built, along with aqueduct channeling water from another catchment area and diverting it into a millrace that eventually fed into the Indian River. This watermill was later repaired in the early nineteenth century (circa 1817). A boiling house with three kettles, a curing house and a distillery was built in close proximity around 1770. Lastly, a cobble road with three bridges was constructed to connect a jetty along the coast with the cane fields, the boiling house, the estate house and the laborer's village. It appears only one alteration was made to this complex during Neave's ownership. Either the initial boiling house was inefficient or incapable of meeting the demands of boiling enough cane juice that Neave ramped up the scale of production. Sometime between 1810 and 1820 a larger boiling house was built with 7 kettles and a distillery. The estate house was located on top of a hill upwind of a slave village. From the front entrance the owner could survey the fields below, boats coming into harbor and the neighboring estates of Chance, Picard and Point Round.

The end result of this accumulation was an estate that could have easily been found on the north coast of Jamaica or the west coast of Nevis. The layout, structure, and organization of the plantation space appears to follow in strict detail successful plantations found elsewhere throughout the British West Indies. In short while this estate was designed to make money for its owner, it was an estate to be seen from a boat and neighboring estates.

6.3.2 Bois Cotlette Estate

Bois Cotlette (Figure 4) was named after the Bois Cotlette tree (*Citharexylum spinosum*). It has been inhabited since the 1750s, if not earlier. It was identified on the Byres Map as '3*' and was listed on the associated property list as a leasehold. An indenture conferred by the British Crown in 1765 leased the land to Louis and Adrien le Ferrier Constance, both creoles of Martinique (DBOD B1 1765). By 1775 both individuals had died and their daughter Therese La Ferrier Constance, a minor, inherited rights to lease the land to be administered by power of Attorney by Joseph Serrant of Point Michel (DBOD 17660). In 1775 a marriage was contracted between Therese and Joseph Bellot of Morne Rouge at which point he became controller of the property and the 98 slaves tasked to work the property (DBOD M2 1775). At that time, the oldest individual living on the site was born in 1725 in Martinique – three years after the owner of the property. The oldest Dominican slave was born in 1752. The youngest Martiniquais slave was born in 1749 (DTSR SM 1817). This provides a fairly firm date for the founding of the estate somewhere between 1749 and 1752.

When the Constances and Joseph Bellot envisioned a sugar estate their most intimate experiences would have been derived from the French colonies of Martinique and Guadeloupe. Plenty of estates on these islands would have provided models for how an estate should be arranged, the organization of labor, and the methods of processing and transportation. Indeed as Bellot and Constance acquired means, such as buildings and labor, they were arranged and organized along lines similar to those described in the French Antilles.

Unlike Sugar Loaf estate, buildings at Bois Cotlette accreted over time. A road running in a roughly north–south orientation with intermittent cobble stone patches splits the estate and currently links it to estates on the southern tip of Dominica and the village of Soufriere to the north. A sugar and coffee estate that also processed cocoa during its almost 300-year history, Bois Cotlette today includes a windmill (*moulin à vent*), the planter's main house (*maison de maître*), coffee racks (*boucan*), a refurbished pulping mill and estate kitchen, and the ruins of two boiling houses, a cattle mill and enslaved laborers' quarter (*cases*). Between the *maison de maître*, the pulping mill and the boiling house, trays of coffee were laid out on racks inside the drying shed (*séchoir*) and were brought out into the sun on the paved stone glacis for drying coffee during the day.

Sometime in the immediate years after British colonization, many of the estates, infused with money from investors began to invest in sugar beginning with Bois Cotlette where they built a windmill and boiling house. Either through bankruptcy or frustration, Bellot and Constance relinquished their ownership of Bois Cotlette to Charles Court who built a cattle mill and boiling house in 1809. By 1817 J.B. Dupigny purchased the estate through a sale of the majority of the 87 slaves that remained on the estate. With only 12 slaves, Dupigny began to acquire means to grow coffee including building the coffee mill, the drying racks and building the glacis. Dupigny married into the Bellot family and by 1825 the estate was producing both coffee and sugar for export. A coffee blight hit Dominica in the 1830s and 1840s and the estate struggled on with sugar alone until a different type of coffee was introduced (Watts 1988). By the 1890s sugar production had largely been abandoned and there was a shift to growing cocoa, which along with limes was seen as being the new salvation for Dominica. Cacao and limes could use the same industrial infrastructure of coffee and sugar without much in the way of reinvestment.

As Bellot, Constance, and Dupigny actualized their enterprise, they did not have to acquire one very important means for sugar production, enslaved Africans. While French subjects were not allowed to own land, they were allowed to own chattel, including cattle and humans. The 1778 indenture that accompanied the

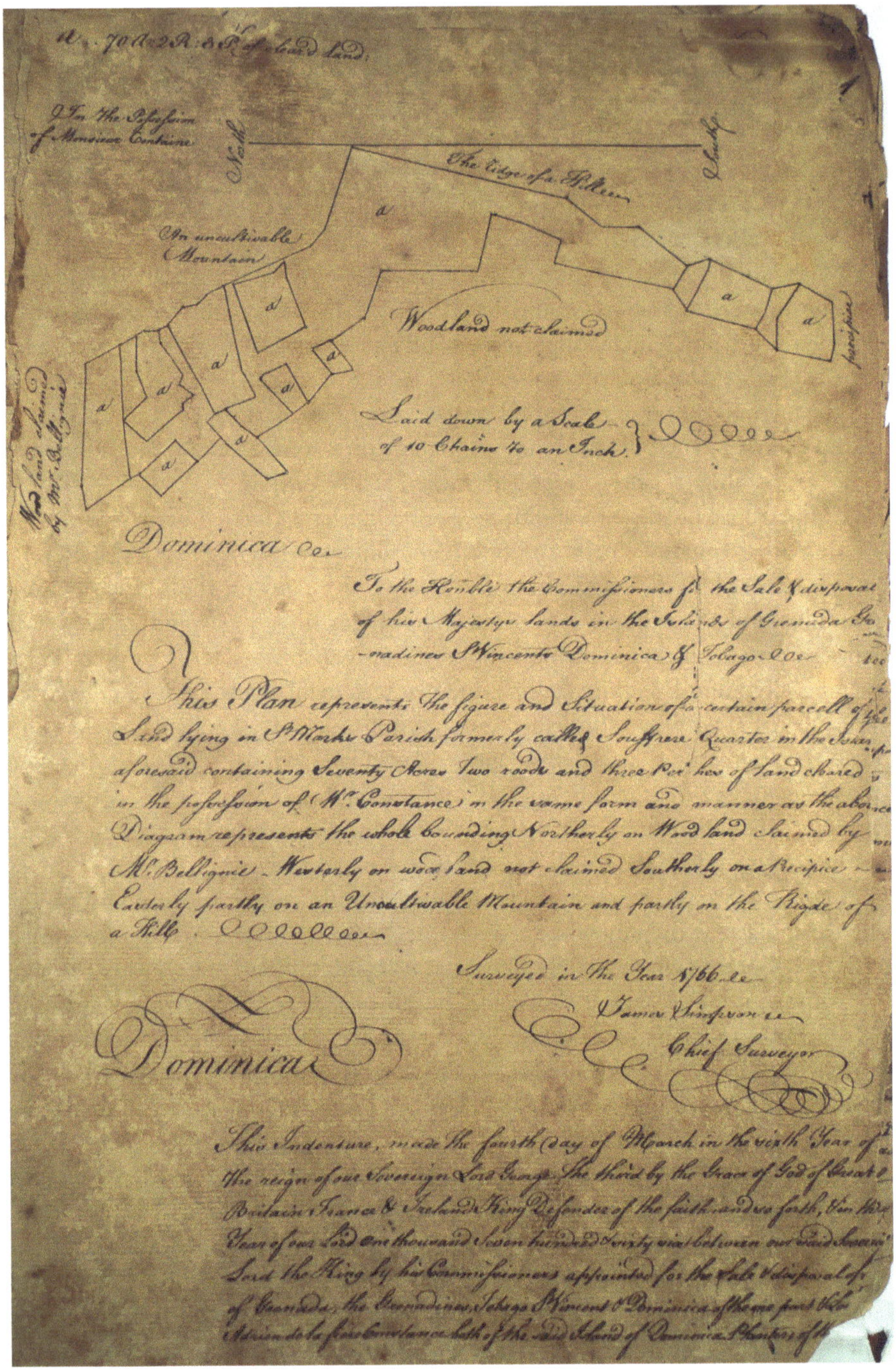

a. 70 A. 2 R. 3 P. of cleard land.

In the Possession of Monsieur Constance

North

South

The Ridge of a Hill

An uncultivable Mountain

Woodland not claimed

precipice

Wood land claimed by Mr. Bellignie

Laid down by a Scale of 10 Chains to an Inch.

Dominica &c.

To the Hon'ble the Commissioners for the Sale & disposal of his Majestys lands in the Islands of Grenada the Grenadines St Vincents Dominica & Tobago &c.

This Plan represents the figure and Situation of a certain parcell of Land lying in St Marks Parish formerly called Souffriere Quarter in the Island aforesaid containing Seventy Acres two roods and three Perches of land cleared in the possession of Mr. Constance in the same form and manner as the above Diagram represents the whole bounding Northerly on Wood land claimed by Mr. Bellignie Westerly on wood land not claimed Southerly on a Precipice Easterly partly on an Uncultivable Mountain and partly on the Ridge of a Hill.

Surveyed in the Year 1766 &c.

James Simpson

Chief Surveyor

Dominica

This Indenture, made the fourth day of March in the sixth Year of the reign of our Sovereign Lord George the third by the Grace of God of Great Britain France & Ireland King Defender of the faith and so forth, in the Year of our Lord One thousand Seven hundred Sixty six between our said Sovereign Lord the King by his Commissioners appointed for the Sale & disposal of [illegible] of Grenada, the Grenadines, Tobago St Vincent & Dominica of the one part & Adrien de la Fosse Constance [illegible] of the said Island of Dominica Planter of the [illegible]

Figure 4. Indenture transferring the leasehold of Adrien and Louis Le Ferrier Constance to Joseph Bellot (1775) Courtesy of the Dominica National Archives.

marriage of Bellot and Constance shows that Bellot came to control 98 enslaved laborers to work the fields of Bois Cotlette. The ability to maintain slaves was crucial for the success of the Bois Cotlette property. There was a legal justification for allowing the French to own slaves and not the land on which they worked. The Oxford English Dictionary defines chattel as "Property Goods, Money; Capital Principal; Live stock" and more broadly "A movable possession; any possession or piece of property other than real estate or a freehold". In short slaves constituted a personal portable possession. This is opposed to real estate which appears in in common law as early as 1605 defined as "Property consisting of land and the buildings on it". Between 1705 and 1748 a change took place in the definition of humans. In 1705 the House of Burgesses in Virginia broke with common practice and established that slaves are real estate, part of the land and a thing transferable by title with the land. This introduced enormous ambiguity especially when it came to inheritance and debt. A 1727 law clarified the 1705 law, establishing that slaves are a potential species for the repayment of debt. In 1748 the House of Burgesses declared that slaves would be considered personal estate. This act was eventually disallowed. The assembly argued that that fixing the slaves to the land led to lawsuits, 'overstock', and the mixing of the population to the point where individuals could not be distinguished. Ownership became ambiguous.

The indenture does not indicate the place of origin or the age of the enslaved laborers. Only gender and task is indicated. A majority of these slaves, 82%, worked as field laborers. A later document, the 1817 triennial slave register, provides greater detail about the composition and origin of the population laboring at Bois Cotlette. According to this document, the vast majority of enslaved laborers living at Bois Cotlette were born in Dominica (75%). The average age of creoles was 25.5 years old. The average age of Africans was 45 years old. This would indicate two things. First this document indicates that Bellot and Constance did purchase a population of enslaved laborers as they re-tasked the estate to grow and process sugar. This constituted no less than 25 % of the population. Second it indicates that the enslaved laborers at Bois Cotlette had children that continued to live on the estate. The demographic trends as represented in the 1817 triennial slave register is one of a community of locals born and raised in the same place and likely the same house.

In contrast to Sugar Loaf, the location of Bois Cotlette was hidden in a valley. Elsewhere I have described the location and intensification of these buildings as a deliberate effort to engage the political objectives of colonial administrators on their own terms (Hauser and Armstrong 2012). While the owners took advantage of British policy of promoting sugar, they also participated in activities that undermined the mercantile system of the empire. That being said, Constance, Court, Dupigny and Bellot built and rebuilt industrial structures to crush cane and process sugar. The owners of Bois Cotlette did not achieve the same success as their competitors to the north in this endeavor. By 1825 while Sugar Loaf was producing about 90 hogsheads of sugar, Bois Cotlette was producing a paltry 2 hogsheads (Dominica Almanac 1825). The debt accumulated by these owners in developing the means to actualize their enterprise inured them to British policy. In short while the Constances and the Bellots attempted to be ungoverned, their attachment to a wider circulation of things kept them indebted to a British entrepreneurial class.

6.4 Discussion: demonstrating success

Given the evidence presented above, owners at both estates might have been premature in claiming that their estates were successes by the second quarter of the nineteenth century. Yet, while both owners struggled, they still attempted to display their success, as partial as it might have been. While certain elements recovered from Bois Cotlette displayed the success of the families who owned it eventually, the entire estate was a show piece in Neave's portfolio.

The most dominant feature of Bois Cotlette is the *Maison de Maître*. When I first visited the site after spending a summer in Guadeloupe and a brief sojourn in Martinique, I was struck by the degree to which it resembled a French estate house, albeit on a smaller scale. The house was constructed out of masonry with a gabled roof and dormers. The internal layout of the house consisted of a central parlor with stone and ceramic tiles and a circumambulating gallery surrounding it. More so measurements of the building did not conform to English feet of the time and appeared to be more in keeping with the French Trois system of measurement. Finally in the kitchen area directly behind the house a cistern composed of five Biot jars sunk into an aboveground brick and masonry restore resembled the ways in which French planters would manage kitchen and drinking water.

Found in the garden associated with this kitchen were a series of ceramics including St Cloud Polychrome faience, Vallauris-type pottery from Southeastern France, and *Coco neg* which might very well represent local production by enslaved laborers or indigenous Kalinago laborers (Figure 4). Found in the same field were English made creamwares, dip molded bottle glass, stoneware jars, and terracotta roofing tiles, these materials bundled together speak to a material assemblage that is imperially ambiguous but provocative as to the kinds of commercial networks that the Constances, Bellot and Dupigny maintained during the course of the nineteenth century.

Underneath and at a 4-degree angle to the foundations of the extent *maison de maître* was a mortared course of stonework; most likely, the foundation of a building associated with the pre-British occupation. Materials recovered from both contexts include Dutch-made pipes, local and European coarse earthenware, French-made faience, European slipware, and white salt glazed stoneware. This is a fairly standard mid eighteenth-century assemblage. In all likelihood, it was the residence of Louis and Adrien le Ferrier Constance. After formal colonization, the village was moved about 100 meters north and a new estate house was built. Materials recovered from these archaeological contexts include creamware, pearlware, faience, dip-molded glass bottles, and English pipes.

Though the owners of Bois Cotlette began to adopt British ceramics on which to eat their meals, they decided to build a house in a way reminiscent of colonial Martinique and cook their food on materials used by their contemporaries in the French world. This would seem an interesting way to highlight to neighbors and competitors the success of their enterprise, yet it seemed to work. In the slave village there was a growing importance of English made creamwares, the reduced frequency of French-made faience. Both enslaved and planters continued to procure cooking wares from where they had all along. While in some cases, such as the presence of Vallauris, it is conceivable that circuits of trade made by caboteurs plying wares between Dominica, Martinique and Guadeloupe provided goods.

Perhaps it is telling that by the last quarter of the nineteenth century, many of the Bellots and Dupignys began to serve in the assembly of the colony act as government officials, and receive foreign dignitaries. While Bois Cotlette probably did not make a significant income for the family it did serve as a kind of corporate headquarters for an island-wide enterprise of sugar estates, coffee estates, merchant houses and other interests. In other words one hundred years after divestment of their land, the descendants of French settlers became the island's first family and the colony's most honorable subjects. Much of this had to do with the expansionary strategies that slavery enabled. Allowing the possibility of sugar, though it was doomed to fail, facilitating the acquisition of means through debt, and the laissez-faire attitude through which success was displayed ultimately governed this population of new subjects.

Sugar Loaf, in part because of its compressed time frame of construction, and the wealth of the absentee owner was a canvas come to life. In the final quarter of the eighteenth century, Sir William Young, President of the Commission for the Sale of Lands in the Ceded Islands and Lieutenant Governor for the island of Dominica (1725-1788), commissioned Agostino Brunias (Figure 5) to paint a series of landscapes to attract potential settlers and investors to the newly acquired island of Dominica. Among the scenes that Brunias captured was a pastoral vision of Dominica *(*1770-1780). Agostino Brunias, trained in Rome and patronized by wealthy tourists (106), painted in a form reminiscent of a post card image that provided a selective kind of realism. Such paintings "distorted the harsh realities of slavery in St Vincent and the Lesser Antilles so as to satisfy his absentee planter clientele (Honeychurch 2004:51). Although "intimately aligned to rhetoric concerning the amelioration of slave conditions, and thus ... deeply implicated in the politics of slavery as early as the 1760s" (Thomas 2010), the images avoided the harsh realities of slave life and instead focused on bucolic, seemingly romanticized images of the everyday. The village at Sugar loaf appears to have been designed to be rendered on an 18th century Brunias canvas. This was an estate to be seen not lived in. Unfortunately for the laborers they lived in it.

At Sugar Loaf discarded ceramics from the kitchen area of the Estate house included English made pearlware and creamware, a small number of Vallauris ceramics and one local cooking pot.

At the slave village almost 87% of Sugar Loaf's kitchenware assemblage (utilitarian coarse earthenwares plus iron kitchenwares) was composed of cast-iron pot fragments. Very few ceramic types used for cooking, such as coco neg, were recovered from that locus. Only 1.22% of the total assemblage was coco neg, a hand built, utilitarian ceramic type possibly made locally in Dominica. The majority of Caribbean made ceramic assemblage was Type 2 or Trois-ilets ware, a higher-fired and thinner-walled coarse earthenware that was probably utilized as tableware and possibly food preparation. This type was probably imported from potteries on Martinique (Kelly and Hauser 1998 and Hauser 2011). The other ceramics recovered in the house area consisted primarily of creamware, pearlware,

Figure 5. Linen Market Agostino Brunias ca. 1770, Courtesy of the Yale Center for British Art.

and whiteware, which combined made up 85% of the imported ceramics. There was also a small percentage of stoneware (2.9% of the imported ceramics) and four sherds (5.9% of the imported ceramics) of French faience (three unidentifiable, one Seine Polychrome) and two small sherds of Chinese porcelain (2.9% of the imported ceramics). The glass artifacts were all from drinking containers and glass bottles. Metal artifacts consisted of nails, fragments of iron cooking pots, as well as a piece of lead shot or lead cutting. Buttons were found in the locus, in addition to a glass pendant with a carved decoration.

In September of 1834- 2 weeks after emancipation- a hurricane hit the island of Dominica and killed three people on Sugar Loaf estate. The village was abandoned and never to be reoccupied. Perhaps this has to do with the laborers voting with their feet. This is unlikely since they were still obligated to labor on the estate as apprentices. It is more likely that with the end of slavery on the horizon Sugar Loaf as a way to display his success ceased to be vital part of Thomas Neave's (son of Richard) portfolio. It, along with other possessions in the Caribbean, had already completed its job. His father received a barony and his enterprises secured his success. In both cases, we have families who became part of the British empire even though their backgrounds suggest agendas slightly askew from those of their colonial administrators.

6.5 Conclusion

In this essay I have shown a couple of things. First that some kinds of archaeological evidence seem to be variations on a theme, while others seem messy, chaotic and not fitting with general patterns described by historians and archaeologists. Second these kinds of evidence can be coordinated with those responsible for its design and implementation. Planters commissioned industrial buildings and enslaved people made pottery and built their houses out of planks and wattle and daub. It is not enough to privilege one form of evidence over another. Rather than disregard Bois Cotlette because it is messy and does not fit with a model where it is a byproduct of imperial design, we should see how variation was a necessary in making such colonial projects work. Such a task requires that we avoid writing history backwards. If we want to depict the island that was successfully colonized by the British we would look at the masonry structure. Yet if we look at the middens of estate houses and the house yards of the enslaved we a see a more complex story of an island and a people still caught up in regional networks but not always according to political design.

One must think of the kinds of cultural knowledge and social networks required to material acquisition. The growing of provisions, the making of goods the sale of those goods on markets that linked disparate people within and between islands. In other words, at Bois Cotlette, the enslaved were engaged in a variety of economic activities including trade, fishing, logging, and the growing of provisions and the hunting of food. These are the same tasks that they were involved in before the British conquered the island. People at bois Cotlette did what they always did. At Sugar Loaf poor income generated from sugar meant that those already marginal and marginalized got even less to support their daily existence. What this shows is that while initially, different colonial agendas resulted in varying strategies on the ground that were reflected in the varying assemblages collected on the two estates, the increasing similarities in assemblages over time suggest the waning influence of colonial design. Instead, what was shared by both plantations – the institution of slavery and local trade networks upon which both planters and slaves relied for their provisions – shaped the contours of everyday life resulting in domestic assemblages that were increasingly similar over time.

Because plantations were both a source of material wealth for the empire and a market for imported goods made in the metropole they are excellent units of observation to study the impact of imperial laws and trade regimes. By identifying the origin of imported and local goods and inferring potential trade circuits through which the items were obtained, we can determine the degree to which laws enacted in London regarding trade were followed by settlers and slaves in the colonies. Today it might be easy to view Caribbean colonies as a consequence of European imperial ambitions. Yet to take such a stance is to potentially overlook the intellectual and material contributions of enslaved laborers hidden in plain sight (Hauser 2011) or, significant to this study, the diversity of agendas of estate owners and colonial elites. These owners' commitments to the slave regime built a potential solidarity where one might not have existed before. On the one hand the British colonization would have intensified solidarities based on linguistic commonality and national identity among French subjects. On the other hand, British colonization allowed these settlers to own slaves and make money based on their labor. In the first instance settlers would have built solidarities with neighboring Martinique. In the second instance they would have built solidarities with Dominican planters.

The Caribbean basin has a material record of slavery. As such it has been a ready canvas for grand narratives in history and anthropology and archaeology. The focus of this chapter has been on the agency of planters and how they had diverse agendas. This is not to deny the agency of enslaved laborers. Analyses of everyday life as retrieved from the house-yards of enslaved laborers make such pasts politically and economically complex. These are issues I will be addressing in future publications.

Acknowledgements

Research on both settlements has been conducted through the assistance of Lennox Honychurch and the Commonwealth of Dominica, University of Notre Dame, and, since 2009, Northwestern University. The author is grateful for the material support provided by these organizations as well as the National Science Foundation and the Direction Regionale des

Affaires Culturelles du Centre (DRAC), Guadeloupe. I am grateful for the assistance of various volunteers who have contributed to this project including Alan Armstrong, Zev Cossin, Lacey Carpenter, Kristin Landau, Jessica Young, Brooke Kenline, Diane Wallman, Khadene Harris, Addison Kimmel, William Keegan and James Delle. The author is especially grateful for research collaborations with Kenneth G. Kelly, Kathryn Caitlin, John Steinberg, Douglas Bolender, and Brian Damiatta which ultimately enabled baseline data for this research. I would like to thank Kenneth G. Kelly, Reginald Auger, Kalyani Menon, Cynthia Robin, Matthew Johnson and the anonymous reviewers for insightful comments on earlier drafts of this manuscript.

References

Atwood, T.

1791 *History of the Island of Dominica.*

Blackburn, R.

1997 *The making of New World slavery: from the Baroque to the Modern, 1492-1800.* London ; New York: Verso.

Brumfiel, E. M.

2003 It's a Material World: History, Artifacts, and Anthropology. *Annual Review of Anthropology* 32:205-223.

Bush, B.

1990 *Slave Women in Caribbean Society, 1650-1838*. London: James Curry Press.

Clement, C.O.

1997 Settlement Patterning on the British Caribbean Island of Tobago. *Historical Archaeology* 31(2):93-106.

Delle, J.A.

1998 *An archaeology of social space: analyzing coffee plantations in Jamaica's Blue Mountains*. New York: Plenum Press.

Delle, J.A.

1999 The Landscapes of Class Negotiation on Coffee Plantations in the Blue Mountains of Jamaica, 1797-1850. *Historical Archaeology* 33(1):136-158.

Dietler, M

1990 Driven by Drink: The Role of Drinking in the Political Economy and the Case of Early Iron Age France. *Journal of Anthropological Archaeology* 9:352-406.

Dietler, M.

1998 Consumption, Agency, and Cultural Entanglement: Theoretical Implications of a Mediterranean Colonial Encounter. In *Studies in Culture Contact. Interaction, Culture Change, and Archaeology*, edited by J. Cusick, pp. 288-315. Carbondale: Center for Archaeological Investigations, Southern Illinois University.

Edwards, B.

1793, 1972 *The history, civil and commercial, of the British colonies in the West Indies*. Volume 1. New York: Arno Press.

Fesler, G. R.

2004 From Houses to Homes: An Archaeological Case Study of Household Formation at the Utopia Slave Quarter, ca. 1675-1775 Dissertation, Anthropology, University of Virginia.

Galle, J.

2006 Strategic consumption: archaeological evidence for costly signaling among enslaved men and women in the eighteenth-century Chesapeake Dissertation, Anthropology, The University of Virginia.

Galle, J. E. and F. Neiman

2003 Patterns of tea and tableware consumption on late eighteenth-century slave quarter sites. In *Society for Historical Archaeology*. Providence, RI.

Gibson, H.

2009 Domestic Economy and Daily Practice in Guadeloupe: Historical Archaeology at La Mahaudière Plantation. *International Journal of Historical Archaeology* 13(1):27-44.

Gleick, P. H.

1996 Basic Water Requirements for Human Activities: Meeting Basic Needs. *Water International* 21(2):83 - 92.

Greene, K.

1990 The archaeology of the Roman economy. Berekley: University of Calofornia Press.

Handler, J. S. and F. Lange

1978 Plantation slavery in Barbados : an archaeological and historical investigation. Cambridge, MA: Harvard University Press.

Hassig, R.

1985 *Trade, Tribute, and Transportation.* Norman: University of Oklahoma Press.

Hauser, M. W., K. G. Kelly and D. V. Armstrong

2007 What to Do With "Other" Ceramics: Inter-Colonial Trade of French Coarse Earthenware. *XXI International Congress of Caribbean Archaeology, St Agustin, Trinidad, 2007.*

Hauser, M.

2008 *An Archaeology of Balck Markets, Local Ceramics and Economies in Eigheenth Century Jamaica.* Gainesville: University Press, Florida.

Heath, B. J.

2004 Engendering Choice: Slavery and Consumerism in Central Virginia. In *Engendering African-American Archaeology: A Southern Perspective*, edited by J. Galle and A. Young, pp. 19-38. Knoxville, TN: University of Tennessee Press.

Heath, B. J. and A. Bennett

2000 "The Little Spots Allow'd Them": The Archaeological Study of African-American Yards. *Historical Archaeology* 34(2):38-55.

Higman, B. W.

1986a Jamaican Coffee Plantations 1780-1860: A Cartographic Analysis. *Caribbean Geography* 2:73-91.

Higman, B. W.

1986b Plantation Maps as Sources for the Study of West Indian Ethnohistory. In *Ethnohistory: A Researcher's*, edited by Guide. W. D., pp. 107-136. Williamsburg, Virgninia: Department of Anthropology, College of William and Mary (Studies in Third World Societies Publication Number 35).

Higman, B. W.

1987 The spatial economy of Jamaican Sugar Plantations: Cartographic evidence from the 18th and 19th centuries. *Journal of Historical Geography* 13(1):17-19.

Higman, B. W.

1988 *Jamaica surveyed : plantation maps and plans of the eighteenth and nineteenth centuries.* Jamaica: San Francisco.

Higman, B. W.

1996 Patterns of exchange within a plantation economy : Jamaica at the time of emancipation. In *West Indies accounts : essays on the history of the British Caribbean and the Atlantic economy in honour of Richard Sheridan*: 211-231.

Honychurch, L.

1995 *The Dominica Story: A History of the Island.* Bridgeport: MacMillan.

Honychurch, L.

2004 Chatoyer's Artist: Agostino Brunias and the depiction of St Vincent. *Journal of the Barbados Museum and Historical Society* 50:104-128.

Ingold, T.

2000 Making Culture and Weaving the World. In *Matter, Materiality and Modern Culture, edited by P.M. Graves-Brown*, pp. 50-71. London: Routledge.

Joyce, R. A. and J. Lopiparo

2005 PostScript: Doing Agency in Archaeology. *Journal of Archaeological Method and Theory* 12(4):365-374.

Keane, W.

2003 Semiotics and the Social Analysis of Material Things. *Language & Communicaton* 23:408-425.

Kelly, K. G.

2004 Historical Archaeology in the French caribbean: An Introduction to a Special Volume of the Journal of Caribbean Archaeology. *Journal of Caribbean Archaeology* (Special Publication #1):1-10.

McDonald, R. A.

1993 *The economy and material culture of slaves: goods and chattels on the sugar plantations of Jamaica and Louisiana.* Baton Rouge: Louisiana State University Press.

McKee, L.

1999 Food supply and plantation social order: An archaeological perspective. In *"I, too, am America": Archaeological Studies of African-American Life.*, edited by T. Singleton, pp. 218-239. Charlottesville, VA: University Press of Virginia.

Meskell, L

2005 Introduction: Object Orientations. In *Archaeologies of Materiality*, edited by L. Meskell, pp. 1-17. London: Blackwell.

Mills, B.

1995 The Organization of Protohistoric Zuni Ceramic Production. In *Ceramic Production in the American Southwest*, edited by B. Mills and P.L. Crown, pp. 200-230. Tucson, AZ: University of Arizona Press.

Pérotin-Dumon, A.

1991 Cabotage, Contraband, and Corsairs: The Port Cities of Guadeloupe and Their Inhabitants, 1650-1800. In *Atlantic Port Cities: Economy, Culture, and Society in the Atlantic World, 1650-1850*, edited by F.W.K.P.K. Liss, pp. 58-86. Knoxville: University of Tennessee Press.

Pulsipher, L.

1990 They Have Saturdays and Sundays to Feed Themselves. *Expedition Magazine* 32(2).

Pulsipher, L.M. and C. M. Goodwin

2001 "Getting the Essence of It:" Galways Plantation, Montserrat, West Indies. In *Island Lives: Historical Archaeologies of the Caribbean*, edited by P. Farnsworth Tuscaloosa: University of Alabama Press.

Singleton, T.A.

2001 Slavery and Spatial Dialectics on Cuban Coffee Plantations. *World Archaeology* 33(1): 98-114.

Stahl, A.B.

2010 Material Histories. In *Oxford Handbook of Material Culture Studies*, edited by D. Hicks and M. Beaudry, Oxford: Oxford University Press.

Thomas, B. W. and L. Thomas

2004 Gender and the Presentation of Self: An Example from the Hermitage. In *Engendering African American Archaeology: A Southern Perspective*, edited by J. Galle and A. Young, pp. 101-131. Knoxville, TN: University of Tennessee Press.

Thomas, N.

1991 *Entangled Objects: Exchange, Material Culture and Colonialism in the Pacific*. Cambridge, Mass: Harvard University Press.

Thomas, S.

2010 Cultivating the slave body: The dance imagery of Agostino Brunias (1730-96) In *Society for Caribbean Studies*. Southampton, England.

Trouillot, M.-R.

2003 *Global transformations: anthropology and the modern world*. New York: Palgrave Macmillan.

Trussell, T.D.

2004 Artifacts of ambition: How the 17th-century middle class at Port Royal, Jamaica, foreshadowed the consumer revolution Dissertation, Anthropology, Univeristy of Texas A & M.

Tupy, M.

2003 *Slavery and Globalization.*

White, C.L.

2005 *American Artifacts of Personal Adornment, 1680-1820: A Guide to Identification and Interpretation. Lanham,* MD: Rowman and Littlefield Publishers, Inc.

Wilkie, L.A.

2000 Culture Bought: Evidence of Creolization in the Consumer Goods of an Enslaved Bahamian Family. *Historical Archaeology* 34(3):10-26.

Williams, E. E.

1994 *Capitalism and Slavery.* Chapel Hill: University of North Carolina Press.

Chapter 7

The spaces in between

Archaeological investigations at St. Nicholas Abbey sugar plantation

Stephanie Bergman and Frederick H. Smith

Department of Anthropology
College of William and Mary
Williamsburg, Virginia
smbergman@email.wm.edu
fhsmit@wm.edu

Abstract

Since 2007 faculty and students from the College of William and Mary in Williamsburg, Virginia have conducted archaeological investigations at St. Nicholas Abbey sugar plantation, which is perhaps the most important heritage site in Barbados. The archaeological research program developed for the site seeks to uncover evidence that will help in the restoration, preservation, and celebration of this important historic landmark. While deeds, maps, paintings, and other documentary sources offer insights into the early history of the estate and its owners, the archaeological investigations aim to shed light on the lives of the many people who made St. Nicholas Abbey one of the island's premier plantations. Over the past four years we have located and surveyed the settlements of planters, enslaved peoples, and free laborers who lived and worked on the estate in the early colonial era. In this paper we summarize the key findings of our archaeological investigations. Moreover, we explore how Barbadians shaped the conceptual and literal in-between spaces of plantation society in the Atlantic world.

Résumé

Depuis 2007, les professeurs et les étudiants du Collège de William et Mary à Williamsburg, en Virginie, ont mené des recherches archéologiques à la plantation sucrière de St. Nicholas Abbey, qui est peut-être le plus important site du patrimoine de la Barbade. Le programme de recherches archéologiques mis au point pour le site cherche à découvrir des preuves qui vous aideront dans la restauration, la préservation et la célébration de cet important monument historique. Alors que les actes, les cartes, les tableaux et autres sources documentaires offrent un aperçu de l'histoire des débuts de la plantation et de ses propriétaires, les recherches archéologiques visent à faire la lumière sur la vie des nombreuses personnes qui ont fait de St. Nicholas Abbey l'une des principales plantations de l'île. Au cours des quatre dernières années, nous avons localisé et prospecté les installations planteurs, des esclaves, et les travailleurs libres qui vivaient et travaillaient sur le domaine à l'époque coloniale au début. Dans cet article, nous résumons les principaux résultats de nos investigations archéologiques. Par ailleurs, nous explorons comment les Barbadiens ont façonné des espaces intermédiaires conceptuel et littéraux dans la société de plantation au sein du monde atlantique.

Resumen

Desde 2007 los profesores y estudiantes de la Universidad de William and Mary en Williamsburg, Virginia, han llevado a cabo investigaciones arqueológicas en el St. Nicholas Abbey plantación de azúcar, que es quizás el patrimonio más importante de Barbados. El programa de investigación arqueológica desarrollada para el sitio trata de descubrir evidencia que ayude en la restauración, preservación y celebración de este hito histórico importante. Mientras escrituras, mapas, pinturas y otras fuentes documentales ofrecen ideas sobre la historia temprana de la finca y sus propietarios, las investigaciones arqueológicas objetivo de arrojar luz sobre la vida de las muchas personas que hicieron St. Nicholas Abbey una de las principales plantaciones de la isla . En los últimos cuatro años hemos localizado y examinó los asentamientos de colonos, pueblos esclavizados y trabajadores libres que vivían y trabajaban en la finca en la época colonial temprana. En este artículo se resumen las principales conclusiones de nuestras investigaciones arqueológicas. Por otra parte, se explora cómo la forma de Barbados. Conceptual y literal en los espacios intermedios de la sociedad de plantaciones en el mundo atlántico.

Keywords

Historical archaeology, Barbados sugar plantations, slavery, abolition, liminality

Mots-clés

Archéologie historique, les plantations de sucre à la Barbade, l'esclavage, l'abolition, liminality

Palabras clave

Arqueología histórica, las plantaciones de azúcar de Barbados, la esclavitud, la abolición, liminality

Since 2007 faculty and students from the College of William and Mary in Williamsburg, Virginia have been conducting archaeological investigations at St. Nicholas Abbey sugar plantation, St. Peter, Barbados. The estate is one of the most prominent heritage sites in the island and is a testament to the early momentum and energy of the British capitalist system in the emerging Atlantic world in the seventeenth century. The plantation great house is one of the oldest standing structures in Barbados (Fraser & Hughes 1982: 9), and is one of only three Jacobean-styled houses still standing in the western hemisphere (Waterman 1946: 141) (Figure 1). The archaeological research program developed for the site aims to uncover evidence that will help in the restoration, preservation, and celebration of this important historic landmark. While deeds, maps, paintings, and other documentary sources offer insights into the early history of the estate and its owners, the archaeological investigations seek to highlight the lives of the many people who made St. Nicholas Abbey one of the island's most substantial sugar plantations. Over the past four years we have unearthed thousands of artifacts, including ceramics, animal bone, beads, buttons, gaming pieces, and clay tobacco pipes, which have helped shed new light on the daily lives of planters, enslaved peoples, and free laborers who lived and worked on the estate in the early colonial era. In this paper we summarize the key findings of our investigations. Moreover, the archaeology at St. Nicholas Abbey highlights how Barbadians participated in the debates over abolition that originated in England, shaping the conceptual and literal in-between spaces of plantation society in the Atlantic world.

Figure 1. The historic, Jacobean-style great house at St. Nicholas Abbey sugar plantation.

7.1 Background

St. Nicholas Abbey is located in the rural eastern half of St. Peter parish, with a small portion extending to the northwest corner of St. Andrew (Figure 2), and is situated approximately eight kilometers from Speightstown, the island's first commercial port which was formally settled around 1630 (Schomburgk 1848: 237). In the short space of twenty years the economic phenomenon known as the Sugar Revolution transformed Barbados forever. Early settlers to the island, John Yeamans and Benjamin Berringer, formed a business partnership in land speculation that fueled the transition to sugar and slavery. By 1647 they accumulated 365 acres for their own profit, dividing the land into two individual plantations (Campbell 1986: 60-63; Lesser 1995). Architectural historians have credited Berringer as the original proprietor of the English-styled mansion (Fraser and Hughes 1982). If this is correct, he died very shortly after it was completed in ca.1661. Ten short

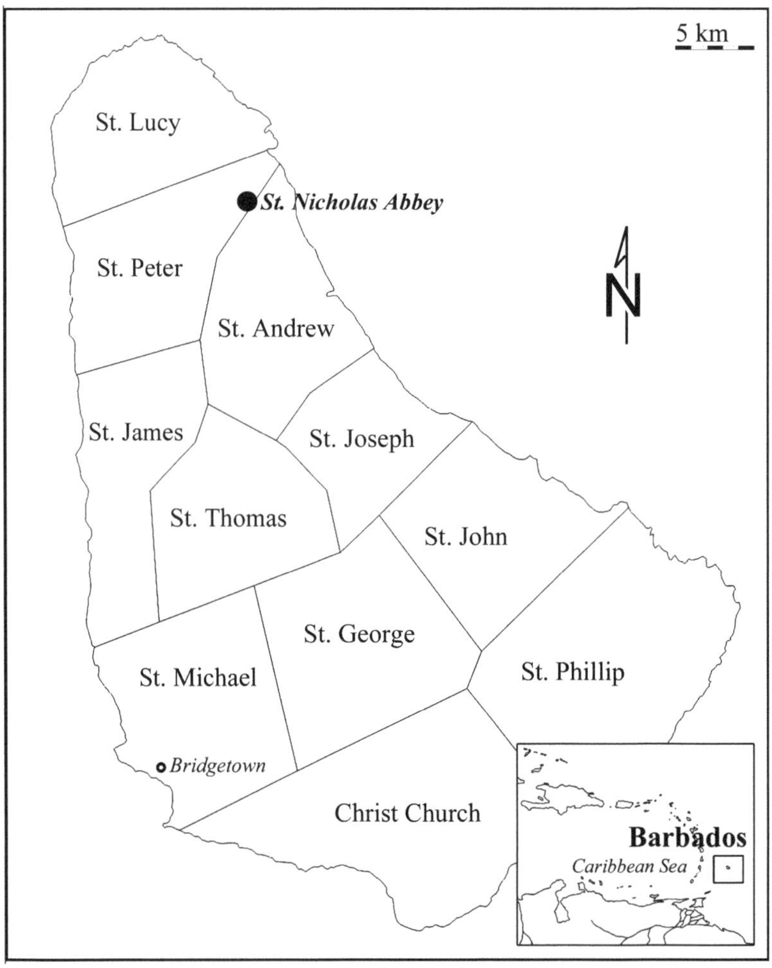

Figure 2. St. Nicholas Abbey is located in the rural eastern half of St. Peter parish, with a small portion extending to the northwest corner of St. Andrew.

weeks after his death Yeamans married Berringer's widow and moved into the newly constructed great house. The scandalous union resulted in the merger of the two plantations, and the resulting core is now known as St. Nicholas Abbey plantation. Though the property passed through several successive owners over the past three-and-a-half centuries, it has remained a single unified sugar plantation into the current day.

The main road from Speightstown leading to St. Nicholas Abbey winds through sugarcane fields while steadily gaining elevation, leading into another popular landmark--Cherry Tree Hill, located within the northwest portion of the plantation. The famed spot provides one of the most remarkable panoramic views of the island and its rugged Atlantic coast. Before reaching the end of the breathtaking vista, a well-marked road turns off to the plantation, providing yet another commanding view of the estate's historic great house. Today, St. Nicholas Abbey is an important heritage site that attracts thousands of visitors each year. The current owners, the Warren family, obtained the plantation in 2006 and have heavily invested in the restoration and preservation of not only the great house, but also the sugar factory and surrounding grounds.

In the late 1640s, Richard Ligon (1657), an English Royalist living in Barbados, observed that the planters lived in houses unsuited for the climate, and simply copied plans from Britain in the building of their homes. St. Nicholas Abbey great house exemplifies Ligon's point. The historic architectural centerpiece is a grand three-storied Jacobean-styled great house with Dutch curvilinear gables and four chimneys and fireplaces. The fireplaces and walled medieval herb garden were almost certainly included in the original plans brought from England, and copied faithfully. The house was constructed of locally quarried coral rubble stone, possibly in the late 1650s (Fraser and Hughes 1982:11-15) and is currently surrounded by perfectly landscaped gardens and fields of sugarcane. The plantation is considered a large plantation by Barbados standards, and by the early nineteenth century it consisted of 420 acres (Handler *et al.* 1989:42), the approximate acreage of the estate in modern times.

Archaeology was first initiated at St. Nicholas Abbey in the mid-1980s, when Jerome Handler, building on his earlier work with Frederick Lange at Newtown Plantation, traveled to Barbados with a team of archaeologists and conducted an archaeological survey of five plantation sites on the island, including St. Nicholas Abbey (see Handler *et al.* 1989). The goal of that research project was to find slave cemeteries and to test a model for locating them on the plantations. Handler's crew conducted a pedestrian survey on nearly eighty acres of the estate and shovel tested an additional seventy acres in search of human skeletal remains. While they were unable to locate any burying grounds associated with enslaved peoples at St. Nicholas Abbey, their research yielded important information about plantation field names that could be used to locate specific archaeological deposits and archaeological material likely associated with village sites for enslaved and free workers.

7.2 Archaeology survey of St. Nicholas Abbey

In 2007, archaeologists from the College of William and Mary returned to St. Nicholas Abbey to conduct archaeological testing at new areas of the plantation and follow-up on surveys done by Handler and his crew in the 1980s. Our archaeological research consisted of two primary goals. The first was to find evidence that could help date the construction of the great house and locate any subsurface remains of outbuildings associated with the plantation. The second goal was to determine the potential for archaeological research at domestic sites of the enslaved and free workers who lived at the plantation. The location of domestic sites of enslaved workers was a key focus for Handler and his team; however, they maintained that domestic village sites on Barbados plantations were difficult to identify archaeologically since they lacked stratigraphic integrity from centuries of cultivation and modern disturbances (Handler et al. 1989:4). Yet, our preliminary study confirmed the presence of discrete cultural features and stratigraphy in most of the areas of the plantation where settlement sites were located. Three distinct slave and ex-slave settlements were identified: A slave village with an occupation that spanned from the mid-seventeenth through the early-nineteenth century, a tenant settlement that was established in the late-eighteenth century, and an emancipation era tenantry that remains a village in the present day. We have determined that the enslaved at St. Nicholas Abbey were relocated to other areas of the estate, a process that began in the late-eighteenth century and was completed when slavery was abolished. Moreover, we surveyed the gullies surrounding St. Nicholas Abbey for caves that may have been used by enslaved and free peoples. We found several caves with scatters of eighteenth and early nineteenth century material culture. As with other cave sites explored in Barbados, the caves surrounding St. Nicholas Abbey contained a sizable amount of bottle glass and other alcohol-related items suggesting that these caves may have served as liminal meeting areas for workers from St. Nicholas Abbey and surrounding estates.

Our research began with a pedestrian survey of the rocky grasslands on Cherry Tree Hill. William Mayo's detailed map of the island in the early eighteenth century shows the plantation had two windmills, an indication of the size and wealth of St. Nicholas Abbey. One mill wall stands near the factory today, and based on construction details, was built contemporaneously with the great house. A second windmill, if it ever existed, has yet to be found. Based on speculation of the current owner we searched Cherry Tree Hill, the highest point on the estate with good and steady winds, for any evidence of a second windmill. While we did not find evidence for a windmill, we did discover a sizeable amount of highly weathered Amerindian (apparently Suazoid) pottery sherds. While most Amerindian sites in Barbados are located along the coast, the presence of Suazoid Amerindian ceramic material at Cherry Tree Hill hints at the possibility that the site, with its commanding view of the coast, served some special purpose, perhaps a ceremonial function, in prehistoric times. A few additional pieces of Amerindian material, including a conch shell adze, were encountered elsewhere on the estate during our investigations suggesting the area saw significant Amerindian activity in prehistoric times.

Next, we searched for evidence that could tell us about the construction of St. Nicholas Abbey great house, identify functional areas around the structure, and uncover information about the lifestyles of the plantation families that lived there. While the great house itself was built directly on bedrock and recent construction of a café had disturbed some areas along the gully behind the house, we did find areas with intact soils and good stratigraphic integrity. We found some archaeological materials, especially ceramics, from the seventeenth century within the immediate vicinity of the house. The evidence consisted mainly of a few fragments of North Devon Sgraffito slipware and a small fragment of what may be English Stoneware or perhaps a German Bartmannkrug. This paucity contrasts sharply with seventeenth-century sites excavated in the port capital of Bridgetown where seventeenth-century material is found in great abundance in archaeological contexts that date to this period (Smith 2001; Smith & Watson 2009). The excavation around the house consisted of a series of 1x1 and 1x2 meter units around the south and east of the house, as well as a series of 1x1 meter units and a visual survey of materials in the gully to the west of the house.

The western area of the property showed little evidence of activity. The area consisted largely of early twentieth century flowerpot fragments supporting early twentieth century drawings that indicate that the area once served as a fernery. Eighteenth and nineteenth-century black glass bottles fragments were also found in this area in substantial amounts suggesting the area may have served some social function as well.

The area near the privy was also tested. We placed excavation units on the outside of the main wall and privy area because we believed the privy area would have a high potential for containing refuse from the main house and compound. Oral testimony and visual inspection confirmed that a portion of this area was used for refuse disposal and burning until very recently. Furthermore, the physical landscape in this portion of the property suggested that it had served historically as a refuse area because it appeared artificially built up in juxtaposition to the natural slope of the land. Two 1x2 meter units were excavated in this area. One located almost directly against the compound wall, and the other into the artificial mound on the slope. These units represented some of the most complex archaeological stratigraphy and deposits, including a heavy concentration of rubble that appears to be from a collapsed, perhaps earlier, privy wall.

A third area of excavation was located in what was the front yard of the main house. This area is a level patch of lawn located just in front of the kitchen building attached to the house. It also appeared to represent an unknown modification of the natural landscape around the house. While the surface of the grass was level to the house entrance, north and west of this feature the ground fell drastically away behind retaining walls that lined spaces currently used for visitor parking. Given these factors, the artificial nature of the landscape and its proximity to the kitchen, this area was thought to have high potential for containing cultural materials. Furthermore, the decision to excavate in the front yard was motivated by the interest of the owners who hoped to reveal the purpose this formalized lawn may have played historically in the social function of the estate. The predominate quantity of artifacts recovered were redware roofing tiles. A stone ledge was found along the southern edge of one of the test units. Possible quarry marks were discovered along the top edge of the stone, and the sharp edge was indicative of a cut stone shape. It is possible that this feature represents a portion of the remnants of quarried stone from the natural bedrock that may have been quarried for the original construction of the house and outbuildings. The materials recovered from these two units suggest that much of the fill was deposited relatively early in the history of the plantation, and may be related to the functional usage of the kitchen building located just to the west of the yard and to sequential modifications to the house.

7.3 Settlements of enslaved and free laborers at St. Nicholas Abbey

We used information about the names of plantation fields, gathered by Handler and his team, to determine the location of settlement sites of the enslaved and free laborers at St. Nicholas Abbey. The plantation's *Mill Yard* is composed of the area surrounding the sugar factory, which is in turn composed of the sugar mill and the boiling house. The location of a field called *Negro Yard* is situated close to the mill yard, which strongly indicates that the area was the former site of the slave village. Although these fields were turned over to sugarcane cultivation, they retained names associated with the locality's original purpose (Handler 2002:125).

In 1686, the enslaved at St. Nicholas Abbey consisted of 157 people and averaged about 183 people between 1817 and 1832 (ranging from 173 to 202) (Handler et al. 1989: 44). At the time of full emancipation in 1838, the existing 489 plantations in Barbados held as much as 85% of the total land area for the island (Gibbs 1987: 29). With no available lands for the establishment of peasantries (Mintz 1974: 131-156), the majority of former slaves in Barbados remained on plantations in tenantries, resulting in a 'located laborer' system (Beckles 2006; Levy 1980). Archaeology at St. Nicholas Abbey sheds light on how the transition from slavery to freedom transpired in Barbados. We surveyed the estate's slave village in addition to two tenantry settlements. Of special note is that our archaeological findings suggest the enslaved at St. Nicholas Abbey were relocated from a settlement near the mill to other areas of the estate, a process that began in the late-eighteenth century and was completed when slavery was abolished.

In the summer of 2009, sugarcane in the southern portion of the *Negro Yard* field had recently been planted, allowing our team to conduct a shovel test survey of the area with controlled surface collections in fields of good visibility, and systematic shovel test pits (50cm-x-50cm) every ten meters. The survey resulted in a surprisingly large amount of artifacts; including many locally produced redwares and a variety of English imports, such as Buckley ware and Staffordshire slipware. The imported ceramics were all produced within the period of slavery, with an increase in late-eighteenth and early-nineteenth century mass produced wares. Additionally, many items of personal adornment, clay tobacco pipes, black bottle glass, gaming pieces, cowrie shells, and stoneware ink jars were also found during the shovel test survey of the site.

Other artifacts recovered from the settlement in *Negro Yard* field include a heavy concentration of architectural materials, including hand wrought nails and slate roofing tiles. These materials were found throughout the site, but an increased concentration in the northern most section of the field, away from the ancillary buildings related to the factory, suggests they were used as housing materials and that the domestic dwellings of the enslaved were situated primarily along this northern edge of the field. This architectural evidence demonstrates that during the slavery era planters at St. Nicholas Abbey intervened, and at least partially provided some expenditure in housing of the enslaved. Finally, the diagnostic ceramics recovered from the settlement represent an earlier occupation than the northern ridgeline, indicating the settlement of *Negro Yard* was gradually relocated to the ridgeline.

Interesting findings came from a ridgeline on the northern edge of *Negro Yard* field near *Tenant* field. Handler and his team noted piles of stone along this ridgeline in their earlier study and individuals confirmed the presence of rubble stone constructed houses in this area, which had only been taken down in the mid-twentieth century (Handler *et al.* 1989:44). It is likely that this area was once a plantation tenantry, and the piles of stones, presumably from former dwellings, were located within a patch of sour grass growing on this ridgeline.

The investigation of the area led to the discovery of a large amount of early historic material culture apparent on the ground surface. For this reason, two test units were placed along the ridgeline to examine the research potential of this area (Figure 3). A 2x2 meter test unit was placed near one of the stone mounds, and the second 1x1 meter test unit was located amidst a thick surface scatter of artifacts discovered beneath the sour grass growth on the opposite side of the cart road. A wide array of material culture was recovered, including ceramics, which were used to develop a TPQ for the site. The results showed that the TPQp90 for Stratum I in both units was in the decade spanning 1820-1830, and Stratum II dated from 1790-1795. These ranges represent the earliest date at which the refuse could have been deposited at the Ridge site, and the mean ceramic date and median occupation date from both test units range from between 1812 and 1814. This site constitutes one of the most well preserved domestic settlements of the plantation, and corresponds to the transition from slavery to freedom.

Another plantation settlement is located in the modern-day village of Moore Hill, a plantation tenantry belonging to St. Nicholas Abbey until the 1980s. We met with many of the residents in the area to learn the history of the village. As the word hill suggests, this village is situated on an area of rising ground, less than a kilometer west of Cherry Tree Hill. This former tenantry has an extant structure that might date to the late period of slavery. The small, unoccupied, dilapidated rubble stone house is still referred to as a "slave hut" by the residents of this community. The house and house spot are currently maintained by the plantation, and probably always have been. The last person to reside in the house was Ethlyn Lopez, born in 1920 (now deceased), who moved to St. Nicholas Abbey

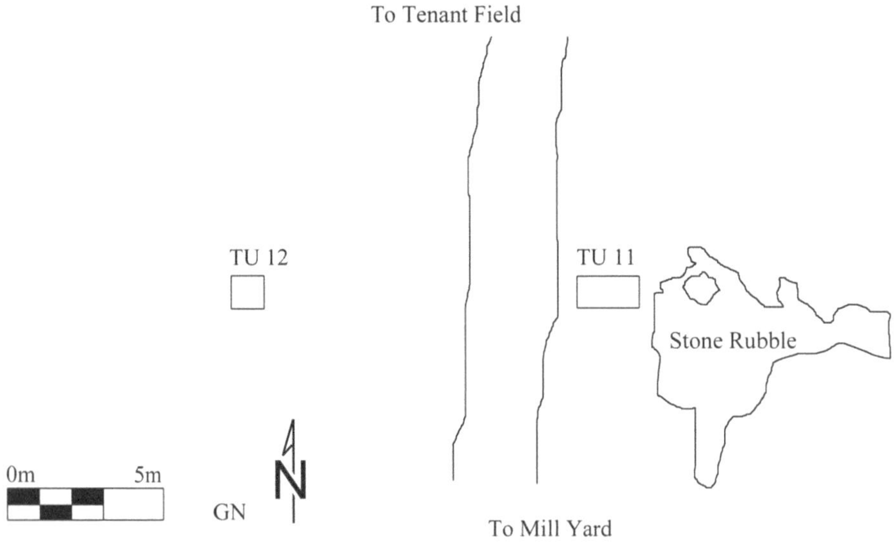

Figure 3. Location of excavation units at the Ridge Site, a well preserved domestic settlement that spans that transition from slavery to freedom at St. Nicholas Abbey sugar plantation.

in 1938 when she became employed by the estate. She recalled renting the house for twenty-four cents a week. According to other neighbors, there were at least five other identical "slave huts" in the tenantry, each aligned in a row, which were vacant for many generations and eventually torn down.

Based on information provided by residents of Moore Hill, this rubble stone house is of identical architectural detail as the ones that once stood on the ridgeline near *Negro Yard* (Figure 4). Houses constructed and repaired by the plantations dates back to the late period of slavery in Barbados. The enslaved or free carpenters and masons who were assigned building these houses either used imported plank wood, or locally obtained and easily worked coral limestone (Handler and Bergman 2009); as is the case with the dwelling houses that were once located on the ridgeline of the *Negro Yard,* and in the former tenantry of Moore Hill.

The structure at Moore Hill was mapped and surfaced collected in 2009. Excavation units were placed within the house as well as the surrounding yard, and shovel test pits were dug near the gully behind the house. No discrete stratigraphy was identified that could determine the date of construction for the site. The historic materials recovered consisted mainly of nineteenth century domestic artifacts; though some earlier wares were also recovered, including English delft and Creamware. It is possible that this tenantry was established at the same time as the settlement on the ridgeline, as these tenantries were located on unproductive, marginal land. It is likely that multiple, smaller settlements would have been needed to meet the physical demands of a community that was nearing 200 people at the time of emancipation.

Figure 4. Rubble-stone constructed house still referred to as a "slave hut" by Moore Hill residents and in Barbados more generally. Identical stone houses used to occupy the Ridge Site near Negro Yard. These house types were introduced during the late period of slavery in Barbados, though it is unknown how common they once were (Handler & Bergman 2009).

It is certain that both of the later-period settlements at St. Nicholas Abbey exhibited a planter-imposed landscape, where the settlement and housing were carefully designed and controlled by the plantation owner/ manager (Armstrong 1990; Armstrong & Kelly 2000; Higman 1998; Wilkie & Farnsworth 2005). The 'improvements' that were occurring in the villages of the laborers at St. Nicholas Abbey conform to common trends throughout the Caribbean region. The imposed landscape model, consisting of orderly spatial arrangements of settlements and permanent building materials, was copied from models in England, where rows of connected cottages with walls of stone or brick and thatched roofs were designed to tie laborers to farms (Higman 1998: 190; Chapman 1991). Barry Higman (1998: 190-194) argued that planters in Jamaica attempted to impose this model on plantation workers to demonstrate their power and to reassure the planter class of the durability of a slave labor system that was entering its final day.

The ideology of power and control expressed by planters in the settlements of the enslaved throughout the West Indies was seldom practiced in the plantation landscape until the abolition of the slave trade in 1807 (Higman 1998). Even then, the extent to which they practiced such control varied considerably during different places and times, from plantation to plantation, and island to island (Farnsworth 2001). In Barbados, it does not appear that ideal model-villages for laborers became prominent until the apprenticeship period, from 1834 to 1838, and only increased after full emancipation (Handler 2002: 121). It is impossible to know how frequently planters in Barbados relocated slave villages from the mill yard to the periphery of estates during slavery. Only a few exceptional cases are documented in Barbados (see Bennett 1955: 127-141).

We have attempted to link the ideological dimensions of the imposed landscape with the families that legally owned St. Nicholas Abbey in the late-eighteenth and early-nineteenth centuries. Sir John Gay Alleyne, the prominent planter, politician, and social reformer who owned the estate from 1746 until his death in 1801, could be responsible for the material and spatial changes of the slave settlements. After his death there was confusion over who was to inherit the property, and by 1810 debts had accumulated and the estate was sold to the Court of Chancery. Brothers Lawrence Trent and Edward Cumberbatch purchased the property in 1816 (Handler et al. 1989: 43), and the property was passed on in 1822 to their niece Sarah who married Stephen Cave, a wealthy banker from Bristol, England. The Cave family remained absentee owners from the period of emancipation until the mid-twentieth century (Campbell 1986). Because Alleyne was a wealthy, liberal social reformer, and since the plantation changed hands several times in the short period leading up to emancipation, we suspect Alleyne was at least partially responsible for the imposed landscape at St. Nicholas Abbey.

Alleyne was a member of the *Barbados Society for the Encouragement of the Arts, Manufactures and Commerce* (known simply as the *Barbados Society of the Arts*), which was founded by the radical planter Joshua Steele in the late eighteenth century. In *White Creole Culture: Politics and Identity during the Age of Abolition,* David Lambert (2005: 41-55) describes the Society and its founder as the leader of a program that sought to restructure plantation life in an attempt to 'improve' the conditions of enslaved peoples. Steele moved to Barbados from Britain in 1780 to overtake the management of several plantations that he owned and remained on the island up until his death in 1796. The most radical, and critiqued, reform he established on his estates was coined the 'copyhold slave system'. Under Steele's system, rents and wages replaced forced coercion, and the enslaved were provided a half-acre to acre of land on the plantation so that they could produce their own food for subsistence as well as exchange (Lambert 2005: 44). Steele published detailed articles about the success of his new liberal system implemented on each of his three estates in the *Barbados Gazattes* (published under "Letters from Philio-Xylon" during the years 1787-88 and reprinted by several abolitionists during the nineteenth century) (see Clarkson 1833, Dickson 1814). It is certain that the British abolitionist debates that were raging at this time shaped the 'improvements' in plantation management. Moreover, after the American Revolutionary War, Barbados lost its primary source of food imports, which made a more liberal system of slavery and self-sufficiency necessary.

The evidence that Alleyne experimented with these liberal reform movements are purely inferential. For one, he was an active member of the *Barbados Society of the Arts*, founded by Steele. Furthermore, Alleyne owned four plantations through inheritance when he was just six years old (Allen 1937: 3), and he went on to manage many more during his lifetime. He served as a plantation attorney at each of the plantations in Barbados where it is known from estate records that rubble-stone slave houses were constructed: At the Codrington plantations in St. John, and Newton estate in Christ Church (Bennett 1955: 100-101; Handler and Bergman 2009: 10-11). At Codrington and Newton, stone slave houses were constructed by 1796, well within the period he served as attorney at each of the estates. Identical rubble-stone houses were also extant until recent times at Alleynedale plantation, St. Peter, also owned by Alleyne.

Lambert (2005) draws on the case study of Joshua Steele to make the argument that debates over the future of slavery came to redefine white creole identities in Barbados between the 1780s and 1830s. As an agent of reformist, metropolitan antislavery pressure, Steele was confronted with opposition from more conservative planters in Barbados. Since his interventions threatened racial and status-based hierarchies, this opposition was expressed in terms of opposing discourses. The first of which tended to embrace the large, poor white population and large slave-owners into a common opposition with free and enslaved "non-whites". The other discourse was a paternalistic one centered on the legitimacy of slave-ownership—the planter ideal. Here, the overarching distinction was one of status rather than race. The tensions between these discourses, or modes of identification, demonstrate the ways that each could configure both loyalty and opposition to metropolitan Britain.

Both the planter ideal and white supremacist modes of identification were in place in Barbados by the late eighteenth century, with the planter ideal affecting plantation management during the first abolitionist movement in the late eighteenth century, and more significantly during the emancipation era. These discourses and the conflicts between them were experienced throughout the island and across the Atlantic. The archaeology at St. Nicholas Abbey shows the extent to which Alleyne strove to express his own loyalty to England while simultaneously trying to legitimize slave ownership. He is even credited with planting the first mahogany trees in Barbados--at Cherry Tree Hill, St. Nicholas Abbey--to celebrate the signing of the Treaty of Paris in 1783. This was not only a symbolic gesture to show that the colony shared the same values as Britain, but was also an attempt to merge a tropical/slave landscape with a British/free one.

While Alleyne openly embraced an English, metropolitan identity, he also actively maintained the popular, local discourse among the more conservative planters. He did this through ameliorative legislation that sought to uplift the poor whites in the island. Alleyne erected and endowed The Alleyne School in the parish of St. Andrew in 1785, the first and only school established for the instruction of poor white boys (Stark 1903: 173). It is clear that Alleyne, as a powerful planter and politician, was active in the maintenance of both race and status at St. Nicholas Abbey and beyond. Planters in Barbados prided themselves as being benevolent and the most 'English' of all the West Indies. This no doubt attests to the development of tenantries, with settlements and houses designed by the planters to represent a free, English landscape.

Yet, it is important to stress that the 'improvements' made on the plantation at St. Nicholas Abbey were far from being 'free' or 'English' for the enslaved that lived in them. It is also revealing that the planter ideal discourse, used to justify slave ownership in the late eighteenth century, became the dominant social system when slavery was abolished in 1834. Houses and land, rents and wages, became the foundation of contracts for emancipated workers in Barbados. Planters used the practice of house evictions to ensure the stipulations provided in the tenant contracts were favorable to the estate. Immediately after emancipation the English Parliament protested these evictions and stipulated that all evictions be reported with adequate justification. As such, some evictions were documented and published in correspondence between Barbados and colonial officials in England (*Parliamentary Papers* 1840: 35), including the account of Mimbo, described as a laborer at St. Nicholas Abbey. Mimbo was ordered to leave St. Nicholas Abbey by the plantation overseer, Thomas S. Harding, on April 6, 1839. She occupied a house located on plantation lands, and the dwelling she occupied was valued at 20L (*Parliamentary Papers* 1840: 35: 44-45).

The slave returns that were mandatory throughout the British Caribbean in 1834 show that Mimbo lived at St. Nicholas Abbey during the slavery period, and she was just barely twelve years at the time of legal emancipation in 1834. Five years later she was evicted from her home because her husband, who had also been employed at St. Nicholas Abbey, refused to perform some work that he had been called to do, resulting in what the overseer stated was his choice of "quitting the estate" (1840: 35: 44-45). Not only did he lose his home, he had to move away from his wife, family, and village. But this alone could not keep him away as he continued to visit Mimbo at St. Nicholas Abbey.

Evidently, this greatly upset the overseer who no longer had any control over the man he already evicted. The overseer wanted to ensure that he could keep this man off his property. As a result, he wielded his power of eviction and banished both from St. Nicholas Abbey. In fall of the same year, three more tenants faced evictions, but magistrates from England intervened and prevented further removals from St. Nicholas Abbey (1840: 35: 45-46).

The *Master and Servants Act* of 1840, passed one year after Mimbo's eviction, formally legalized house evictions and imprisonment for not working to the demands of the plantation (Gibbs 1987). As a result, family and community relations that were established during slavery came under new threats of both voluntary and forced separation with emancipation. The documentary and archaeological evidence from St. Nicholas Abbey highlights the actions that plantation tenants pursued to maintain community relations.

7.4 Spaces in between

Though the archaeology of plantation settlement sites demonstrates increased planter control, the spaces in between these sites offer significant information from places where the reach of planters was the most minimal. Archaeological investigations in the gullies that run through the plantation lands at St. Nicholas Abbey offer important insights into the social practices that plantation laborers engaged in. The gully between St. Nicholas Abbey and Moore Hill contains a series of caves, many of which possess a large amount of material culture, including ceramics and black bottle glass. Perhaps these caves, as liminal spaces on the landscape between adjoining plantations served as meeting areas for enslaved and later free workers from other estates. The privacy these spaces afforded likely allowed greater mobility between villages and the encouragement of activities that were not permitted in the public sphere of white authority.

Following emancipation in 1834, the island of Barbados was left in a stage of rebuilding. The planters continued to build new houses and settlements for their laborers copying English designs, creating a coercive bond to the lands many had grown deeply attached to in slavery. At the same time, the formerly enslaved sought their idea of what emancipation society should become. The use of the landscape at St. Nicholas Abbey speaks to the actions many pursued to maintain community and family relationships. Families were often separated from their social and physical attachments in the decades immediately following emancipation; much as they did during slavery. Whether this happened through eviction, such as the case of Mimbo and her husband, or by choice in the equally dramatic cases when some individuals left the plantations in search of relative autonomy; returning to these communities would become increasingly necessary and difficult.

Gullies are thus viewed as highly fluid places that physically and socially connected many of the communities in the plantation-dominated landscape of Barbados. As somewhat rugged and uncultivated areas, they provided a private space where people could travel without restriction and relationships between members from several plantations and villages could be maintained. Much like today in St. Peter where rum shops sit at the crossroads between estates, the caves may also have served in earlier times as established meeting spaces for estate residents. The historical archaeological study of Mapps Cave, a cavern and sinkhole complex in St. Philip, Barbados used by enslaved peoples in the seventeenth-nineteenth centuries, is one of only a few to highlight the use of caves by enslaved peoples (Smith 2008). While domestic tablewares dominated the Mapps Cave site, alcohol related materials represented a significant proportion of the Mapps Cave artifact assemblage and indicated that alcohol drinking was one of the primary activities that occurred at the site. Mapps Cave is located on Bayleys sugar plantation, but is centrally located between two other large estates. According to Smith, the evidence indicates Mapps Cave, a liminal space on the plantation landscape, provided enslaved peoples from Bayleys and surrounding sugar estates with a temporary refuge from the rigors of plantation life, and the use of alcohol at Mapps Cave enhanced those feelings of escape.

The Gullies surrounding St. Nicholas Abbey may have served as clandestine corridors between surrounding sugar estates. Through these corridors, information was spread and regional community ties were reinforced. As with Mapps Cave, the caves situated in the gullies surrounding St. Nicholas Abbey appear to have provided more extensive periods of social interaction and social integration among workers from regional estates. The presence of black bottle glass fragments and pieces of stoneware drinking mugs hints at the likelihood that alcohol drinking was one of the main activities to occur at these pivotal sites. As a social performance, alcohol drinking would have helped strengthen regional social bonds and foster the expression of regional identities. The presence of twentieth century beer bottle glass at the cave sites demonstrates the ongoing use of gullies as corridors and meeting spaces.

7.5 Conclusions

St. Nicholas Abbey sugar plantation is perhaps the most important heritage site in Barbados. As a symbol of the Barbadian sugar revolution and a product of early British colonialism in the New World, St. Nicholas Abbey's historical significance transcends the physical boundaries of Barbados. Archaeological investigations have shed new light on St. Nicholas Abbey's prominent role in the emerging Atlantic world. The site is well preserved and archaeological deposits are largely intact. Furthermore, the archaeological investigations reveal a continuous occupation of the St. Nicholas Abbey property from prehistoric Amerindian settlement all the way up to the present. The majority of materials we have collected, however, are from the seventeenth through nineteenth centuries when St. Nicholas Abbey was an extremely active sugar-producing estate.

The archaeological work at St. Nicholas Abbey is enhancing the interpretation of this important historical landmark, as well as expanding scholarly research and public education at the site. Our primary aim is to pursue archaeological work at St. Nicholas Abbey that speaks to the interests of Barbadians and foreign visitors alike. Of significance to this goal are the archaeological findings that reveal the conceptual and literal in-between spaces of plantation society in the Atlantic world. These liminal spaces extend far beyond the settlement sites of St. Nicholas Abbey and are the sites where identities were negotiated, especially in the eighteenth and nineteenth centuries.

References

Allen, L.R.

1939 Records of the Family of the Alleynes of Barbados. *The Journal of Barbados Museum and Historical Society* 21:1-27.

Armstrong, D.V.

1990 *The Village and the Great House: An Archaeological and Historical Examination of Drax Hall Plantation, St. Ann's Bay, Jamaica.* University of Illinois Press, Chicago.

Armstrong, D.V. and K. Kelly

2000 Settlement Patterns and the Origins of African Jamaican Society: Seville Plantation, St. Ann's Bay, Jamaica. *Ethnohistory* 47(2):369-397.

Beckles, H. McD.

2006 *A History of Barbados: From Amerindian Settlement to Caribbean Single Market.* Cambridge University Press, New York.

Bennett Jr., J. H.

1955 *Bondsmen and Bishops: Slavery and Apprenticeship on the Codrington Plantations of Barbados, 1710-1838.* University of California Publications in History, Berkeley and Los Angeles 62:1-176.

Campbell, P.F.

1986 Nicholas Plantation and Some of its Associations. In *Chapters in Barbados History.* Barbados Museum and Historical Society, Bridgetown.

Chapman, W.

1991 Slave Villages in the Danish West Indies: Changes of the Late Eighteenth and Early Nineteenth Centuries. *Perspectives in Vernacular Architecture* 4:108-120.

Clark, G. D.

1833 *Proposals for the formation of a West India Free Labour Company for Effecting the Abolition of Slavery and Affording Equitable Protection....* London.

Dickson, W.

1814 *Mitigation of Slavery, In Two Parts. Part I: Letters and Papers of the Late Hon. Joshua Steele,* pp. 1-7, 132-136, 177-183. *Part II: Letters to Thomas Clarkson, Esq. M.A.*, pp. 193, 338-353. London.

Delle, J.A.

1998 *An Archaeology of Social Space: Analyzing Coffee Plantations in Jamaica's Blue Mountains.* New York University, New York.

Farnsworth, P.

2001 'Negroe Houses Built of Stone Besides Others Watl'd + Plastered,' The Creation of a Bahamian Tradition. In *Island Lives: Historical Archaeologies of the Caribbean,* edited by P. Farnsworth. The University of Alabama Press, Tuscaloosa.

Fraser, H. and R. Hughes

1982 *Historic Houses of Barbados, A collection of Drawings, with Historical and Architectural Notes.* The Barbados National Trust, Bridgetown.

Gibbs, B.

1987 The Establishment of the Tenantry System in Barbados. In *Emancipation II, Aspects of the Post-Slavery Experience in Barbados; A Series of Lectures to Commemorate the 150th Anniversary of Emancipation,* edited by W.K. Marshall, pp.27-33. University of West Indies, Department of History, and Barbados National Cultural Foundation, Bridgetown.

Great Britain Parliament, House of Commons

1841 Papers Relative to the West Indies. 1840: Part II: Barbados. *Parliamentary Papers.* Volume 35 (282):1-255.

Handler, J. S.

2002 Plantation Slave Settlements in Barbados, 1650s to 1834. In *The Shadow of the Plantation,* edited by A.O. Thompson, pp.123-160. Ian Randle Publishers, Kingston, Jamaica.

Handler, J.S. and S. Bergman

2009 Vernacular Houses and Domestic Material Culture on Barbadian Sugar Plantations: 1650-1834. *Journal of Caribbean History* 49 (1&2):1-36

Handler, J.S., and F.W. Lange

1978 *Plantation Slavery in Barbados: An Archaeological and Historical Investigation.* Harvard University Press, Cambridge.

Handler, J.S., M. Conner and K. Jacobi

1989 *Searching for a Slave Cemetery in Barbados, West Indies. A Bioarchaeological and Ethnohistorical Investigation.* Research Paper No. 59, Center for Archaeological Investigations, Southern Illinois University, Carbondale.

Higman, B.W.

1998 *Montpelier, Jamaica: A Plantation Community in Slavery and Freedom, 1739 to 1912.* The University Press of the West Indies, Kingston, Jamaica.

Lambert, D.

2005 *White Creole Culture, Politics and Identity during the Age of Abolition.* Cambridge University Press, Cambridge.

Lesser, C.H.

1995 South Carolina Begins, the Records of a Proprietary Colony, 1663-172. Manuscript on file in the South Carolina Department of Archives and History, Columbia.

Levy, C.

1980 *Emancipation, Sugar and Federalism: Barbados and the West Indies: 1833-1876.* University of Florida Press, Gainesville.

Ligon, R.

1657 *A True & Exact History of the Island of Barbados.* London.

Marshall, W.K.

1987 Villages and Plantation Sub-Division. In *Emancipation II, Aspects of the Post-Slavery Experience in Barbados; A Series of Lectures to Commemorate the 150th Anniversary of Emancipation,* edited by W.K. Marshall. University of West Indies, Department of History, and Barbados National Cultural Foundation, Bridgetown.

Mintz, S.W.

1974 *Caribbean Transformations.* Aldine Transaction, New Brunswick and London.

Schomburgk, Robert H

1848 *The History of Barbados.* Frank & Cass, London.

Smith, F.H.

2008 *The Archaeology of Alcohol and Drinking.* University Press of Florida, Gainesville.

2001 *Volatile Spirits: The Historical Archaeology of Alcohol and Drinking in the Caribbean.* Unpublished Ph.D dissertation, Department of Anthropology, University of Florida, Gainesville.

Smith, F.H., and K. Watson

2009 Urbanity, Sociability, and Commercial Exchange in the Barbados Sugar Trade: A Comparative Colonial Archaeological Perspective on Bridgetown, Barbados in the Seventeenth Century. *International Journal of Historical Archaeology* 13(1): 63-79.

Stark, J.H.

1893 *Stark's history and guide to Barbados and the Caribbee Islands, containing a description of everything on or about these islands of which the visitor or resident may desire information ...* London.

Waterman, T.T.

1946 *The Mansions of Virginia.* University of North Carolina Press, Chapel Hill.

Wilkie, L.A. and P. Farnsworth.

2005 *Sampling Many Pots: Archaeology of Memory and Tradition at a Bahamian Plantation.* University Press of Florida, Gainesville.

Chapter 8

Post-emancipation lifeways at Green Castle Estate, Antigua

Samantha Rebovich Bardoe

Heritage Department
Antigua and Barbuda National Parks Authority
samantha.bardoe@gmail.com

Abstract

Following emancipation in Antigua, the colonial legislature and planters tried to continually coerce the formerly enslaved by enacting laws and creating new means of social control to force free laborers to continue to live and work on sugar plantations. Yet, Antiguan laborers found innovative ways to resist colonial ideologies during the periods of both slavery and freedom. This paper examines domestic assemblages associated with enslaved and free laborers at Green Castle Estate, Antigua and offers insights into how Afro-Antiguans subverted the power of planters to create unique cultural traditions and meaning of their own accord. Most notably, changes in consumption and daily practice point to ways Antiguan laborers tried to shape their lives despite the subversive forces that hindered them.

Resumé

Après l'émancipation à l'Antigua, la législature coloniale et des planteurs essayés continuellement de contraindre les anciens esclaves en décrétant des lois et en créant de nouveaux moyens de contrôle social afin de forcer les travailleurs libres à continuer à vivre et travailler dans les plantations sucrières. Cependant, les travailleurs antiguais ont trouvé des moyens innovants de résister aux idéologies coloniales au cours des périodes de l'esclavage et de la liberté. Ce document examine les assemblages domestiques liés aux esclaves et aux travailleurs libres du domaine de Green Castle (Antigua), Antigua et offre des perspectives sur la façon dont les Afro-Antiguais ont renversé la puissance des planteurs en créant des traditions culturelles uniques. En particulier, dans changements dans les modes de consommation consommation et les pratiques quotidiennes indiquent comment les travailleurs antiguais ont essayé de modeler leur vie en dépit des forces subversives qui les ont gênées.

Resumen

Después de la emancipación en Antigua, la legislatura colonial y los plantadores intentados para forzar continuamente esclavizado antes decretando leyes y creando nuevos medios del control social de forzar a trabajadores libres a continuar viviendo y trabajando en plantaciones del azúcar. Con todo, los trabajadores de Antigua encontraron maneras innovadoras de oponerse a ideologías coloniales durante los períodos de esclavitud y de libertad. Este papel examina a las ensambladuras domésticas asociadas a esclavizado y libera a trabajadores en el estado verde del castillo, Antigua y ofrece penetraciones en cómo los Afro-Antiguans derribaron la energía de plantadores de crear tradiciones y el significado culturales únicos sus los propios acuerdo. Especialmente, los cambios en la consumición y la práctica diaria señalan a los trabajadores de Antigua de las maneras intentados para formar sus vidas a pesar de las fuerzas subversivas que las obstaculizaron.

Key words

plantation archaeology, slavery, post-emancipation

Mots-clés

archéologie des plantations, l'esclavage, post-émancipation

Palabras clave

arqueología de plantaciones, esclavitud, después de la emancipación

Slavery was abolished in the British Empire in 1834. Nonetheless, throughout the Caribbean, a system of apprenticeship was put in place in which the formerly enslaved would serve as apprentices under their former masters for four years before gaining full freedom in 1838. In Antigua, however, planters voted for full emancipation in 1834, setting the stage for a social experiment that would be watched throughout the Caribbean. In the case of post-emancipation life in Antigua, planters and colonists were concerned with keeping the *status quo* of slavery by maintaining control over the newly freed labor force and ensuring that the profitability of sugar plantations was maintained. For the formerly enslaved, though, freedom offered opportunities that were previously denied during the period of slavery and archaeological excavations at Green Castle Estate demonstrate that following emancipation Afro-Antiguans took hold of opportunities to forge new lifeways for themselves.

8.1 Slavery and freedom in Antigua

Antigua was settled in 1632 by English settlers for agricultural production. By 1655 sugar was introduced to the island and quickly became the cash crop of choice among English planters. Slavery took hold quickly in Antigua, too. By 1708 the island accounted for over half of the slave population of the Leeward Islands. Throughout the first quarter of the eighteenth century, Antigua became characterized as an island of large sugar plantations as land was consolidated among wealthy planters, agricultural production moved exclusively to sugar production, and the number of enslaved laborers on each estate increased dramatically. By the end of the first quarter of the eighteenth century, Antigua had cemented its position as an island of wealthy planters who created large sugar plantations that were worked by gangs of enslaved laborers. In the third quarter of the eighteenth century, Antigua reached its peak in sugar production. The slave population of the island reached its height at 37,808 people in 1774 (Sheridan 1960: 127). At the same time, the consolidation of estates continued, resulting in Antigua's sugar industry being reliant on a number of wealthy planters with large estates.

During the period of slavery, enslaved laborers who lived and worked on these large sugar estates were able to create lifeways that subverted the dominance of Antiguan planters. For instance, enslaved laborers developed internal markets in which they sold surplus foodstuffs and crafts such as locally-made Afro-Antiguan earthenwares (Gaspar 1985). In addition, many enslaved laborers attended schools sponsored by churches and missionaries to acquire literacy and encouraged their children to attend school as well (Blouet 1990). Throughout the landscapes of slavery in Antigua, enslaved laborers created niches in which they could exert some control over aspects of their own lives.

Despite the promise of freedom that accompanied the shift to emancipation in 1834, there was great anxiety among Antiguan planters as to how Antiguan society would operate following emancipation. Therefore, in the years prior to emancipation, Antiguan planters enacted a series of legislative acts restricting the rights of laborers by prohibiting Sunday markets, limiting how laborers could appeal for missed wages, and by creating strict laws relating to social conduct. These measures were passed to help ensure that the formerly enslaved would continue to work on sugar plantations following emancipation.

In large part, the continued success of the sugar enterprise on Antigua has been attributed to the unique system of strong coercion immediately following emancipation (Bolland 1996; 1999). Though Antiguan planters advocated immediate emancipation, the Antiguan legislature developed a series of contracts that legally bound laborers to estates for specific periods of time (Boland 1996: 109). Antigua is also credited with introducing the wage/rent system in the British Caribbean in which planters served as both employers and landlords as formerly enslaved individuals continued to live in cabins inhabited during slavery and work provision grounds on estates (Bolland 1996: 109).

The Antiguan legislation was considered so harsh that colonial overseers in London overruled the Antiguan legislation and enacted a series of less harsh (though only slightly) labor laws (Bolland 1996: 109). Under these acts, oral labor contracts were only valid for a year and could be terminable at a month's notice (Bolland 1996: 109). In addition, under these changes, the existence of a tenement was eligible as legal evidence of the existence of a tenancy contract between the laborer and his landlord (Bolland 1996: 109). Limits were set on the length of workdays, too, with laborers working nine hours a day for a wage of nine pence a day, with one day off every week or two (Bolland 1996: 109). Though these new acts were an improvement of labor and living conditions over those originally passed by the Antiguan colonial legislature, wage laborers were still very impoverished under this system and it has been argued that the *material* conditions of life for the formerly enslaved would not have changed much immediately following emancipation (Bolland 1996: 109).

8.2 Green Castle Estate

In 1677 Major Samuel Martin moved his family to Antigua where he founded Green Castle Estate in St. Mary's Parish (Gaspar 1985: 66). The original property purchased by Martin was approximately 550 acres of land, but at the height of productivity at Green Castle in the eighteenth century, the plantation consisted of 600 acres of land, at least 400 of which were dedicated to sugar planting (Gaspar 1985: 96; Sheridan 1960: 132). Major Samuel Martin was instrumental in the colonial government of Antigua as he was a member of the Assembly by 1686 and was made Speaker of the Assembly in 1689. In 1697, he was listed as a member of Council (Oliver 1894: 1xvi). Samuel Martin's position in the local government may have contributed to the rapid success of his plantation. Green Castle was an estate that greatly profited in the last decades of the seventeenth century, as Major Martin quickly added to his landholdings, increased his enslaved population, and profited handsomely off the sugar trade. By the end of the seventeenth century, the estate boasted two windmills, highlighting the scale of production underway.

While Green Castle quickly arose as one of the largest and most profitable sugar plantations on the island, the management skills of Major Samuel Martin are called into question as he was killed by his enslaved laborers on December 25, 1701 (Gaspar 1985: 185). According to historic accounts of the incident, the laborers rebelled because he did not grant them their Christmas holiday, killing Major Martin with their field hoes while he was still sleeping (Gaspar 1985: 185). Other accounts contend that his refusal of the holiday marked the culmination of a series of harsh treatments committed by Major Martin against his enslaved laborers (Dyde 2000: 44). Still other documents reveal the surprise of members of Antigua's elite planter class at the event, commenting that Major Samuel Martin must have performed some grave mistreatment of his workers since they came from the most gentle of the African tribes (Dyde 2000: 44). While Major Samuel Martin was killed in his bed, his wife and children fled into the sugar field where they were kept safe.

Following the death of Major Samuel Martin, it is unclear what repercussions were taken against the conspirators who killed him. Additionally, it is unclear what impact Major Samuel Martin's murder had on productivity and life at Green

Castle Estate in its immediate aftermath. In the first decades of the eighteenth century, various managers oversaw the estate, including relatives and friends of the Martins, as Major Martin's eldest son, Samuel, finished his education abroad (Sheridan 1960: 128).

In 1750, when Colonel Samuel Martin returned to Green Castle Estate after an extended stay in England, he found the plantation in disarray. His sugar fields were in squalor, he had lost some of his enslaved laborers due to disease and death, and his sugar works were nearly in ruins. Rather than abandon his plantation, Colonel Martin began a process of reform and restoration that would make Green Castle Estate one of the most profitable sugar plantations in Antigua. Martin's attention to management on his plantation represents a shift away from the violent nature of slave society as it was practiced in Antigua throughout the first half of the eighteenth century. Instead, Martin's approach is a turn to paternalism (Sheridan 1960; Zacek 2007).

In 1750, Martin published the first edition of *An Essay Upon Plantership* in which he put forth his plans for sound plantation management. The *Essay* would go through seven editions and be reprinted twice following the publication of the final edition. Throughout the *Essay Upon Plantership*, Colonel Martin did not just provide recommendations for plantation landscaping, agricultural processes, and techniques in fertilizing, but also contributed a rather large portion of the text to the proper treatment of the enslaved laborers including their living conditions, appropriate workloads and task assignments, proper medical care, and adequate provisioning gardens. Martin definitively linked the treatment of the enslaved laborers with levels of production output. Thus, proper plantation management and good treatment towards laborers would result in increased sugar production leading to reduced costs and overall greater profit.

Throughout the period of social change from slavery to freedom in Antigua, sugar production continued at Green Castle Estate. When Samuel Martin died in the late eighteenth century, the estate was inherited by one of his heirs, Sir Henry Martin. Henry Martin seemed to share a passion for planting and plantation improvement with Samuel Martin as historic accounts speak to how he continued to develop ways to increase the efficiency of labor and production at Green Castle Estate (Murray 1825:261). Henry Martin may also have shared some concern for the welfare of enslaved laborers at the estate as he approved the opening of a day school for enslaved children at the estate in the early nineteenth century (Blouet 1990: 632).

Following emancipation, the historical record does not offer many insights into the nature of life and production at Green Castle Estate, though sugar production continued at the plantation through the first half of the twentieth century. Samuel Martin offered his enslaved laborers incentives to remain on the estate, such as provisions grounds and, given the lack of free land for settlement following emancipation, it is highly likely many of the laborers that had been enslaved at Green Castle Estate continued to live and work there following emancipation. In this context, the formerly enslaved at Green Castle were able to take advantage of opportunities available under the new system of freedom to improve their lives and exercise agency in forging a new pattern of lifeways in post-emancipation Antigua.

8.3 Excavations at Green Castle Estate

The history of Green Castle Estate provides a fascinating backdrop for a diachronic study of the lives of Afro-Antiguans during the periods of slavery and freedom because of the social struggles that occurred at the site. One of the advantages of the archaeological evidence recovered from Green Castle Estate is the opportunity to compare assemblages that date to the periods of slavery and post-emancipation. This is an innovation for plantation archaeology in Antigua because it provides evidence of the daily lives of enslaved laborers and wage laborers. Previous plantation research on Antigua has only examined the lives of wage laborers in the late nineteenth century (Gonzalez Scollard 2008) or the planter's house (Fox 2009). The landscape of Green Castle Estate, wherein there are distinct areas of domestic refuse dating to the periods of slavery and emancipation, allows for a comparative approach that examines how lifeways changed for Afro-Antiguans from the period of slavery to freedom.

Archaeological fieldwork began at Green Castle Estate in the summer of 2007. Initial pedestrian survey of the site resulted in the designation of seven loci within the area of potential archaeological interest. These loci were identified through the use of historic representations of the plantation, local knowledge of the estate, and the presence of surface features within the site. As this project is interested in comparing the lifeways of laborers during the periods of slavery and freedom in Antigua, loci with archaeological remains that might be associated with the enslaved and wage laborer populations of the estate were given priority for subsurface testing.

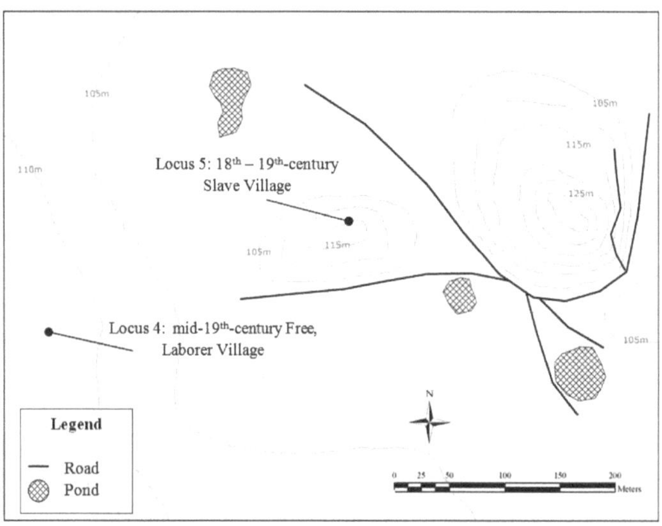

Figure 1. The Green Castle Survey Map demonstrates the movement of wage laborer households away from those of enslaved laborers.

In the summer of 2007 a shovel testing program was initiated to determine the presence, nature, and extent of subsurface deposits at Green Castle Estate. Three loci were targeted in this program in the hopes that substantial archaeological deposits would be present and warrant additional excavation. Loci 2, 4, and 5 were tested during the 2007 shovel testing program and informed the excavation of units during the following field season. Shovel tests in all three loci revealed the presence of intact archaeological deposits. The deposits at Loci 2 and 4 were relatively shallow (between 20-40 cm deep) while at Locus 5 shovel testing revealed deposits as deep as 50-70 cm.

In the summer of 2008, unit excavations were conducted in Loci 2 and 4 with the goals of identifying the presence of distinct house features, developing a greater sense of the spatial distribution of artifacts within each locus, and beginning to collect data relating to the daily practices of enslaved and wage laborers at the estate. Six units were excavated in Locus 2 resulting in scant archaeological deposits dating to the nineteenth century. This area had been targeted for archaeological investigation because it was designated as the site of the slave village in an 1804 watercolor painting of the estate by Nicholas Pocock. The archaeological evidence does not support this interpretation because the artifact assemblage dates to the post-emancipation period and therefore excavations in Locus 2 were halted.

Unit excavations at Locus 4 were also conducted during the summer of 2008 resulting in the identification of discrete domestic deposits dating to the third quarter of the nineteenth century. The archaeological evidence corroborated the local knowledge that this was a site of domestic activity among wage laborers in the second half of the nineteenth century. A total of six units were excavated during the summer of 2008 and an additional 14 units were excavated in this locus during the 2009 field season. No distinct house features were identified in the excavations, yet the artifact assemblage from this locus consistently dates to the second half of the nineteenth century and suggests this area of the estate was used as domestic quarters for wage laborers in the post-emancipation period.

Unit excavations at Locus 5 were conducted during the 2009 field season in an attempt to identify the domestic spaces of enslaved laborers. The locus was targeted because of the presence of distinct terracing along the hillside, possible building remains and the presence of cultural deposits, as evidenced by shovel testing. A total of 20 units were excavated along two terraced platforms of Locus 5 resulting in the recovery of an artifact assemblage that dates to the late eighteenth century. In addition, a single building feature was identified. As multiple, distinct house or building structures were not identified in archaeological investigations, excavations in both Locus 4 and Locus 5 focused on obtaining a representative sample of the archaeological deposits by sampling across the area of each locus.

In my discussion of the archaeological assemblages from Green Castle Estate, I focus on the material recovered from unit excavations in Locus 4 and Locus 5. These excavations provide discrete archaeological deposits that can be closely associated with the post-emancipation lifeways and the enslaved laborer lifeways, respectively, on the plantation.

8.4 Post-emancipation lifeways at Green Castle Estate

The archaeological deposits associated with wage laborers at Green Castle Estate demonstrate the ways in which the daily lives of wage laborers differed from those of enslaved laborers. These differences point to how the daily lives of laborers changed in the years following emancipation. The formerly enslaved took great advantage of the new opportunities available to them such as greater access to markets, increased autonomy in their domestic lives, and more educational opportunities. Archaeological evidence of daily practice demonstrates how Afro-Antiguans actively changed their lives in the post-emancipation period in spite of continued coercion and restraint by the colonial legislature.

Artifacts relating to foodways are ubiquitous in domestic contexts and the archaeological assemblages from Loci 5 and 4 at Green Castle Estate are no exception. Items relating to foodways comprise 77.91% (3484) of the Locus 5 (enslaved laborer) assemblage whereas they comprise 70.00% (1612) of the Locus 4 (wage laborer) assemblage. While in both cases these types of artifacts comprise the majority of the artifact assemblages, the composition of these assemblages differs between the two periods and might point to ways in which the lives of free laborers changed from those of enslaved laborers.

First, there are considerable differences in the distribution of items relating to foodways within subcategories such as food storage, food serving and food preparation (Table 1). For instance, items relating to food preparation comprise an overwhelming 51.55% (1796) of the foodways artifacts from Locus 5 (slavery) whereas only 7.26% (117) of the foodways artifacts from Locus 4 (wage labor) fall within that category. This suggests there was a substantial shift in the ways in which Afro-Antiguans prepared food in the period of slavery and after emancipation, as evidenced from the archaeological deposits in Loci 5 and 4. Additionally, there is a drastic change in the amount of artifacts relating to food storage over these two periods as well. While items relating to food storage only comprise 8.90% (310) of the foodways artifacts from Locus 5, they comprise 32.51% (524) of foodways items from Locus 4.

While there is not as dramatic a shift in the overall percentage of artifacts relating to food serving from the periods of slavery and freedom (items relating to food serving comprise 35.30% [1230] and 46.59% [751] of the foodways assemblages from Locus 5 and Locus 4, respectively), there are distinct changes in the artifacts used for food serving. The vessel types used for food serving do not change significantly over time (Table 2), however, there are considerable changes

	Locus 5 (Period of Slavery)		Locus 4 (Post-Emancipation)	
	Number of Artifacts	Percentage	Number of Artifacts	Percentage
Food-Faunal	148	4.25%	220	13.65%
Food Storage	310	8.90%	524	32.51%
Food Serving	1230	35.30%	751	46.59%
Food Preparation	1796	51.55%	117	7.26%

Table 1. Comparison of foodways artifacts from Loci 5 and 4.

		Locus 5 (Period of Slavery)		Locus 4 (Post-Emancipation)	
Artifact Class	Vessel Type	Number of Artifacts	Percentage	Number of Artifacts	Percentage
Ceramic	Bowl	173	14.07%	94	12.52%
	Lid	3	0.24%	0	-
	Plate	200	16.26%	74	9.85%
	Saucer	8	0.65%	3	0.40%
	Serving Dish	3	0.24%	5	0.67%
	Teacup	16	1.30%	2	0.27%
	Unid.: Tableware	649	52.76%	462	61.52%
	Unid.: Teaware	127	10.33%	60	7.99%
Glass	Drinking glass	1	0.08%	0	-
	Stemware	1	0.08%	0	-
	Tableware, unid.	44	3.58%	48	6.39%
Metal	Spoon	0	-	3	0.40%
	Utensil Handle	5	0.41%	0	-

Table 2. Vessels relating to food serving in Locus 5 and Locus 4.

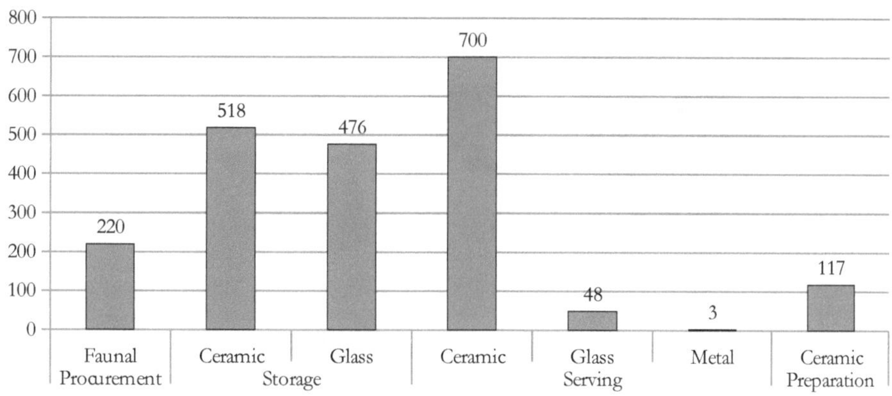

Figure 2. Sub-categories of artifacts relating to foodways from Locus 4.

to the decorative techniques used on ceramics which might point to differences in the availability of particular items over time, but also to the increased consumer power Afro-Antiguans had following emancipation.

Serving items dominate the artifacts relating to foodways from Locus 4 and include a variety of tablewares such as bowls, plates, and serving dishes, as well as teawares such as teacups and saucers. Of the identified tableware vessels, bowls are the most prevalent (94) yet plates are also relatively common (74). Such an assemblages points to two distinct changes in how people ate and dined following emancipation. First, the prevalence of serving items points to greater consumer power to buy ceramic and glass items for dining and, second, it also suggests a preference for more fancy and permanent dining wares over organic materials such as the calabash.

Artifact Type	Vessel Type	Number of Fragments
Ceramic-Tableware	Bowl	94
	Plate	74
	Serving Dish	5
	Unid.: Tableware	462
Ceramic-Teaware	Saucer	3
	Teacup	2
	Unid.: Teaware	60
Glass	Tableware, unid.	48
Metal	Spoon	3

Table 3. Vessels relating to food serving from Locus 4 excavations.

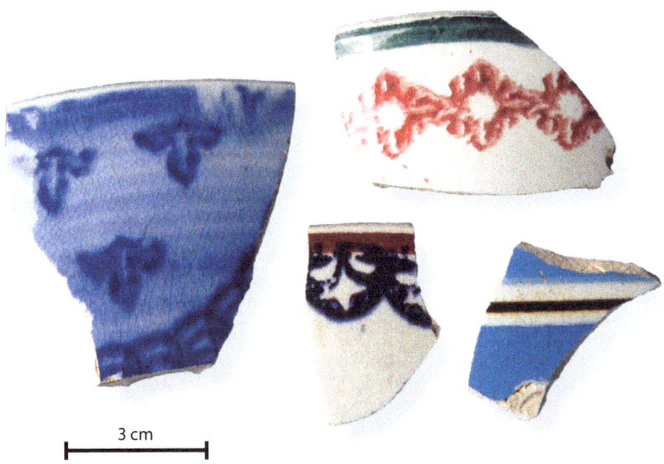

Figure 3. Locus 4 ceramics include a hand painted pearlware bowl fragment, two sponge painted bowl fragments and one annularware bowl fragment.

In addition, a large proportion of items relating to foodways consist of storage items such as jugs, pitchers, storage jars, and a variety of glass jars and bottles (Table 4). These items comprise 32.51% (524) of the foodways assemblage at Locus 4, and include a variety of types of materials ranging from coarse earthenwares and stonewares to glass bottles in a variety of shapes and sizes such as olive green "wine-style" bottles, case bottles, and bell jars (Figure 4).

In addition to the evidence for food storage, preparation, and serving, faunal evidence recovered from Locus 4 gives some insights into what types of foods free laborers had access to and were consuming (Figure 5). Nearly half (45.45% [100]) of the faunal assemblage consisted of shells, 13 of which were from the West Indian Top Shell (*Citarrium pica*). Fish were also represented in the faunal collection, including 13 fish vertebra and the maxilla of a parrot fish. Only 6 pieces of mammal remains and 2 rodent remains were recovered from Locus 4. Due to

Artifact Type	Vessel Type	Number of Fragments
Ceramic	Bottle	1
	Jug	2
	Lid	1
	Mug/Can	7
	Pitcher/Ewer	1
	Storage Jar	1
	Unid: Utilitarian	35
Glass	Bell Jar	1
	Bottle, beer	59
	Bottle, case	1
	Bottle, liquor	7
	Bottle, mineral	75
	Bottle, unid.	221
	Bottle, wine style	106
	Container, unid.	6

Table 4. Items relating to food storage from Locus 4 excavations.

Figure 4: Storage vessel fragments include salt-glazed stoneware sherds.

their minute nature, 44.55% of the faunal remains were unidentifiable. In general, the large percentage of sea creatures in the faunal collection points to an increase in the practice of supplementing diets through local fishing. As laborers could no longer rely on provisions of salted fish from planters, it is likely they fished more themselves or turned to local fisherman to purchase fish to supplement the provisions they grew in their provision plots and house gardens.

These shifts in foodways point to several changes in the lives of free laborers that occurred following emancipation. First, the artifacts relating to foodways reflect a much greater use of imported European ceramics such as pearlwares, whitewares, and stonewares. While this shift might reflect a greater availability and access to

Figure 5: Faunal remains from Locus 4 include mammal bone fragments and West Indian Top Shell (Cittarium pica) fragments.

imported ceramics, the nature of these ceramics points to a change in the practices surrounding foodways.

Second, the amount of items relating to food serving and storage suggests a greater interest in these aspects of foodways as opposed to food preparation. Several changes in laborer lifeways following emancipation lend insights into why there is an emphasis on food serving and storage. Freed wage laborers could no longer rely on receiving provisions from planters as they did during the period of slavery. Although at Green Castle Estate enslaved laborers had access to provision grounds, the presence of artifacts relating to food storage following emancipation suggests a greater concern with preserving foodstuffs. Historical accounts also stress how the formerly enslaved were responsible for growing their own foodstuffs following emancipation. "Now, they provide themselves with what they like; and are therefore better, if less abundantly fed" (Sturge and Harvey 1838:47-48). Even if wage laborers were given the opportunity to grow food items they preferred, the lack of food rations received from planters was a problem that some free laborers could not overcome. At least one post-emancipation court case highlights how a laborer resorted to stealing food because he had been sick and could not earn his wages, nor grow food items, nor afford to purchase food (Sturge and Harvey 1838:35). Additionally, the challenge of providing food for elderly Afro-Antiguans who could not work to earn a wage was a widespread social problem following emancipation: "The most painful feature in the state of Antigua at the present moment is, the destitute condition of the old and infirm, owing to the absence of a legal provision for them, and to the present distress from the long period of drought" (Sturge & Harvey 1838: 33). It becomes clear that following emancipation, as laborers were responsible for providing themselves with food, a greater interest in food storage would be necessary and we see this occurring at Green Castle Estate, as evidenced by the high presence of food storage vessels in the Locus 4 assemblage.

Third, the high percentage of items relating to food serving suggests greater importance was placed on the act of dining in the period following emancipation. As some women were given more freedom to remain home to do domestic work, the dynamics of how domestic work was performed must have changed as well. Whereas in the period of slavery, greater emphasis seems to have been placed on the activities surrounding food preparation, in the post-emancipation period, items relating to food serving have priority in the archaeological record. Food preparation was still a vital component of foodways, yet as the nature of households changed, domestic activities were divided along gender lines and a greater distinction between work on the plantation and work at home was created. In this light, it appears the act of dining might have become a more important activity relating to foodways than the act of food preparation.

Although there is a low emphasis on food preparation, as evidenced by only 7.26% (117) of the food-related artifacts being used for food preparation, this does not completely suggest the importance of food preparation was undermined following emancipation. Wage laborers may have shifted the types of vessels they used for cooking, such as turning to cast iron pots instead of locally-produced Afro-Antiguan wares, yet still maintaining a strong cultural tradition around food preparation. In fact, following emancipation, a greater appreciation for foodways in general may have been fostered, as it became an aspect of life that was now completely controlled by the formerly enslaved.

Other changes in the lives of free laborers can be interpreted from the assemblages at Green Castle Estate, specifically with regard to personal adornment. One of the greatest shifts the historical record notes in the practices of the formerly enslaved is in the area of personal adornment. As free laborers acquired greater purchasing power, clothing and accessories appear to have been a favored way to exercise that power.

Archaeological evidence for personal adornment in Locus 4 is small, but striking. Four fragments of metal boot heel cleats were recovered, along with two clothing clasps and four grommets (Figure 6; Figure 7). A variety of buttons, manufactured from shell, glass, metal, and bone were excavated, along with two wound glass beads (Figure 8). Both beads are spheroid in shape and one was manufactured from dark olive glass while the other is made of an opaque, white glass (Figure 9). All of these items are related specifically to clothing and dress and suggest that clothing was an area in which wage laborers invested to display their social status as free laborers. In addition, remnants of bluing powder, used in laundering clothes, was recovered from Locus 4. This might suggest that alongside increased use of clothing, especially fancy dress for Sundays and special occasions came further domestic responsibilities, such as washing more clothing, which accompanied the ownership of fine items.

Items relating to personal and recreational activities account for 3.56% (82) of the Locus 4 assemblage and present interesting insights into the lives of wage laborers at Green Castle Estate. Only 33 British tobacco pipe fragments were recovered from Locus 4, suggesting that smoking became a less popular activity

Figure 6. Metal boot heel cleat fragment.

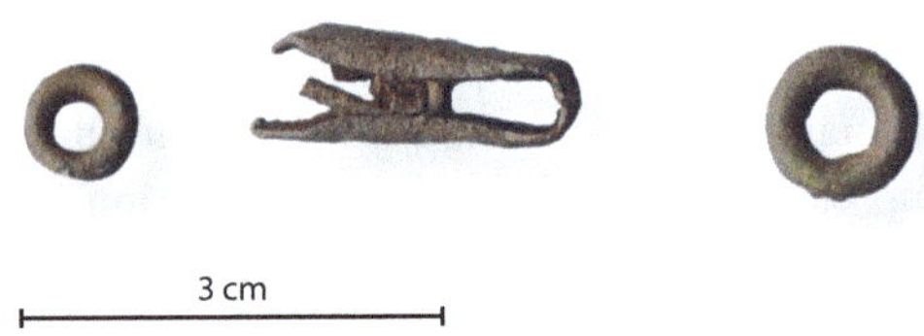

Figure 7. Metal clasp and two grommets for clothing.

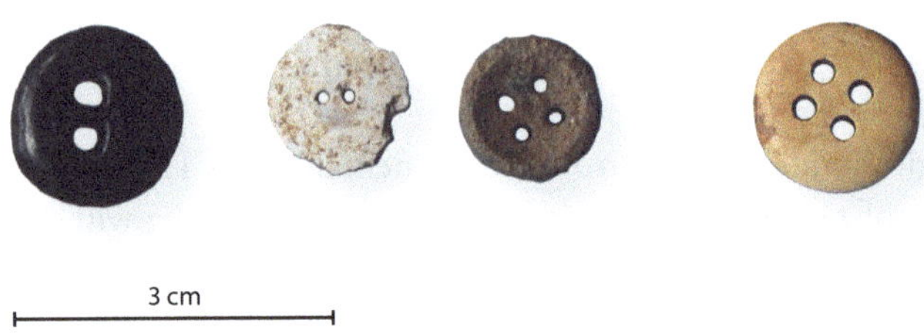

Figure 8. Buttons excavated from Locus 4 include buttons made from glass, shell, metal, and bone.

Figure 9. Glass Beads from Locus 4 include a dark olive, wound bead and an opaque white, would glass bead.

Figure 10. Copper alloy thimble.

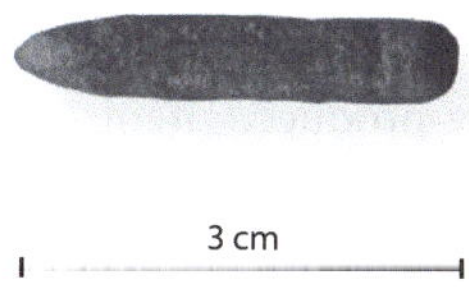

Figure 11. Lead pencil fragment.

Figure 12. Iron alloy keyhole.

following emancipation. Nine chert and flint fragments were also excavated and were probably used as strike-a-lights for smoking or starting fires for domestic uses. Yet wage laborers engaged in other activities. Sewing, as evidenced by one copper thimble, was practiced by at least one laborer (Figure 10). Additionally, several of the free laborers at Green Castle were probably literate as one lead pencil, three glass ink bottle fragments, and 10 pieces of writing slate were recovered (Figure 11). One fired lead musket ball was also excavated. Though the carrying of weapons was illegal following emancipation, laborers may have had access to firearms for hunting.

Interestingly, an iron alloy keyhole was recovered in excavations and it was probably part of a small chest or cabinet (Figure 12). This points to an interest in safeguarding items such as money or items of value. The presence of this keyhole leads to some interesting questions about the nature of social relationships within the wage laborer village. On the one hand, the keyhole might indicate that some households were wealthier than others and therefore felt a need to safeguard valuable items to prevent stealing from within the village. Alternatively, laborers may have collectively owned a safe box to keep money and other items inside to protect the assets of the community as a whole from planters or other individuals. The keyhole is interesting in that it points to lifestyles that are increasingly material and that greater value becomes placed on the material objects that wage laborers are now able to acquire such as money or other items of importance.

8.5 Conclusions

The dynamics of social life in Antigua during the periods of slavery and freedom created a world in which planters continually tried to coercively control the lives of laborers, both enslaved and free. In spite of this, in both the periods of slavery and post-emancipation, Afro-Antiguans were able to create strong cultural traditions that asserted a unique, Afro-Antiguan identity in the face of colonial ideologies. The activities of daily life among Afro-Antiguan laborers, though, changed dramatically from the period of slavery to freedom and each period demonstrates how Afro-Antiguans manipulated their social positions, and took advantage of opportunities presented to them, to create better lives for themselves and their families.

The archaeological evidence from Locus 5 and Locus 4 demonstrate that there are differences in the artifact assemblages that suggest significant changes in some areas of daily life for Afro-Antiguans over the periods of slavery and freedom in the eighteenth and nineteenth centuries. This evidence points strongly to a shift from the presence of locally-produced items, namely Afro-Antiguan ceramics, to imported ceramics. While this change was influenced by the availability of imported ceramics in Antigua and by the relatively limited purchasing power of Afro-Antiguans, the extent of the differences of the assemblages also points to changing attitudes towards consumption, the influx of capitalist social relations, and an increasing consciousness of modernity.

This data from Antigua provides a strong point of comparison for examining how freedom manifested differently throughout the British Caribbean. As Antigua shifted to full freedom first, it provides a historical precedent for how English planters may have expected the social relations of freedom to develop on other islands. Yet, research in Jamaica, for instance, demonstrates that the negotiations of freedom were very specific to the social relations of particular locales. The greater availability of land not dedicated to sugar production, the history of maroon settlements, and the development of larger, free settlements provided landscapes in which the formerly enslaved could, in some cases, forge different paths towards finding freedom; paths that were not available in Antigua (Armstrong 2010; Armstrong & Kelly 2000; Kelly et al. 2011).

As is evident, the shifts in the landscapes of Antigua and the material culture of Afro-Antiguans over the periods of slavery and freedom on the island are not just reflective of changes in lifeways among laborers but also highlight how labor relations and the social relations of production and consumption between planters and laborers changed during this time period as well. These shifts point to ways in which Antiguans created a post-emancipation society that translated the rhetoric of freedom into the practice of emancipation on the island. The ways in which emancipation unfolded in Antigua are unique within the context of the British Caribbean and reflect the complex negotiations of social life that accompanied this shift within this particular locale.

References

Archival Sources

Antigua and Barbuda National Archives, St. John's, Antigua (ABNA) The Laws of Antigua

Published Sources

Armstrong, D.V.

2010 Degrees of Freedom in the Caribbean: Archaeological Explorations of Transitions from Slavery. *Antiquity* 84(323):1-15.

Armstrong, D.V. and K. G. Kelly

2000 Settlement Pattern Shifts in a Jamaican Slave Village, Seville Estate, St. Ann's Bay, Jamaica. *Ethnohistory* 47(2):369-397.

Blouet, M. Olwyn

1990 Slavery and Freedom in the British West Indies, 1823-33: The Role of Education. *History of Education Quarterly* 30(4):625-643.

Bolland, O.N.

1996 Systems of Domination after Slavery: The Control of Land and Labour in the British West Indies after 1838. In *Caribbean Freedom: Economy and Society from Emancipation to the Present*, edited by H. Beckles and V. Shepherd, pp. 107-123. Markus Wiener Publishers, Princeton.

1999 The Politics of Freedom in the British Caribbean. In *The Meaning of Freedom: Economics, Politics, and Culture after Slavery*, edited by F. McGlynn and S. Drescher, pp. 113-146. University of Pittsburgh Press, Pittsburgh.

Dyde, B.

2000 *A History of Antigua: The Unsuspected Isle*. MacMillan Education, Ltd., London.

Fox, G.

2009 Preliminary Archaeological Investigations at Betty's Hope, Antigua: The Plantation as System and Socioenvironmental Change in the English Caribbean and Atlantic World. *Paper presented at the XXIII Congress of the International Association for Caribbean Archaeology*, Bolans, Antigua.

Gaspar, D.B.

1985 *Bondsmen and rebels: A Study of Master-Slave Relations in Antigua with Implications for Colonial British America*, The Johns Hopkins University Press, Baltimore.

Gonzalez Scollard, E.

2008 *Raising Cane: Sugar, People and the Environment in Nineteenth-Century Antigua, West Indies*. Ph.D. dissertation, City University of New York. University Microfilms, Ann Arbor.

Kelly, K.G., M. Hauser and D.V. Armstrong

2011 Identity and Opportunity in Post-Slavery Jamaica. In *Out of Many, One People: The Historical Archaeology of Colonial Jamaica*, edited by J.A. Delle, M.W. Hauser and D.V. Armstrong, pp. 243-257, University of Alabama Press, Tuscaloosa.

Martin, S.

1750 *An Essay Upon Plantership*. 1st ed. Printed by R. Mearns, Antigua.

Murray, J.

1825 *Six Months in the West Indies in 1825*. 2nd ed. Thomas Davison, Whitefriars, London.

Oliver, V.L.

1894 *The History of the Island of Antigua.* Mitchell and Hughes, London.

Petersen, J.B., D.R. Watters and D.V. Nicholson

1999 Continuity and Syncretism in Afro-Caribbean Ceramics from the Northern Lesser Antilles. In *African Sites Archaeology in the Caribbean*, edited by J.B. Haviser, pp. 157-195. Markus Wiener, Princeton.

Sheridan, R.B.

1960 Samuel Martin, Innovating Sugar Planter of Antigua, 1750-1776. *Agricultural History* 34(3):126-139.

Sturge, J. and T. Harvey

1838 *The West Indies in 1837; being the Journal of a Visit to Antigua, Montserrat, Dominica, St. Lucia, Barbadoes, and Jamaica; undertaken for the Purpose of Ascertaining the Actual Condition of the Negro Population of the those Islands.* 2nd ed. Hamilton, Adams, and Co., Paternoster Row, London.

Zacek, N.A.

2007 Cultivating Virtue: Samuel Martin and the Paternal Ideal in the Eighteenth-Century English West Indies. *Wadabagei: A Journal of the Caribbean and its Diaspora.* 10:8-31.

Conclusion

The context of plantation archaeology in the Lesser Antilles

Multi-disciplinary, multi-cultural, pluri-national

Kenneth G. Kelly

Department of Anthropology
University of South Carolina
Columbia
kenneth.kelly@sc.edu

Abstract

This chapter reviews the themes introduced in this book, recognizing that plantation archaeology has great potential in the Caribbean region. This potential is best realized by considering multiple factors, such as specific historical context, temporal context, and cultural context in order to develop a more sophisticated and nuanced understanding of the commonalities, and the variation present in the plantation colonies of the Caribbean. Methodologies employed in archaeological research must also be considered, as they influence the sorts of historical and anthropological questions that can be addressed.

Résumé

Ce chapitre passe en revue les sujets traités dans le présent livre, prenant en compte l'énorme potentiel de recherche en archéologie des plantations/habitations aux Antilles. La réalisation de ce potentiel implique l'inclusion de nombreux éléments, par exemple - le contexte historique spécifique, le contexte temporel et le contexte culturel, afin de développer une compréhension subtile et nuancée des points communs et des différences présents dans les colonies Antillaises. Il faut tenir compte aussi des méthodologies employées car celles-ci peuvent influencer le choix des questions historiques et archéologiques abordées dans les études.

Resumen

El presente capítulo revisa los temas presentados en este libro, reconociendo el gran potencial de la arqueología de los ingenios en el Caribe. Para realizar este potencial lo mejor es de tener en cuenta múltiples factores, como los contextos históricos, temporales y culturales específicos con el fin de desarrollar una comprensión más sofisticada y matizada de las permanencias y de las variaciones que existen en las colonias de plantación del Caribe. Las metodologías empleadas en la investigación arqueológica también deben ser considerados, ya que influyen en el tipo de preguntas históricas y antropológicas que se pueden abordar.

Key words

plantations, archaeology, history

Mots-cléts

plantations, archéologie, histoire

Palabras clave

plantación, arqueología, historia

The study of plantations is ideally suited to the approaches of historical archaeology. Historical archaeologists pride themselves on their ability to explore the worlds of the subaltern, the marginalized, the undocumented: indeed, the majority of people who were living at any particular time. They are also proud of their ability to 'read between the lines,' making the material world, as it is constructed, negotiated, and resisted, speak about broader processes, such as racism, capitalism, imperialism, and so forth that lie at the core of the modern world. Plantations, especially as they developed in the Caribbean, are remarkable settings as they embody, and indeed, construct, social processes such as racism and imperialism, and they are populated by a majority of subaltern, 'voiceless' people. When considered in this light, clearly the Caribbean plantation is one of the ideal realms for historical archaeology to work its magic.

Beginning in the late 1960s archaeological methods began to be applied to plantation sites in the Caribbean region (Handler & Lange 1978), and we are now seeing the fruits of this work, as a greater and more diverse variety of plantation sites are excavated. The earliest plantation studies explored plantations that might be considered archetypal—large sugar estates in economically important colonies such as Jamaica (see Armstrong 1990 for an example of work conducted in the early 1980s and Higman 1998 for long term study that began in the early 1970s). Much of the pioneering work that was done on these plantations was conducted from the theoretical perspective of African Diaspora studies. These projects were largely geared toward exploring the contribution of enslaved Africans and their descendants to the construction of creole societies in the slaveholding colonies. This approach was highly successful, as many aspects of slave life were brought to light, including the creativity associated with the manufacture of material culture using African and other antecedents, the skills associated with surviving in impoverished conditions, and the ways daily life was organized, both socially and spatially.

Plantation archaeology has continued to evolve, broadening from its earlier focus on the responses of enslaved people to their conditions, to the archaeological explorations of the space of the plantation and how the various parties present on plantations attempted to use space to guide the actions of themselves or others (see Delle 1998, Armstrong & Kelly 2000, Pulsipher 1994, Wilkie & Farnsworth 2005 for some examples). The developing maturity of the historical archaeological contribution to the understanding of plantations is seen in the range of contributions in this volume. Whereas early efforts to explore plantations were focused on characterizing the 'plantation world' by reference to results from a single site (necessarily, as only a very limited number of sites had been investigated), now we see that archaeologists are taking explicitly comparative approaches that are open to, and even seek out, the diversity of plantation experiences within the broad structural framework of the Caribbean plantation. This comparative approach has even begun to push the boundaries of the 'Caribbean' plantation, by investigating plantations that operated on what appears to be the same model in French Guyana (Losier 2012, Le Roux et al. 2009, Barone-Visigalli 2010) and Brazil. It is only a matter of time before this comparison is further expanded to include the plantation colonies of the Indian Ocean.

Context and plantations

Bringing a comparative approach to plantation studies is important as it allows us to appreciate the role that context plays in the expression of daily life and its experience. The context that must be considered includes a range of variables, from environmental setting in both coarse and fine scale, to economy, to political administration, to social factors such as the cultures of the plantation owners and laborers. Interestingly, these last factors have not been considered in their full complexity until recently, and even then they are by no means universally considered. As we see in the case of Hauser's contribution to this collection, political administration, or lack thereof, can have important ramifications in the way plantation societies develop.

Culture is at least as important, and yet has played little role in most plantation interpretations. In cases when culture has been included, it has usually been in reference to the culture(s) of the enslaved laborers, and has attempted to consider the role of 'African-ness' or African ethnicities in the expression of adaptation and resistance to slavery. In earlier plantation studies, certain aspects of slave practice, such as foodways or housing, were seen as examples of a generic 'African' expression of culture—what were called 'Africanisms' (following Herskovits 1941). That rather crude perspective has now been replaced with a more sophisticated and nuanced view of African people being distinct in time and place. For example, particular African ethnicities have been suggested to play a significant role in the choices made in manufacturing low-fired earthenware cooking pottery (Mathewson 1972; Ebanks 1984, 2003; but see Hauser 2008) or in the expression of particular ritual activities such as the so-called Bakongo cosmogram (Ferguson 1992, 1999; Mouer et al. 1999, etc.), to name two cultural practices. This sort of interpretive sophistication is needed to avoid essentializing and homogenizing the cultural practices of a diverse range of Africans who would have possessed different kinds of knowledge depending on their place of origin, age, gender, and the era in which they lived. In other words, a young woman from the area of present-day Dakar, who was captured in the mid 17th century would have had a very different set of culturally constructed knowledge than a middle aged man captured in the region of Calabar in the early 19th century. While this would seem to be obvious, this distinction has not been was widely observed as it should be.

Even more remarkable, the influence of context on the planter group and the way they created their world has been widely ignored, with the exception of the studies of 'capitalism' and its penetration into the plantation system. If it seems natural that temporality and African ethnicities might play a role in cultural expression, it should be so for Europeans as well. Yet until recently this has not been explicitly considered, and even now it is only very rarely explored (Hicks 2007, Kelly 2011, Hauser this volume). Certainly we implicitly, if not explicitly, acknowledge the factor of temporality in that the plantations set up in the first wave of non-Spanish Caribbean colonization (1620s-1660s) were different in organization than those that followed in the late 17th and early 18th centuries (Hicks 2007). The work of archaeologists in Cuba demonstrates that 19th century plantations there are also distinct from their earlier counterparts elsewhere in the Caribbean (Singleton and De Souza 2009). Yet we have been less willing to acknowledge the role culture plays in the plantation. Should we not expect that French planters would have a particular set of ideas (their culture) that framed the ways in which they conceptualized plantation colonies? Should we not expect that there might be some differences between those culturally constructed ideas and the mindset of English, or Dutch, or Danish colonists?

The role that specific historical events, yet another form of context, play in the manifestation of colonial plantation life is also important. In the contributions in this volume we see that attention to this sort of detail, within the broad strokes of a common Caribbean history, highlights the agency of planter and laborer. By looking at an island such as Dominica that only became a formal colony rather late in the scheme of Caribbean history, processes that would otherwise be obscure come to light, such as the role of identity and performance in cementing colonial control over a disparate population used to being on the margins of government (Hauser this volume). Also, in this sort of setting we see how lessons learned in nearly 150 years of Caribbean colonial practice are employed in attempting to establish a sugar plantation economy out of whole cloth. Clearly, the British colonial government of Dominica was able to profit from the accumulated knowledge of plantation ventures in Jamaica, Barbados, St. Kitts, Nevis, and elsewhere in pushing for sugar production.

The role of historical and geographical context is also seen in the discussion of the end of slavery in Antigua by Rebovich Bardoe. The profit maximizing decisions undertaken by Antiguan planters to reduce their costs through granting immediate emancipation to a highly circumscribed population is fascinating, and without parallel in the Caribbean. Clearly the planters recognized that the population of emancipated slaves would have nowhere to go, and no option but to continue to work for on the plantations, because the island is relatively small, with little in the way of unclaimed or uncultivated land. This lack of options was reinforced through the imposition of restrictive and coercive legislation that further limited alternatives. Historical archaeology provides an excellent means by which the consequences of this exploitative policy can be seen in the daily lives of the laboring population. To the best of my knowledge, the consequences of this sort of management strategy has only been explored in one other setting, that of post-emancipation Jamaica, where two laboring households of the mid 19th century were compared (Kelly 1989). In that case, while management strategies, either more paternalist, or more exploitative, were seen to have definite consequences for the residents of the plantation, other factors such as ethnicity complicated the accuracy of the interpretations (Kelly et al. 2009).

In considering context, we must also include theoretical and methodological contexts. We also see in these contributions a commitment to multiple theoretical perspectives. Whereas pioneering approaches to plantation archaeology frequently had as their departure point the acculturationist perspectives that saw the plantation as a setting where enslaved Africans and their descendants acculturated to the dominant society, plantation archaeology today routinely views African adaptation in the framework of creolization or ethnogenesis. In this perspective, the cultures that developed in the cauldron of plantation slavery were something new, and embodied new identities that were distinct from both the African ancestries of the enslaved, and from the European cultures of the enslavers. Other theoretical perspectives are also employed to explore different aspects of the plantation world. World systems perspectives investigate broad economic relationships between the European metropoles and the Caribbean periphery as plantations produced wealth for the core (Fox this volume). Plantations are also explored as early manifestations of the capitalist or proto-capitalist system, and can be viewed as a quasi-industrial form of exploitation (Delle 1998). This exploitation had its costs, in many ways. Certainly the human cost, in terms of the suffering and hardship endured by literally millions of Africans as they were captured and the survivors taken across the Atlantic to be enslaved, was enormous, and unimaginable in the true meaning of the word. The suffering of their descendants is also a clear aspect of the human cost. But so to is the widespread environmental change and degradation that occurred as a result of the plantation system, with entire ecosystems destroyed, or altered through the introduction of new species. These environmental costs are only now really beginning to be explored, through the work of Fox and others on Antigua and Barbuda in particular.

Methodology

The plantation studies in this volume all bring together a range of methodological perspectives geared toward understanding daily life on plantations. The methodologies range from the focus on zooarchaeological remains, to human graves, to ceramics, and to housing, to name some of the most frequently employed. In each of these cases, the archaeological data were combined with historical evidence. In some cases, the historical evidence was detailed and specific to the site being investigated, but in many, if not most cases, the historical data was not specifically related to the site in question. While unfortunate, this is not surprising, as many plantations have surprisingly little in the way of documentary materials associated with them. It is a rare situation where there are more than depictions on maps, or some rather generic economic data. Furthermore, given the nature of the populations under study, which are in many cases the enslaved workers or their descendants, the lack of specific documentation is not surprising as these groups were rarely able to record their own observations of their lives, and those who could write typically ignored them. Therefore, the historical archaeology of plantations is often an archaeology with a well developed historical context, but without the specificity we might like to see.

The chapters collected here all deal with aspects of plantation life, whether it is the experiences of the enslaved or the elite. In studying these settings, we see many different theoretical foci and goals. One other area, often not considered in theoretical or methodological discussions, in which we see some differences lie in the excavation strategies employed by each researcher. Broadly speaking, we see that there two primary approaches in current Caribbean archaeology: what we might call 'North American research' methodologies and 'French cultural resource management' strategies (see chapters in Siegel and Righter 2009 for an island by island review of the range of archaeology conducted in the Caribbean). As my earlier chapter in this book discusses, there are some major differences I encountered in working in the French West Indies. In the chapters here, we see that, outside of excavations targeted at specific features believed to have been graves (Varney), the excavation strategies employed by Hauser, Rebovich Bardoe, Bergman and Smith, and Wallman all commenced with the use of historic maps and other documents to define areas for pedestrian survey and shovel testing, followed by the excavation of one or more relatively small (1 m^2 or 2 m^2) test units, either singly or in larger groups, to recover representative assemblages of artifacts and to identify features associated with structures or other aspects of the built landscape. In some cases these features were located, and in other cases they remained elusive. But in either case, artifact assemblages were obtained that enabled the authors to make interpretations about chronology, occupation, spatial disposition, and function, and to use those interpretations to further explore the bigger theoretical issues such as creolization or agency. This can be contrasted with the French CRM approach, which resulted in the collection that was analyzed and reported in the chapter by Tomadini et al. In fact, that collection, derived from distinct refuse deposits, is much larger than many of the collections obtained in the other ways, and therefore permits the sorts of robust analyses that large sample sizes permit. Yet the data from other areas of the site that could contribute to understanding differential uses of the site, and perhaps provide evidence of who occupied which structures, were not collected in a way that facilitates their study. So we see that two different methodologies can have significant impacts upon the sorts of interpretations or conclusions that can be derived from the respective collections. This means that we need to be cognizant of the fact that while neither one nor the other methodology is innately superior or inferior, the methodologies affect the interpretation, and assemblages collected through different methods are not necessarily able to be compared easily.

Concluding thoughts

Plantation archaeology has been around for nearly 40 years in the Caribbean, and it has grown exponentially since the late 1980s, following the pioneering work of Handler and Lange, Armstrong, Higman, and Pulsipher. Now there is scarcely an island in the region, no matter how small or peripheral to the main thrusts of the Caribbean plantation economy, that is not home to some sort of archaeological work on their plantations. This proliferation of research has certainly demonstrated many commonalities amongst the plantations of the region, but it has also opened our eyes to the sometimes subtle, and other times dramatic differences between islands, time periods, and crops. We are also moving beyond a focus on simply the institution of slavery and the lives of enslaved people, although historical archaeology is ideally placed to do that, but to querying the entirety of the plantation experience, from the people on it, to the impacts the system had upon the local and regional environments, and the world economies. Clearly, plantation archaeology, as demonstrated by the contributions to this volume, has come a long way, and will continue to generate insights into the Caribbean world of the 17th, 18th, 19th, and early 20th centuries. New and exciting perspectives are being brought to bear on the plantations of the region, as we see from the work on Antigua, Barbados, and Dominica, and the potential of historical archaeology is now being felt ever more strongly on Guadeloupe and Martinique. As the research reported in the chapters collected here shows us, there is much to learn, and the international and interregional interactions that the continuing International Association of Caribbean Archaeology meetings provide are essential to bringing these perspectives and results together. It is my hope that the exchanges that come from these meetings, and from focused publications such as this one, will continue to make the culturally rich Caribbean basin a place where the richness of archaeological collaboration shines in the strength of our interpretation and understanding of the past.

References

Armstrong, D.V.

1990 *The Old Village and the Great House: An Archaeological and Historical Examination of Drax Hall Plantation, St. Ann's Bay, Jamaica.* Urbana, University of Illinois Press.

Armstrong, D.V. and K.G. Kelly

2000 Settlement Patterns and the Origin of African Jamaican Society: Seville Plantation, St. Ann's Bay, Jamaica.' *Ethnohistory* 47(2): 369-397.

Barone-Visigalli, E.

2010 *Histoire et archéologie de la Guyane française: Les jésuites de la Comté. Habitations St. Régis et Maripa.* Matoury, Guyane, Ibis Rouge.

Delle, J. A.

1998 *An Archaeology of Social Space: Analyzing Coffee Plantations in Jamaica's Blue Mountains.* New York, Plenum Press.

Ebanks, R.

1984 Ma Lou, An Afro Jamaican Pottery Tradition. *Jamaica Journal* 17: 31-37.

Ebanks, R.

2003 History of Jamaican Ceramics, 1655-1840. Unpublished M. Phil. Thesis, Department of History and Archaeology, Mona, University of the West Indies.

Ferguson, L.

1992 *Uncommon Ground: Archaeology and Early African America, 1650-1800.* Washington D.C., Smithsonian Institution Press.

Ferguson, L.G.

1999 'The Cross is a Magic Sign': Marks on Eighteenth-Century Bowls from South Carolina. In *'I, Too, am America': Archaeological Studies of African-American Life*, edited by Th.A. Singleton, pp.116-131, Charlottesville, University Press of Virginia.

Handler, J.S. and F. Lange

1978 *Plantation Slavery in Barbados: An Archaeological and Historical Investigation.* Cambridge, Harvard University Press.

Hauser, M. W.

2008 *An Archaeology of Black Markets: Local Ceramics and Economies in Eighteenth-Century Jamaica.* Gainesville, University Presses of Florida.

Herskovits, M.

1941 *The Myth of the Negro Past.* Boston, Beacon.

Hicks, D.

2007 *'The Garden of the World:' An Historical Archaeology of Sugar Landscapes in the Eastern Caribbean.* Oxford, Archaeopress.

Higman, B.W.

1998 *Montpelier, Jamaica: A Plantation Community in Slavery and Freedom, 1739-1912.* Kingston, Jamaica, The Press University of the West Indies.

Kelly, K.G.

1989 Slaves no more: An archaeological comparison of two post emancipation house sites on Drax Hall and Seville Estate, St. Ann's, Jamaica. Unpublished Master's Thesis, Department of Anthropology, College of William and Mary.

Kelly, K.G.

2011 *La Vie Quotidienne*: Historical Archaeological Approaches to the Plantation Era in Guadeloupe, French West Indies. In *French Colonial Archaeology in the Southeast and Caribbean,* edited by Kenneth G. Kelly and Meredith D. Hardy, Gainesville, University Press of Florida, 189-205.

Kelly, K.G., M.W. Hauser and D.V. Armstrong

2011 Identity and Opportunity in Post Slavery Jamaica. In *Out of Many, One People: The Historical Archaeology of Colonial Jamaica,* edited by J.A. Delle, M.W. Hauser and D.V. Armstrong, pp.243-257, Tuscaloosa, University of Alabama Press.

Le Roux, Y., R. Auger and N. Cazelles

2009 *Les jésuites de l'esclavage Loyola: l'habitation des jésuites de Rémire en Guyane française.* Québec, Presses de l'Université du Québec.

Losier, C.

2012 Approvisionner Cayene au cours de l'ancien régime: étude archéologique et historique de l'économie et du réseau commercial d'une colonie marginale, la Guyane (XVIIe et XVIIIe siècle). Unpublished Ph.D. dissertation, Department of History, Université Laval, Québec.

Mathewson, R. D.

1972 Jamaican Ceramics: An Introduction to 18th Century Folk Pottery in West African Tradition. *Jamaica Journal* 6(2): 54-56.

Mouer, L. D., M.E.N. Hodges, S.R. Potter, S.L.H. Renaud, I. Noel Hume, D.J. Pogue, M.W. McCartney and T. E. Davidson

1999 Colonoware Pottery, Chesapeake Pipes, and 'Uncritical Assumptions.' IIn *'I, Too, am America': Archaeological Studies of African-American Life,* edited by Th.A. Singleton, pp.83-115, Charlottesville, University Press of Virginia.

Pulsipher, L.M.

1994 The Landscapes and Ideational Roles of Caribbean Slave Gardens. In *The Archaeology of Garden and Field*, edited by N. F. Miller and K.L. Gleason Philadelphia, pp. 202-221, University of Pennsylvania Press.

Siegel, P.E. and E. Righter (editors)

2011 *Protecting Heritage in the Caribbean.* Tuscaloosa, University of Alabama Press.

Singleton, Th.A. and M. A. Torres de Souza

2009 Archaeologies of the African Diaspora: Brazil, Cuba, and the United States. In *International Handbook of Historical Archaeology*, edited by T. Majewski and D. Gaimster, pp. 449-469, New York, Springer.

Wilkie, L.A. and P. Farnsworth

2005 *Sampling Many Pots: An Archaeology of Memory and Tradition at a Bahamian Plantation.* Gainesville, University Press of Florida.